Love's Labour's Lost

LOVE'S LABOUR'S LOST

A Guide to the Play

JOHN S. PENDERGAST

Greenwood Guides to Shakespeare

Greenwood Press
Westport, Connecticut • London

Library of Congress Cataloging-in-Publication Data

Pendergast, John S., 1963–
    Love's labour's lost : a guide to the play / by John S. Pendergast.
       p. cm.—(Greenwood guides to Shakespeare)
    Includes bibliographical references (p.   ) and index.
    ISBN 0–313–31315–6 (alk. paper)
    1. Shakespeare, William, 1564–1616. 2. Love's labour's lost—Handbooks, manuals, etc. I.
Title. II. Series.
    PR2822.P46   2002
    822.3'3—dc21   2001033693

British Library Cataloguing in Publication Data is available.

Copyright © 2002 by John S. Pendergast

Library of Congress Catalog Card Number: 2001033693
ISBN: 0–313–31315–6

First published in 2002

Greenwood Press, 88 Post Road West, Westport, CT 06881
An imprint of Greenwood Publishing Group, Inc.
www.greenwood.com

Printed in the United States of America

The paper used in this book complies with the
Permanent Paper Standard issued by the National
Information Standards Organization (Z39.48–1984).

10 9 8 7 6 5 4 3 2 1

Copyright Acknowledgments

The author and publisher gratefully acknowledge permission for use of the following material:

Photograph *A Pleasant Conceited Comedie Called Loues Labors Lost* (the title page of the 1598 Quarto) used by permission of the Folger Shakespeare Library.

Photograph *De Octo Orationis partium* (the title page for Lily's Grammar) used by permission of the Folger Shakespeare Library.

Excerpts from *Libretti of Love's Labour's Lost.* Copyright © 1973 by W.H. Auden and Chester Kallman. Reprinted by permisison of Curtis Brown, Ltd.

CONTENTS

PREFACE

Few of Shakespeare's plays conjure the passionate response afforded to *Love's Labour's Lost* (*LLL*). At one point perhaps the least loved of Shakespeare's comedies, the play is now a very popular one. Whereas critics have always been fascinated by it, today many critics see the play as one of Shakespeare's most unique and personal works. The play's newfound popularity suggests that it conforms to modern taste in the same way it once conformed to Renaissance tastes. More than any other of Shakespeare's plays, *LLL* reflects a passionate love of language that, for some critics, turns it into an extended poetic meditation on the power and limitations of language. At the same time, however, the play has met with much negative criticism. *Love's Labour's Lost* holds a unique position in Shakespeare's canon: as one of Shakespeare's most vilified plays, its critical and theatrical heritage has been limited to a few moments of illumination, but for the most part the play has been ignored until the twentieth century. Many critics, even into the early twentieth century, insisted that this must be the first play written by Shakespeare, a conclusion erroneously based on an assumption that its exuberance and unique dramatic development must suggest a young playwright. However, what has been more recently discovered is nothing less than a lost gem.

Nonetheless, the play is one of Shakespeare's most demanding, and its difficulty is responsible for its earlier lack of attention. The following exchange, occurring at III.i.67–77, is typical both of what makes the play so inventive and enjoyable and what makes it a seemingly daunting work:

Moth: A wonder, master! here's a costard broken in a shin.

Armado: Some enigma, some riddle: come, thy l'envoy; begin.

Costard: No enigma, no riddle, no l'envoy; no salve in the
            mail, sir: O, sir, plantain, a plain plantain! no
            l'envoy, no l'envoy; no salve, sir, but a plantain!

Armado: By virtue, thou enforcest laughter; thy silly
            thought my spleen; the heaving of my lungs provokes
            me to ridiculous smiling. O, pardon me, my stars!
            Doth the inconsiderate take salve for l'envoy, and
            the word l'envoy for a salve?

Has Costard taken "salve" for "l'envoy"? If so, what exactly does that mistake entail? The words sound nothing alike, so how could the mistake occur? Obviously, something is going on linguistically that an Elizabethan audience would find humorous, but that is now lost on modern readers and viewers. The first line is easy enough to explain: most editors agree that a "costard" is another word for head and, as we find out a few lines later, what has happened is that Costard has tripped and hurt his shin, but, in typical Elizabethan fashion, the two words reflect off each other and afford Shakespeare the opportunity to "quibble," as Samuel Johnson called such silly punning. A "l'envoy" is simply a conclusion or moral to a story, as Armado goes on to explain, and an "enigma" means simply a dark or obscure idea. For Costard, however, the words are exotic sounding, and for him they insinuate some kind of cure for his illness, such as a "plantain," or a healing leaf. This kind of exchange, so typical of all of Shakespeare's comedies but of *Love's Labour's Lost* in particular, is what makes the play so interesting to modern critics but also renders it so representative of Shakespeare's time. It is also one of the features of the play that makes a reference and critical guide to the play so necessary.

Despite the fact that the play has become a favorite of critics and directors alike, it has also inspired a great deal of criticism that is now seen as foolish or simply misconceived. As Alfred Harbage noted in 1961, "*Love's Labour's Lost* seems to act upon them [critics] as catnip upon perfectly sane cats, and possibly the fault lies in the play itself" (19). Perhaps it does; certainly the play defies its audiences' expectations at almost every turn: here is a comedy without a happy ending, a comedy built out of words and exchanges rather than plot, but which contains no songs (unless one counts the ending songs), but does contain elaborate plays-within-the-play. A highly formal play, it ultimately defies its own form. As a result, the play seems to beg for interpretation, often at the expense of the play qua play. To make sense of what has been written about *LLL*, I have sifted through decades of criticism, and I have paid especially careful attention to those ideas that have influenced later critical appraisals as well as those statements that have influenced the play's theatrical reputation.

Ultimately, perhaps the most important comment made about the play came from Samuel Johnson, who wrote that there is no "play that has more evident marks of the hand of Shakespeare" (182). The previous exchange illustrates why this is undoubtedly true: Shakespeare took great delight in the power of language to mirror nature, to mystify, to create new worlds and ideas, and to entertain. The play taps into an energy of the time in a way no other play does. Again, it is Johnson who best explains why:

> He wrote at a time when our poetical language was yet unformed, when the meaning of our phrases was yet in fluctuation, when words were adopted at pleasure from the neighboring languages and while the Saxon was still visibly mingled in our diction. . . . In that age, as in all others, fashion produced phraseology, which succeeding fashion swept away before its meaning was generally known or sufficiently authorized; and in that age, above all others, experiments were made upon our language which distorted its combinations and disturbed its uniformity. (Johnson 115)

Johnson was describing a general characteristic of Shakespeare's genius, but he could have been describing *Love's Labour's Lost* specifically. Throughout the play, language is continually in fluctuation and words are continually being adopted from "neighboring languages": in the previous exchange, for example, Costard, who seemingly does not know French or Latin, is not really intimidated by Armado's use of those languages; instead he is fascinated by them and quickly learns to appropriate the newfound words for his own use. This pattern recurs throughout the play and constitutes one of its major themes. It is also telling that Johnson used the word "fashion": no other Shakespeare play better parodies "fashionable" behavior than *LLL*. Note, for example, the description of Armado from early in the play as "A man in all the world's new fashion planted" (I.i.163), which ironically follows the young men's declaration to withdraw from the world. *Love's Labour's Lost* was written at a time when sonnets were the literary fashion of the day: a little later in the play, the braggart Armado pleads: "Assist me, some extemporal god of rhyme, for I am sure I shall turn sonnet. Devise, wit; write, pen; for I am for whole volumes in folio" (I.ii.172–175). Finally, Johnson notes that Shakespeare's age was noteworthy for how it "distorted" and "disturbed" linguistic uniformity. The example also serves to illustrate this point—the meaning of "costard," "l'envoy," and "plantain" all get distorted in the course of a few lines. There are virtually no exchanges in the play that are allowed to stand without some commentary or challenge by other characters. In fact, the whole play questions itself as a play, most notably in its concluding lines when Costard notes the limitations of theatrical time to tell an "old comedy" and in the final songs, which change from dramatic to lyrical mode.

In the following chapters, I have focused on those critical issues that are most important for modern readers while attempting to give an overview of the history of criticism on the play. At the same time, however, I have tried to avoid allowing the criticism to overshadow the play's dramatic structure and its brilliance as a performance script. All too often criticism of the play has done just that, sometimes even treating the play as a complex code system that only existed as a text to be read, and read by a limited few who saw in the play specific topical references or allusions. For these reasons, I have not attempted to forward an original thesis on the play, except to draw together common strands of opinion that serve to clarify and deepen the appreciation of readers. Modern textual practices have exposed the limitations of purely "topical" or thematic readings of Renaissance plays and have revealed their complexity as both literary texts and performance scripts. As a result, I will treat the play as both text and script, with Chapters 1, 2, 4, and 5 dedicated to the textual nature of the play, while Chapters 3 and 6 will focus on its performative and dramatic nature. Readers should be careful, however, of mistakenly seeing the two aspects as necessarily distinct; as I suggest in the pages that follow, *LLL* is a particularly striking example of the two coming together to produce a complicated and aesthetically pleasing work of art.

Given the play's linguistic density, I have relied on the Arden Shakespeare edition of the play, edited by R.W. David. The Arden editions of Shakespeare's plays have traditionally focused on linguistic and philological issues, providing the most extensive glosses on difficult or controversial passages. The Arden edition is also, however, a bit outdated in its critical approaches to the play, and therefore I have supplemented my discussion with references to other editions. (For a detailed discussion of the various editions of the play available, see the next chapter.) For all other Shakespeare plays, I have relied on the *Riverside Shakespeare*, 2nd edition.

I have modernized spelling and punctuation only where the original might cause confusion. I have also regularized the spelling of the title to *Love's Labour's Lost*, as it appears on the first folio, rather than *Love's Labor's Lost*, as it appears on the first quarto. My choice is, however, an arbitrary one with no bearing on the meaning of either the title or the play.

WORKS CITED

David, Richard W., ed. *Love's Labour's Lost*. Arden Shakespeare. 2nd series. London: Routledge, 1994.

Harbage, Alfred. "*Love's Labor's Lost* and the Early Shakespeare." *Philological Quarterly* 41 (1962): 18–36.

Johnson, Samuel. *Samuel Johnson on Shakespeare*. Ed. H.R. Woudhuysen. London: Penguin, 1989.

Love's Labour's Lost

1

TEXTUAL HISTORY

Until the 1950's there was an assumption that *Love's Labour's Lost* was one of Shakespeare's earliest, if not the earliest, plays. The primary reasons for this assumption were twofold. First, the language and linguistic density of the play suggested for some critics a playwright still learning his art and showing off his newfound skills. Second, the play is essentially plotless, that is, plotless as long as one's definition of plot is simply storytelling. Both assumptions are unfounded and are dealt with in more detail later in this book. Modern critics tend to date the play between 1594 and 1595, putting it in the era that produced *Titus Andronicus, The Taming of the Shrew, The Two Gentlemen of Verona, King John*, and, probably, the sonnets. Earlier dates for composition rely upon generalizations about its seeming deficiencies, but specifying an earlier date leads to innumerable problems; why, for example, if this play is early, do other early plays not share its enthusiasm for puns and verbal dexterity? If its lack of plot is suggestive of a young, not yet theatrical savvy playwright, why then are other early plays, such as *The Comedy of Errors* and *Taming of the Shrew*, so plot driven? If Shakespeare failed to develop the characters in the play in a satisfactory way, where or when did he acquire the skills to create Kate or King Richard III? Finally, why does the play perform so well and show such a sophisticated understanding of dramatic form?

DATING *LOVE'S LABOUR'S LOST*

Our first clue as to the date of the composition lies in the title page (see Photo 1), which reads: "A PLEASANT / Conceited Comedie / CALLED,

A

PLEASANT

Conceited Comedie

CALLED,

Loues labors loſt.

As it vvas preſented before her Highnes
this laſt Chriſtmas.

Newly correčted and augmented
By *W. Shakeſpere.*

Imprinted at London by *W.W.*
for *Cutbert Burby.*
1598.

Photo 1. Title Page of 1598 Quarto.

/ Loues labors lost. / As it was presented before her Highnes / this last Christmas. / Newly corrected and augmented / *W. Shakespere.*" The title page also tells us that the text was "Imprinted at London by W.W. / for Cutbert Burby. / 1598." Although there is some evidence that the quarto was proofread before printing, there are still numerous problems, such as false starts and the inclusion of revised and uncorrected versions of the same passages. Several of these problems will be dealt with in more detail later. In addition, the speech prefixes in the quarto are often generic tags such as "King," "Braggart," "Page," "Lady 1–3," and so on, which suggests that Shakespeare at some point thought of his characters as types more than as individual personalities. If this is indeed the case, we have strong evidence for a later substantial revision. Thus, we must consider the play as composed not in a single year or theatrical season, but over time with the result that the play as it now stands bears the mark of Shakespeare's hand both as a composer and a reviser.

It is likely that the quarto derived from some earlier source. The phrase "newly augmented" suggests not only that the play was likely revised but, possibly, that an earlier, now lost, quarto existed, and most scholars agree that the first quarto was preceded by an earlier one. The editor of the 3rd Arden edition of the play, H.R. Woudhuysen, notes that in 1656 the publisher Edward Archer created "An Exact and perfect Catalogue of all the Plaies that were ever printed"; in it he mentions a play titled *Loves Labor Lost* by one "C Will. Sampson" (Woudhuysen 301). Walter Greg notes that if this is indeed an earlier quarto of *LLL*, then the initials "W.S." could be mistaken, either by Archer or by an earlier printer, for Will Sampson (301). However, we do not know if this *LLL* is our play or a different play inspired by Shakespeare, or perhaps even a version preceding Shakespeare's play and serving as a source for it. Nor do we know when William Sampson's play was originally written. However, what the evidence does suggest is the often confusing nature of Renaissance authorship and the tradition of revision and inspiration that makes authorial attribution and dating so difficult. The suggestion that the play was revised, and internal evidence strongly suggests that it was, makes composition and dating questions even more complicated since any single line or allusion in the quarto as we now know it could either be from the earlier draft or unique to the later version. For reasons we will see, the most likely date for the original version would be between 1594 and 1595, followed by a 1597 revision, possibly for court performance.

TOPICAL ALLUSIONS AND THE MASQUE OF THE MUSCOVITES

Based on internal textual evidence, the earliest the play could have been written is 1594. This conclusion, by no means universally accepted, is based on the large number of topical allusions that concentrate around 1594. (In the next chapter we will outline some of the problems inherent in employing topical allusions.) For example, Berowne's remark at V.ii.460–462 may be a reference to the ill-fated performance of *The Comedy of Errors* on December 28, 1594, during the revels at the Gray's Inn Christmas held between December 20, 1594, to about March 4, 1595. Berowne says:

> here was a consent,
> Knowing aforehand of our merriment,
> To dash it like a Christmas comedy.

The *Gesta Grayorum*, first published by William Canning in 1688, describes the ceremonies in a way reminiscent of *LLL*. The Christmas season of 1594 was the period of the most elaborate revels (xiii). At one point over eighty-one named individuals were involved in the masque (xiv). In an editorial note to this passage in his Arden edition, R.W. David warns us to be careful of relying too heavily on this single allusion since the custom of Christmas plays was "general." However, the whole business of the Muscovites throughout the act is also reminiscent of the same Gray's Inn entertainment. In general, the revels were intended as training in "all the manners that are learned by the nobility," in the words of one mid-sixteenth-century report of the revels (quoted in David xxv). There is another possible allusion to the ceremony in Berowne's complaint at I.i.48, "Not to see ladies," for in the *Gesta Grayorum* one of the counselors complains: "What, nothing but tasks? Nothing but working days? No feasting, no music, no dancing, no triumphs, no comedies, no love, no ladies?" (quoted in Woudhuysen 5). These topical allusions do not necessarily mean a date of composition of 1594. The Masque of Muscovites could also refer to the visit of the Russian ambassador in 1582, but it is unlikely the play was written that early (Taylor 1). Rupert Taylor also uses the presence of Blackmoors in the Masque as evidence of a topical allusion to the Gray's Inn revels of 1594. In his study of the date of the play, Taylor quotes extensively from the *Gesta Grayorum* and focuses primarily on the presence of the emperor of Russia and his struggles against the Tartars (3).

These historical allusions strongly point to a date of 1594 for the original composition of the play, and most critics accept that date. However, there has not always been a clear critical consensus, and some division still exists. The most often made argument against 1594 is that it does not make the play early enough for some critics who insist on seeing it as one of Shakespeare's earliest plays. Arguments against that position are made elsewhere in this book. However, one can make a very good argument against solely using topical references for dating literary works, as Alfred Harbage does: "Catch-phrases derived from current events do not mean that the writing where they occur has to do with those events, and if the phrases appear in revised writing, they tell us nothing of original date and source of inspiration" (23). Phrases can lie "deeply buried" in a national or social unconscious long after the events with which they were originally associated occurred, especially in the mind of a writer. With this warning in mind, we will proceed to analyze the various topical allusions found in the play and the historical events and personages behind them, keeping in mind that such attributions merely suggest that persons or events were in the national consciousness, at least at the time of writing if not the time of performance.

HENRI IV, KING OF NAVARRE

The fact that Shakespeare gave his young male characters "real" historical names suggests certain dates of composition; however, trying to date the play through a supposed French allusion is as tricky as any other attempt at defining a contemporary reference. Geoffrey Bullough points out that Henri IV, King of Navarre, was the source for Shakespeare's Navarre. Queen Elizabeth had a loose alliance with Henry, who in 1589 had 4,000 English troops sent to him under the command of Lord Willoughby. Navarre's "liaison officer with the English was one Marshal de Biron" (428). Bullough conjectures that Dumain was named after Charles, Duc de Mayenne, one of Henry's opponents. Also appearing in French records of the time are persons named Boyet, Longueville, and Marcade (429). Complicating the appropriateness of these allusions is the fact that Henry of Navarre converted to Roman Catholicism in July 1593. Given the English political and religious sentiments at the time, his conversion would have not only made him the focus of controversy but likely would have lost him whatever English sympathy he might have had before. However, an attempt on his life late in 1594 might again have made him a more sympathetic character. It seems likely that before 1594 any character based on the King of Navarre would have been made an unattractive one, but since the play may possibly date from before either the period of his conversion or after the assassination attempt, these events cannot be used to date the play with any accuracy.

Ultimately there is no reason to assume that these historical figures presented Shakespeare with anything more than topical names. There is nothing in their biographies to suggest that Shakespeare intended to model his play on their actions, nor is the play a political allegory. The "real" history, in fact, has Dumain as an enemy of Henry, not his friend. But, as we will see, the existence of these historical figures does shed some light on Shakespeare's intention in writing the play.

STYLISTICS

There are other kinds of evidence used to date a given text. For example, similarities in language from one play to another can suggest that the two plays were written at roughly the same time. For example, the descriptions of "dark-eyed Rosaline" at I.ii.83 and II.iv.14 suggest a possible connection with *Romeo and Juliet*, which is usually dated at 1595. Additionally, the masked courting scenes in *Romeo and Juliet, The Merchant of Venice* (1596–97) and *Much Ado about Nothing* (1598–99) all suggest similarities with one another. *Richard II* (1595), *Romeo and Juliet*, and *A Midsummer Night's Dream* (1594–96) all contain marked stylistic and thematic similarities with *Love's Labour's Lost*. Given that these three plays are usually dated between 1595 and 1596 and also keeping in mind that stylistic similarities cannot define a specific date, we can see broadly where the play falls in Shakespeare's canon.

Love's Labour's Lost is Shakespeare's most heavily rhymed play, followed by *A Midsummer Night's Dream* and then *Richard II*. The play contains 1,028 rhyming pentameter lines and 579 lines of blank verse— or "one line of blank verse to 1.8 rhyme" (Taylor 10). Much of the rhyme occurs in deliberate patterns—for example, in triplets, quatrains, and the quatrain-couplet six-line stanzas used in *Venus and Adonis*, published in 1592–93. There are no quatrains in the undoubtedly earlier plays, *Henry VI, Titus*, and *Richard III*. They do, however, occur in *The Comedy of Errors, Two Gentlemen of Verona*, and *Merchant of Venice*, all likely written before *LLL*. Taylor suggests that although these facts do not help to date the play precisely, they do preclude it from the earliest group of plays (16). The heavy use of rhyme also suggests a possible link with the narrative poems *Venus and Adonis* and *The Rape of Lucrece* (1593–94). Between August 1592 and the spring of 1594 the London theaters were closed due to an outbreak of the plague. During this time Shakespeare was possibly busy writing or revising the narrative poems, both of which included dedications to the Earl of Southampton. It is also likely that *LLL* was written at this time since Shakespeare was probably preoccupied with poetic diction and rhetoric.

Alfred Harbage calls the attempt to date the play according to "lyrical attributes" the "new orthodoxy," and, according to Harbage, such attempts are wrong. For Harbage, the language of *LLL* does not have the lyrical quality assigned to *Richard II, Midsummer Night's Dream*, or *Romeo and Juliet*, the plays of the lyrical group (24). Rather, language such as the following from Act IV.i.93–100 suggests an earlier play:

> *Princess:* What plume of feathers is he that indited this letter?
> What vane? what weathercock? did you ever hear better?
>
> *Boyet:* I am much deceived but I remember the style.
>
> *Princess:* Else your memory is bad, going o'er it erewhile.
>
> *Boyet:* This Armado is a Spaniard, that keeps here in court;
> A phantasime, a Monarcho, and one that makes sport
> To the prince and his bookmates.
>
> *Princess:* Thou fellow, a word:
> Who gave thee this letter?
>
> *Costard:* I told you; my lord.

To Harbage this is not the poetry of the lyrical group. Rather, it sounds more like the verse in Act I, scene iii of *The Comedy of Errors.* "It is hard to believe that, having adapted so perfectly to his purpose blank verse and the heroic couplet in the plays of the lyrical group (and in parts of *LLL* itself) Shakespeare would have relapsed to doggerel, and considered it appropriate for the witty exchange of royal and noble speakers" (24). Harbage's learned opinions are worth consideration, especially since he acknowledges that parts of *LLL* reflect a sophisticated lyrical style, but he makes the mistake many other critics also make who insist on seeing the play as inferior due to "doggerel": he fails to note that one of Shakespeare's main intentions in the play was to draw a distinction between doggerel and lyrical language, and he could only do so if he included doggerel in the mouths of many of his characters. The doggerel of the play is artistic and dramatic doggerel, not a symptom of a lack of artistry. Therefore, rather than dating the play early to suggest a novice playwright, the play should be dated a little later, when Shakespeare had learned to command language to serve his dramatic purposes.

EVIDENCE FOR AN EARLY DATE

Despite the arguments of critics who insist that the play is not among the earliest of Shakespeare's plays, there has been a long tradition, one that still thrives in some critical agendas, that this is Shakespeare's first play. This assumption is generally based on the opinion of one of Shakespeare's first critics, Charles Gildon, who wrote in 1710 that "since it is one of the worst of Shakespeare's Plays, nay I think I may say the very worst, I cannot but think that it is his first." *Love's Labour's Lost* is undoubtedly a relatively early play; even a date of 1594 would put it before the works generally seen as Shakespeare's most mature work. The question remains as to how early and what its relationship is to other early plays. In many ways *LLL* is a unique play in Shakespeare's canon, yet the aspects of the play that help to date it also show how typical it really is of his canon as a whole. For example, the verse in the play represents some of Shakespeare's most ornate and self-conscious writing, and in turn the role of language in defining characters and marking the class or societal differences between them is a common theme throughout Shakespeare's career. Likewise, the often troubled relationship between the sexes is the subject of most of his comedies. In *The Early Shakespeare*, A.C. Hamilton notes that like the two other early comedies studied in his book (*The Comedy of Errors* and *Two Gentlemen of Verona*), Shakespeare makes use of both classical and contemporary dramatic traditions. For example, Hamilton notes that Shakespeare borrowed frequently from John Lyly. Also, these early plays are as much like a masque or opera in structure as drama in their sparse plot structure and emphasis on diction and the melody of words. Hamilton provides a close analysis of Act IV, noting that the "entire act may be organized into a larger dramatic spectacle" (135) that is centered around an "elaborately organized series of inner plays" that unmask each lord in turn. For Hamilton, this structure is exemplary of the early plays. The best "sketch" of the early Shakespeare, for Hamilton, is seen in the description of Berowne as one whose eyes "begets occasion for his wit . . . " (II.i.69–76). This description serves as a "self-advertisement," possibly suggesting that *LLL* is a pastoral work in which Shakespeare is declaring himself a poet, comparable to Spenser's Colin Clout in *The Shephearde's Calendar* (141) and following a long tradition of pastorals as the first work in a poet's career. Most of the play takes place in a park, a great many of the dominant images and poetic conceits are concerned with nature versus artifice, and the young protagonists are learning how to manage their literary talents. All these attributes are typical of Renaissance pastoral, but of course Hamilton's argument fails if the play is not as early as the others he studies in his book. (Like *LLL*, *The Two Gentlemen of Verona* has been reappraised in recent years and is now seen as a contemporary of *LLL*.) Nonetheless, Hamilton is correct in his citing of these themes as dominant ones in the play.

Alfred Harbage joins Dover Wilson, E.K. Chambers, and Richard David in believing that the play was first performed for a court or great house performance early in Shakespeare's career (18). Harbage suggests that the play was written for one of the child acting troupes of the time, either the Chapel Children or the Paul's theater, the latter of which is Harbage's preference (31). He bases this assumption on five structural qualities of the play: (1) the grouping and balancing of characters, (2) the deference to the unities, (3) the "fairly equitable" distribution of lines among the characters, (4) the emphasis on language over action, and (5) the use of set pieces rather than an integrated plot (29). Add to this the large number of parts calling for non-adult actors (five women and a boy) and the absence of an overtly comic court jester character and *LLL* does begin to look similar to child dramas of the time. Undoubtedly the play was revised at a later date, since, given what we know with certainty about the play's performance history, it was performed in front of both conventional and courtly audiences. However, there is no written record of the play's performance by one of the child companies.

If the play was originally written early in Shakespeare's career, then it would be quite natural for it to reflect his education. *The Comedy of Errors*, for example, is a revision of plays Shakespeare could easily have read in his grammar school, Plautus's *Menaechmi* and Amphitruo. However, unlike *The Comedy*, *LLL* does not rely on another source; the plot is unique to Shakespeare. However, in a monumental study of Shakespeare's early influences, T.W. Baldwin argues that *LLL* is essentially an adaptation of Lyly's *Gallathea* and *Endimion*, and reflects a similar composition style to that used in *The Comedy of Errors*. Since Shakespeare's adaption of the two plays is very general, Baldwin argues that Shakespeare must have adapted them from his memory of a staged play. Lyly's plays were performed during the winter season of 1587–88, and therefore Shakespeare must have gotten his inspiration then (629). Further, since the Spanish Armada, an event that likely provided the name of Armado, occurred in July 1588, a date not much later than 1588 must be accepted. However, it should be added that an event such as the Armada would remain in an audience's and writer's mind for a long time afterward. Artistic minds do not so soon forget events that might be of future dramatic interest. For these reasons, Baldwin argues that any date as late as 1595, putting it in the midst of the lyrical plays, is false, since, Baldwin argues, there is "no evidence for a 'lyrical group' " in Shakespeare's writing and *LLL* is "rhetorical, not lyrical" (635). On this point Baldwin is in agreement with Alfred Harbage.

Not all comparisons to other early plays have been favorable. For example, Blaze Odell Bonazza, in *Shakespeare's Early Comedies: A Structural Analysis*, believes that structurally the play is Shakespeare's weakest. For example, Bonazza argues that "the weakness of plot construction that started with Act II continues to the last scene in Act IV" (71). Ultimately we are "forced to conclude that either the playwright was not concerned with constructing a complex but integrated plot or that he had not yet found the formula which would permit the synchronizing of disparate stories into a unified plot structure" (72). For Bonazza, the play compares negatively to *Midsummer Night's Dream* where Shakespeare does show a command of plot and structure. The play is too dependent on long acts and scenes, illogical arrivals, departures, and coincidences; finally, the overall language of the play is subordinated to character and plot (74). Although Bonazza's comments are dated and overly harsh, they do reflect an often unstated opinion about the play from those critics who relegate it to early in Shakespeare's career: that at best it shows linguistic ability, but as a play it is not a success.

However, such a conclusion does not fit with the known facts of its reception among Shakespeare's contemporaries: the title page tells us that the play was performed in front of Queen Elizabeth and later for Queen Ann. Likewise, a contemporary report of the play, written by Robert Tofte as part of his poem *Alba: The Month's Minde of a Melancholy Lover* (1598), reflects a different opinion about the play: he seems to have enjoyed the play, as did the rest of the audience.

> LOVES LABOR LOST, I once did see a Play,
> Ycleped so, so called to my paine,
> Which I to heare to my small Ioy did stay,

Giuing attendance on my froward Dame,
My misgiuing minde presaging to me Ill,
Yet was I drawne to see it gainst my Will.
This Play no Play, but Plague was vnto me,
For there I lost the Loue I liked most:
And what to others seemde a Jest to be,
I, that (in earnest) found unto my cost,
To every one (saue me) twas Comicall,
Whilst Tragick like to me it did befall.

The "others" in the audience found the play humorous, even if Tofte's melancholic disposition did not allow him to do so. Everything about Tofte's report suggests a play that was popular with a general theater-going audience; it is even possible to further conjecture that by making a reference to the play and subtly comparing his own "loss" of love to a "froward Dame" to the main theme of the play, Tofte is assuming some knowledge of the play years after its first appearance.

REVISION

All evidence for an early date of composition must be seen in light of the considerable evidence for a later revision. It is possible that this later revision was done to make the play more topical, but whatever the reason for its reworking, the revision suggests a play that saw some revival later in its life. One fact that must be considered in dating the play is the supposed first performance in front of Queen Elizabeth; as the title page reads, the play was "presented before her Highnes / this last Christmas. / Newly corrected and augmented." As Woudhuysen notes in his edition of the play, "From 1570 the title-pages of some eighteen plays assert that they were presented before Queen Elizabeth; of these, five got into second or later editions within thirty years of first publication. In three out of these five, the circumstances of the original performance before the Queen are repeated without significant altera-tion—*The Shoemakers' Holiday* (1600) went on claiming it was acted before the Queen on New Year's Day at night in 1610, 1618, 1624, 1631 and 1657." What this suggests is that we do not know with certainty when this performance took place or how many times it was performed for the Queen.

Given the evidence, it is likely that the later revisions to the play were done for the sake of a court performance. T.W. Baldwin, who as we saw

favors an early date, notes that some later revision probably occurred to
the play. For Baldwin, any direct topical allusions would likely be from
a later revision for a courtly audience; for example, the reference to
"piercing a hogshead" at IV.ii.84 is possibly a reference to Harvey's
Pierce's Supererogation, which was most likely published in 1592. (For
more on this controversy, see David xxxii–xxxix.) Given that the text
existed early enough to have influenced Shakespeare's original draft of
the play (and to his credit Baldwin is skeptical that there is necessarily
a connection), the passage was probably added around 1598. Of the
Gray's Inn festivities, Baldwin is again skeptical since the "Russian
theme" and fascination with Russians was common long before the
Gray's Inn festivities of 1594 (639). Given these facts, Baldwin comes
to the conclusion that the play was revised in the second half of 1598
(647).

As the argument goes, as part of that revision Shakespeare inserted
the Show of the Nine Worthies. Baldwin conjectures that Shakespeare
originally intended that at the end of the fourth act the king and his
companions were to escort the ladies from the park to their tents, but
what really happens is that Berowne says, "Then homeward every man
attach the hand/Of his faire Mistres." At this point in the play, however,
the men have not identified their ladies. The Show of the Worthies
"breaks the sequence of thought, at whatever time it was introduced"
(660). Without the show, the last act becomes more dramatically man-
ageable and its size more proportioned to the rest of the play and the
traditional structural role of last acts. However, with the masque, the
play becomes highly ornate and ceremonial, suggesting a courtly masque.
Much like the presentation of the "rude mechanicals" in *MND*, the
Masque and the following Nine Worthies performance suggest a self-
effacing commentary on courtly entertainment. Courtly masques and private performances of plays were notoriously elaborate and expensive,
and sometimes amateurish, spectacles, and both of the performances in
LLL make dramatic sense primarily when seen as commentaries on
courtly entertainment. The fact that they can be excised from the play
with little or no injury to the basic story line reaffirms the belief that
they were later additions.

In her *Riverside Shakespeare* introduction to the play, Anne Barton
observes that the text undoubtedly underwent revision, and notes two
sections, IV.iii.292–314 and V.ii.817–22, as likely candidates for revision given that in both cases Shakespeare seems to have later revised his
words a few lines later. Because they enter so late in the play and serve

no real dramatic purpose, it is likely that the characters of Holofernes and Sir Nathaniel are also later editions. One of the strongest pieces of evidence for revision or for a later date comes from J.W. Lever, who argued in 1952 that Shakespeare had read and referenced John Gerard's *Herbal*, which was first published in 1597. The first stanza of the song by Spring at the end of the play reads, "When daisies pied, and violets blue,/And lady-smocks all silver-white." Gerard writes: "Milke white Ladie smockes that stalkes rising immediately for the root . . . These kinds of Cuckowe flowers . . . " (Barton 212). Although Shakespeare uses "silver-white" rather than "Milke white," his use of "cuckoo-buds of yellow hue" does strongly suggest that he had read this text and remembered the language when it came time to revise the play.

The last line in the play is perhaps the best example of revision, either deliberate or accidental. "You that way; we this way" appears only in the folio edition of the poem. The line could either be Shakespeare's addition or it may be an unauthorized addition, possibly by a typesetter or a stage manager, meant to clear the stage, added accidently either from a marginal note from a prompt text or by a performance-minded editor. Another change is noted by R.W. David, who cites the difference between the folio's "That were to climb o'er the house to unlock the little gate" and the quarto's "Climb o'er the house to unlock the little gate" as evidence of an honest mistake probably on the part of the type-setter. There is nothing in these revisions that suggests a specific date of composition.

PRINTING HISTORY

Love's Labour's Lost was first published in a quarto version in 1598 by William White and later in the first folio in 1623. (A facsimile of the quarto was published in 1888 with an introduction by Frederick J. Fur-nivall.) The folio version is very similar to the first quarto, with only a couple of notable exceptions. The quarto is noteworthy as the first pub-lished play to feature Shakespeare's name as author. As Woudhuysen notes, earlier published plays named the company that acted the play rather than its author, the exception being *2 Henry VI*, which has neither Shakespeare's name nor his company on its title page. In the same year the quarto was published, Shakespeare's name also appeared on the two quartos of *Richard II* and on the second quarto of *Richard III*, all three histories being published by a different publisher, Andrew Wise. That same year his name also appeared on the title pages of the second and third quartos of *Richard II* ("By William Shake-speare"), and on the second quarto of *Richard III* ("By William Shake-speare"). In 1599, Shakespeare is for the first time listed as the author of a work he only contributed to, *The Passionate Pilgrim*. The collection of poems was said to be "By W. Shakespeare" but actually only contained poems from *Love's Labour's Lost*. It would be reasonable to conclude that by 1598 Shakespeare was beginning to make a name for himself as a playwright and publishers found him to be a marketable commodity. Like *Romeo and Juliet, LLL* was never entered into the Stationers' Register.

The 1598 quarto, of which fourteen copies still exist, is generally considered one of Shakespeare's best and most reliable quartos. Nonetheless, the quarto does contain several textual problems, not the least of which is the inclusion of two versions of Berowne's defense of love at 4.3. The first quarto was likely set from "foul papers," a writer's rough draft or working draft, and as a result contains several mistakes. The two versions of the play reflected in the quarto and later folio give us a glimpse of Shakespeare revising his own work. Both plays were published by Cuthbert Burby and therefore to some extent the claim to newness on their respective title pages could be merely a sales pitch. On the other hand, the dating problems associated with the play suggest that Shakespeare possibly returned to the play over a span of several years and that the play as it was published in the first quarto might actually resemble a carefully revised and augmented edition of the play.

EDITING AND THE PROBLEM OF REVISION

One of the major problems of the quarto is that in Act II, scene i there is great confusion about which of the ladies is being wooed by Berowne and Dumain. The problem is that Berowne seems to flirt with two women, first Katherine and then Rosaline. Dumain seems interested in Rosaline and Berowne in Katherine, yet the rest of the play makes it clear that Shakespeare intended Berowne to woo Rosaline and Dumaine Katherine. There are two explanations for the confusion. First, Shakespeare may have intended the confusion and meant for the ladies to be masked, but apparently Shakespeare did not adequately revise the scene once he moved the mask scene to Act V, scene 2. Another view is that Shakespeare simply had not decided on the ladies' names, and that the confusion made it into print (Wells 138). What both of these alternatives suggest is that the quarto was faulty, not an uncommon occurrence by Elizabethan printing standards, and that some corrections needed to be made for the folio. Renaissance proofreading was not very thorough, at least by modern standards, due to many factors, not the least of which is a lack of education on the part of the printers, who often only caught particularly egregious errors. Even the more literate proofreaders, who took care to read the manuscript, even if they did so quickly, often "cared little whether a combination of letters made a word, but cared more that a combination of words made sense" (Werstine 40). Proofreaders also often ignored or overlooked simple typographical mistakes (41).

The issues surrounding how the quarto came to be revised for the folio are enormously complicated and beyond the scope of this discussion. Anyone wanting to wade further into the debate should start with Wells's overview. He summarizes the three possibilities, the last of which suggests a now lost corrected and more authoritative edition of the play. In the first, championed by John Dover Wilson in his New Shakespeare edition of 1923, the corrections were the result of someone involved in the theater who needed to clean up the text, and that the corrections may not be the result of Shakespeare's hand (something all three alternatives leave open—we simply do not know who made these corrections). The second possibility, championed by Walter Greg, in *The Shakespeare First Folio* (Oxford, 1954) and *The Editorial Problem in Shakespeare* (Oxford, 1942), suggests that someone in a publishing house made the corrections in an attempt to "fix" the old quarto for the publication of the folio. Finally, Wells's own opinion suggests that someone with access to a more authoritative text than the quarto made the revisions. This last alternative seems to be best supported by the evidence. Nonetheless, we must remember that Elizabethan printers made numerous mistakes, and therefore we can never know with certainty where Shakespeare's hand ends and the printer's begins. Modern readers often take for granted that the text they read is the text as written by the author, but such stability is foreign to Renaissance textual practices. In addition to sloppy editing and an overall relaxed attitude toward consistency and accuracy, Renaissance printed plays were sometimes written solely by the author, who controlled what went into them and what was taken out, and sometimes were recorded performances, separated from the intentions of the writer by any number of factors such as actors ad-libbing or forgetting lines to last-minute revisions by a director or stage manager. In short, it is the arduous task of an editor to recreate the most likely and pleasing version of an author's work.

It is always important to remember when reading Shakespeare that all printed editions of the plays take editorial liberties with the original quartos (and later folios) in an attempt to make the play more "readable." Take the following example of IV.iii.247–250, quoted in the original spelling and punctuation of the quarto:

> O who can giue an oth? Where is a booke?
> That I may sweare Beautie doth beautie lacke,
> If that she learne not of her eye to looke:
> No face is fayre that is not full so blacke.

To these lines the king responds:

> O paradox, Blacke is the badge of Hell,
> The hue of dungions, and the Schoole of night.

Undoubtedly, there are punctuation problems with this passage in the quarto. Why the seeming random capitalization? Is the comma after "dungeons" necessary? However, one influential edition of the play, the New Cambridge Edition, edited by Sir Arthur Quiller Couch and John Dover Wilson, punctuates the passage according to an a priori opinion, specifically that "Schoole of night" refers to an "actual coterie," in the words of Ernest Strathman in his essay on this passage (177), and that Shakespeare is making a topical reference to that school. According to this belief, the "School of Night" is a reference to Raleigh's infamous school and secret organization centered around agnostic and mystic practices. Believing that this is the case, the New Cambridge editors take the liberty of capitalizing "Night" and removing the comma after "dungeons," so that the passage reads:

> O paradox! Black is the badge of hell,
> The hue of dungeons and the School of Night.

If allowed to stand as it appears in the quarto, "blacke" becomes the figurative teacher of "night," just as it is the "badge of hell" and the "hue of dungeons." As soon as editors try to impose modern grammatical conventions to the messy quarto or folio versions of plays, biases often become the guiding light rather than simplicity or clarity. The Signet edition (like the Arden) reads: "O paradox! Black is the badge of hell, The hue of dungeons, and the school of night" (lines 253–254 in Signet). Although the Signet editor does not highlight "School of Night" by capitalization, he does lower the uppercase "S" from the quarto and makes

"O paradox" a separate explanation. Oddly, the Norton edition (textually based on the Oxford) changes "Schoole" to "style," which has no support from either the quarto or folio. These examples remind us that no editorial decision is bias free, and each is closely tied with critical opinion. In the case of the New Cambridge, the whole play becomes a potential topical allusion to a school that, according to Ernest Strathman, probably never existed.

In addition to editing for grammatical meaning, editors must also contend with questionable augmentation of texts. *Love's Labour's Lost* is particularly affected by additions, most likely by Shakespeare as he revised the text. These revisions led some critics to ask what Shakespeare originally intended for the now lost, original work. Henry David Gray, in *The Original Version of Love's Labour's Lost, with A Conjecture as to Love's Labour's Won*, carefully reconstructs what he sees as the "original," pre-1597 play, basing his argument on obvious textual mistakes and unusual or sudden entrances or exits. According to Gray, removing what are possibly additions of 1597 cuts the play to half its length (19). The number of prose lines still remains high, reminding us of the influence of John Lyly's prose comedies, discussed more in the next chapter. Some of Gray's suggested cuts are as follows:

Act I, i—Gray cuts lines 1–10 and questions 24–33; ii remains

Act II, i—omits lines 1–20. (Minor characters may have been introduced in a proposed second scene.)

Act III, i—the scene remains as printed

Act IV, i—omits lines 1–4 and omits from line 110 to end of scene

ii—omits whole scene and Berowne's sonnet in next scene

iii—questions Longaville's sonnet, lines 60–73, inserts Berowne's sonnet after line 219; omits lines 220–281; questions lines 305–308; omits lines 318–354; questions lines 363–365 and 370–380.

Predictably, given the final shape of the play, the most changes occurred to Act V. Gray omits all of scene i, and, in scene ii, he questions lines 315–334 and omits line 462, 492–509, and lines 515–549. He questions as "doggerel" lines 543–549 and cuts "Bigness of Pompey" in 453–455. Lines 559–564 and 565–634 are, to Gray, possibly rewritten by someone other than Shakespeare. Lines 882–888 constitute the original ending. The play that remains is 1,912 lines long, of which 541 lines are prose,

346 are blank verse, with 778 pentameter lines (22). Although Gray's attempt at restoring a "lost play" is admirable, many of his methods, such as cutting what seems superfluous or awkward, is highly questionable, as is his refusal to see "doggerel" as an important dramatic part of the play. Nonetheless, he reminds us that what we read as *Love's Labour's Lost* is the product of revision and editorial adulteration.

Most editors take it for granted that the original quarto requires some revision to be readable to modern readers and audiences. This assumption leaves no room for the possibility that the quartos might be right despite seeming contradictions or awkwardness. It should not be forgotten that often quartos and folios were play texts or performance scripts. This point is made passionately by Homer Swandler in "*Love's Labor's Lost*: Burn the Parasols, Play the Quarto!" Swandler sees the quarto of 1598 as the "original script" of *LLL*. All editions since that of Lewis Theobald in 1734 have made changes to Shakespeare's script and "unscripted" the quarto (53). To support his assertion that this is a problem, Swandler cites several examples. For example, at I.ii.136, Costard says, "Come Jaquenetta, away," and yet in the Quarto he does not leave, though she does. The quarto stage direction states "exeunt." To make sense of the contradiction, modern editors often give the line to Dull—it is Dull and Jaquenetta who leave. However, Swandler argues that this violates Dull's character since elsewhere in the play he does not speak unless necessary (53). Stage actions can take care of any ambiguities—one possibility is that Costard speaks the line, starts to move Jaquenetta off stage, but is stopped by the jealous Armado, who speaks next, "Villain, thou shalt fast for thy offences ere thou be pardoned" (146). As a rule, when the text seems to not make sense literally, actors can be trusted to invent comic business that makes sense of the script theatrically (53).

It is also not uncommon for modern editors to take lines or speeches out of the mouths of characters and assign them to other, more convenient characters. This is a "particularly audacious editorial act" in the words of Swandler (54). This practice is illustrated in another exchange from the first scene:

> *Longaville:* Marry, that did I.
>
> *Berowne:*   Sweete lord and why?
>
> *Longaville:* To fright them hence with that dread penalty.
> A dangerous law against gentility!
> Item. If any man be seen to talk with a woman within
> the terms

of three years, he shall endure such public shame as the
rest of the

court can possibly devise.

Berowne: This Article my liege yourself must break . . . (I.i.124–
132)

Despite the original stage directions, modern texts give the other four
lines ("A danger law against . . . ") to Berowne. However, dramatically
it seems obvious that "A dangerous law" is a criticism of Longaville,
not a comment by him (56). This example is characteristic because it
illustrates the importance of distinguishing between a play script and a
literary text. For Swandler it can be argued that the characters are more
surprising and theatrical in the quarto due to its inherent contradictions
and seeming discrepancies. In this scene, for example, leaving the lines
as in the quarto suggests a tension between characters. In all, Swandler
points to five moments in the play in which modern editors have reas-
signed speeches, and in each case he can find a dramatic reason for using
the quarto as it was originally published. His final example, the Rosaline–
Katherine triangle, is his most persuasive. Leaving the "confusion" in
the text results in a more dynamic (and "realistic") view of Berowne,
who first makes a play for Katherine in the first "duet," then for Rosaline,
and then back to Katherine, and, finally, settles on Rosaline (66–68). As
any editor of any modern edition of the play will attest, this seeming
confusion must be rectified for a reader, who, without the benefit of stage
action and interaction, will easily become confused by the static text.
"To edit Shakespeare's sonnets and narrative poems is to undertake a
literary task. To edit his scripts is to undertake a theatrical task" (72).
Finally, Swandler concludes that editors should trust "the original texts
far longer and more deeply" than they usually do and that they should
"explore and test theatrical texts with theatrical methods in theatrical
arenas" (73). As readers we should do the same. Doing so will allow us
to avoid many of the negative opinions about the play that less theatrically conscious critics have had.

In addition to the problems of textual editing already noted, *LLL* presents a special problem: the extensive use of Latin throughout the play.
Shakespeare was well trained in Latin, receiving an education in it that
would rival the average classics graduate today (Binns 119). We must
acknowledge that, if he wanted to, he could have gotten his Latin correct
in his plays. Yet in *LLL* there are numerous mistakes in the Latin, leading
to an important editorial question: are the errors in Latin deliberate—

that is, for dramatic effect—or the result of corruption on the part of printers or scribes? Furthermore, the lack of spelling conventions in Renaissance English does not hold for Latin—it was fixed in terms of spelling due to the existence of the original classical texts. Since passages of original Latin, (i.e., Latin composed by Shakespeare) are infrequent in the plays and absent in *LLL*, there is even less room for mistakes. In *LLL* and *Merry Wives of Windsor*, "Latin, and especially its misuse and misunderstanding, contributes to the characterization and is a source for comic effect, bringing into the plays familiar echoes of the dust pedantry of the schoolroom" (120).

The first example of a problem presented by Latin is the use of "Celo" at IV.ii.5 in both the quarto and folio. Certainly, from the context, Holofernes means "heavens." Is there a mistake in the line and, if so, is it Shakespeare's or the printer's? Most modern editors either correct the line or try to find an explanation for why it is seemingly butchered. However, according to the conventions of Elizabethan spelling, this is not a "mistake": if "e" and "ae" are treated as the same sound, then "celo" is the same as "caelo" and therefore there is no confusion. Another problematic use of Latin is at IV.ii.92–93 when Holofernes seems to garble a line from Mantuan's first eclogue: *"Fauste, precor gelida quando pecus omne sub umbra Ruminat,"* translated, "I pray thee, Faustus, when all your entire flock is resting in the cool shade . . . " What Holofernes says, however, as printed in the quarto, is *"Facile precor gelida quando pecus omne sub umbra. Ruminat . . . "* ("Easily, I say, you are making a mess of everything under the shade; it ruminates.") Is this Shakespeare's mistake, or a printing mistake? The editor of the Signet edition corrects the original from Mantuan: *"Fauste, precor, gelida quando pecus omne sub umbra ruminat."* The Arden and Riverside retain the first word from the quarto and read *"Facile precor gelida quando pecus omne sub ruminat."* R.W. David wisely notes that "a line so well known and so recently notorious could hardly be misquoted by Shakespeare. Surely the blunder is Holofernes"—it would be consistent with his character (81). Thus, the quarto is "correct," dramatically, except for the double l in "gelida," which is not detectable in speech. Thus, those who know Latin and had studied Mantuan in school would easily understand the intended joke. Ironically, editors who insist on Holofernes's correct pronunciation end up "fixing" a passage that is not broken. The extensive use of Latin, and to a lesser extent French, Spanish, and perhaps Italian, added to the extensive word play and use of colloqualisms by the lower-class characters, makes *LLL* a particularly difficult text to edit. Many of these issues only surface as problems when the play is treated as a text rather than as a performance piece. Whereas *LLL* is one of the most representative plays of Shakespeare's time and place due to its linguistic exuberance, it is likewise a representative commentary on modern textual practices and fixations on "correctness": all critics and editors are, to some extent, like Holofernes, arguing over the correct way to pronounce "debt."

On January 22, 1607, Nicholas Ling appropriated from Cuthbert Burby the publishing rights for *LLL* as well as *Romeo and Juliet* and *The Taming of the Shrew*. The following November these three plays, along with *Hamlet*, became the property of John Smethwick, one of the eventual publishers of the first folio of 1623. The first folio version follows the 1598 quarto with little variation. There are some important corrections in the folio, namely in regards to speech prefixes and headings. There is also the addition of the final line of the play, "You that way; we this way" and about 250 relatively minor variants. The best discussion of the differences between the first quarto and the folio is to be found in Stanley Wells's "The Copy for the Folio Text of *Love's Labour's Lost.*"

EARLY EDITIONS OF THE PLAY

As we have noted throughout, editors can have a profound, and sometimes troubling, influence on the reception of Shakespeare's text. Starting with the first folio, collected works of Shakespeare have been the most widely read and, as a result, the most carefully edited. Given the popularity of collections, it is no surprise that through them the most lavish attempts have been made to model Shakespeare's image. The first critical edition of Shakespeare's plays, (i.e., one that added critical apparatus and attempted to edit them into a coherent picture of Shakespeare) was Nicholas Rowe's edition of 1709. Rowe was the first to add the list of dramatis personae that modern readers take for granted, and he was the first to consistently divide plays into acts and scenes and to mark entrances and exits. However, despite his additions to the text, Rowe's edition remained true to the original quartos and folios.

Unlike Rowe's generally unabridged texts, Alexander Pope's edition of 1723 cut whole pages from the text, relegating them to the bottom of the page. Although he used Rowe's edition as his guide, he believed that a critic should find what is best about a work or writer and praise that. He excised a great deal of Shakespeare's text with the hope of making

the plays more acceptable to refined tastes. Those sections he felt were
not tasteful he placed at the bottom of the page, out of context, and those
he felt were most problematic he marked with a dagger to note that he
wished he had the authority to cut out altogether. Pope believed *LLL*
was the worst play, but he did, however, praise Berowne's speech in Act
IV—"But love is first learned in a lady's eyes." Those passages Pope
wished he had the authority to leave out occur most frequently in *LLL*,
including the Masque of the Muscovites. As Irene Dash notes, in Pope's
hands *LLL* became a "thin comedy" (14). In fact, by the third printing
of his edition, Pope threw out *LLL* altogether (along with *Comedy of
Errors, Titus Andronicus,* and *Winter's Tale*).

One of Pope's rivals was Lewis Theobald, whose *Preface to the Works
of Shakespeare,* published in 1734, was the object of much criticism and
scorn from Pope, who labeled Theobald the "piddling Theobald." To a
certain extent Pope was correct: Theobald was very meticulous in his
editing, paying careful attention to textual variants. In this way Theobald
could be called the first "professional" Shakespearian to edit the text.
Theobald responded to Pope in a later edition of his collected works of
Shakespeare by making some 200 corrections to Pope's edition. His arguments with Pope were primarily over style—where Pope was polite
and gentile, Theobald was more scholarly and objective. Fortunately,
with a few exceptions, Theobald set the standard for modern editions of
Shakespeare with their lengthy footnotes and scholarly glosses. Given
this attention to linguistic details, it should come as little surprise that
LLL presents a special challenge to modern editors.

Pope hoped to make Shakespeare more polite and refined, a tradition
that remains today for many critics—for example, those who hold the
belief that still circulates, despite the evidence to the contrary, that either
Shakespeare attended Oxford or was himself a front for a gentlemanly
writer. Although none of the editors considered here is guilty of such
fancy, the earliest critics and editors of Shakespeare's work did attempt
to use Shakespeare to support more conservative aesthetic agendas. For
example, Samuel Johnson, in his edition of the play in 1765, noted of
LLL:

> In this play, which all the editors have concurred to censure, and
> some have rejected as unworthy of our poet, it must be confessed
> that there are many passages mean, childish, and vulgar; and some
> which ought not to have been exhibited, as we are told they were,
> to a maiden queen. But there are scattered, through the whole, many

sparks of genius; nor is there any play that has more evident marks
of the hand of Shakespeare. (182)

Like Pope, Johnson hoped to make Shakespeare more palatable to
eighteenth-century tastes; in short, he wished to make him an eighteenth-
century writer. Like Pope, Johnson omitted many lines of bawdy or sex-
ually connotative language. Again, as Irene Dash notes, many of these
lines not only rid the play of suggestive language, but caused a distortion
in how the audience came to understand many of the characters. In
Pope's edition, the most damaged character was the princess, who had
many of her lines relegated to the bottom of the page, including a great
deal of the honest but bawdy discussion of the men by the women.

MODERN EDITIONS

Given the complicated linguistic nature of *LLL*, modern editors since
Theobald and Pope have found the play particularly challenging. Of all
of Shakespeare's plays, *LLL* is the one for which first-time readers will
find a good scholarly edition indispensable. Modern editions of the play
begin with the Variorum Shakespeare project, edited by Horace Howard
Furness, of which *LLL* is Volume XIV. Published in 1904, it compiled
all the significant critical opinion of the play to that date to create what
is still one of the most complete textual studies of the play. Furness's
brief introduction compares the play to *Much Ado About Nothing* both
in terms of the reliance upon the quarto as the primary source of the
play and in the comparison of Berowne and Rosaline to Benedick and
Beatrice. Furness also includes a very brief overview of the debt Shakespeare owed to John Lyly. The appendixes, consisting of brief excerpts
from applicable criticism, include sections on the date of composition,
sources of the plot, and English, German, and French criticism, as well
as a bibliography.

The Yale edition, edited by Wilbur L. Cross and Tucker Brooke, was
published in 1925. Obviously now dated, this edition nonetheless contains excellent endnotes to a few problematic passages, but overall it
does not put a lot of emphasis on textual or editorial issues. It contains
brief appendixes on the sources of the play, the original text and revisions, the history of the play, the text and "Suggestions for Collateral
Reading," as well as a glossary. In their notes on the sources for the
play, the editors make an interesting observation regarding Marlowe's
Massacre at Paris as a possible source for Shakespeare's use of the

names Navarre and Dumain, and also point out that in Marlowe's play the two are enemies (128).

The original New Cambridge edition, published in 1923 and edited by Sir Arthur Quiller-Couch and John Dover Wilson, set the standard for textual editing of the play. Although in the introduction the editors arrive at the questionable conclusion that the play is necessarily a topical one and that "most, if not all, of its characters were meant by Shakespeare to be portraits or caricature of living persons" (xvi), they do an excellent job of summarizing the scholarship on the subject as it stood in 1923. The textual notes at the end of the edition are excellent, as is the exhaustive section entitled "Copy for the text of 1598," which argues that the quarto of 1598 was a prompt book.

In 1962, John Dover Wilson revised the Cambridge edition. In his "Preface to the Second Edition," he outlines the changes that he instituted in the new edition, including extensive changes in punctuation and the "regularizing" of Latin, a decision based on the theory that the mistakes in Latin, primarily by the pedants, were mistakes originating in the printing shop and not intended by Shakespeare. Wilson also wisely tempers many of his and Quiller-Couch's original conclusions about the topicality of the play, although he develops a new theory that Holofernes is in fact a caricature of Thomas Harriot (xvi–xviii). The "Copy" appendix remains largely unchanged, except for a revision in the original argument regarding the quarto's relation to a prompt book. The glossary is greatly expanded.

Given the advancements and achievements of the Arden 2nd and 3rd editions, the 1st series has very little to recommend it, except as an historical example of topical criticism gone mad, citing Lodge's *Looking-Glass for London and England* (1591–92) as a possible source for some of Shakespeare's language in the play (xiii). In addition, the editor, H.C. Hart, has included an insightful discussion of the language of the play in the context of late sixteenth-century literature (xxix–xlii). In keeping with the Arden's tradition of providing in-depth philological notes, Hart's textual notes are extensive and served as the basis for the second Arden edition. Although also now somewhat dated, the 2nd Arden *Love's Labour's Lost* (1951) is indispensable for issues of language and a thorough treatment of topical allusions. For this reason, it is the edition I have relied on for this book. Edited by R.W. David, who comes to the somewhat suspect conclusion that "all the evidence, then, goes to show that *Love's Labour's Lost* was a battle in a private war between court factions" (xliii), it still remains the best overall textual edition of the play, a trait common to the first two series of Arden editions. David's introduction includes a thorough discussion of the textual history of the play, which effectively outlines the evidence for revision and the textual problems of the first quarto, a discussion of the date of composition (David favors the 1593–94 season), and sections on both the probable sources and the "topical context."

The 3rd series Arden *Love's Labour's Lost*, edited by H.R. Woudhuysen, newly edits and glosses the play, with the result that there is less emphasis on topical allusions and philological concerns and more on paraphrasing and contextualizing of challenging passages. In addition, Woudhuysen has incorporated much of the criticism of the play that had been written since the earlier Arden. Woudhuysen's lengthy introduction includes requisite sections on the plot, date, and sources, but he also adds sections on the relationship between words and things in the play as well as discussion of the influence of Sir Philip Sidney on the themes and plot of the play. Finally, Woudhuysen includes appendixes on textual variants, the etymology of Moth's name, and a list of rhymes and compound words in the play.

The Signet Classic Shakespeare edition (1965) includes "Shakespeare: Prefatory Remarks" by Sylvan Barnet and an introduction by John Arthos, who edited the text. As with the Signet series in general, this is a good edition for first-time readers of the play, as Arthos treats most of the technical questions, such as dating and topical sources, briefly, and in his introduction focuses on the theme of love. His notes are much briefer than most other editions, and he generally focuses on glosses of difficult passages. The best feature of the Signet edition texts are the short excerpts from significant critical commentaries; in this edition he includes Walter Pater's influential discussion of the play, Northrop Frye's definition of comedy, and an essay each from Richard David and John Arthos on the play in performance. Finally, Arthos includes a fairly exhaustive "For Further Reading" section, revised and brought up to date for the early 1980s.

The Oxford Shakespeare edition of *Love's Labour's Lost*, edited by G.R. Hibbard, was published in 1990. The introduction opens with a survey of the stage history of the play, attributing its newfound popularity on its "unfinished state . . . in which the text has come down to us" (10). The most extensive section of the introduction, entitled "The Play," is a thorough analysis of the play's dramatic structure. Hibbard seems most interested in issues pertinent to performance or the theater, and to that end he emphasizes the tone of the play and the dramatic develop-

ment or motivation of many of its characters. Also included is an overview of "The Date and 'Source' " and "The Text." In keeping with
modern editorial practices of the play, the text is based on the quarto
with the folio variants noted. The extensive textual notes provide glosses,
paraphrases, and grammatical analysis. Included as an appendix is an
interesting "Note on the Music" by John Caldwell.

The New Folger Library series, edited by Barbara Mowat and Paul
Werstine, is designed to give students a well-edited text of Shakespeare's
plays, usually based on the earliest printed text. Their *LLL* is therefore
based on the first quarto, with significant variations from the folio edition. The Folger series is helpful because of the inclusion of both act
and scene summaries and facing page textual notes. The prefatory material is aimed at novice readers and includes a section on "Reading
Shakespeare's Language" and a brief biography. The edition concludes
with an essay by William Carroll ("*Love's Labour's Lost*: A Modern
Perspective") that emphasizes Shakespeare's dramatic use of language.
Also included is a helpful "Further Reading" section.

An excellent single edition of Shakespeare's plays, *The Riverside
Shakespeare*, includes a very good introduction by Harry Levin covering
the historical context and language of the plays and an introduction to
twentieth-century criticism by Heather Dubrow. The influential introduction to *LLL* is by Anne Barton. She notes that the play is "perhaps the
most relentlessly Elizabethan of all Shakespeare's plays" (208). After
acknowledging that the play is verbally rooted to Shakespeare's age, she
notes that "it can communicate its quality and concerns to a modern
audience which, although it may not be able to explain just why 'a
costard broken in a shin' (III.i.70) should be funny, responds to the
freshness and brilliance of the comedy just the same" (208). Barton goes
on to note the similarities between *A Midsummer Night's Dream* and
Love's Labour's Lost and to discuss the theme of gender as it relates to
the action and language of the play. She contrasts how the men use
"unexamined conceits" while the women are literal minded (210). In the
end, the play is about contradictions: it is about the power and beauty
of language, but ends on a note of suspicion about it (211).

The Norton Shakespeare (1997) is based on the Oxford Shakespeare,
using its textual notes and variants. The footnotes and introductions are
original to the Norton edition, and *LLL* is prefaced by Walter Cohen.
Under the guidance of general editor Stephen Greenblatt, the Norton has
a decided new-historicist inclination, which is illustrated in Cohen's preface. Although not to be recommended for novice readers, the Norton has

a great deal to offer readers who seek to better understand the cultural and historical contexts of the plays. Greenblatt's "General Introduction" and Andrew Gurr's essay on the Shakespearian stage are particularly helpful and insightful. Cohen's introduction to the play likewise focuses on the political figures who serve as the backdrop for the play, and Cohen noted the "ambivalence" with which Shakespeare treats these events.

WORKS CITED

Arthos, John, ed. *Love's Labor's Lost*. Signet Classic Shakespeare. New York: Signet Classic, 1988.

Baldwin, T.W. *Shakespeare's Five-Act Structure: Shakespeare's Early Plays on the Background of Renaissance Theories of Five-Act Structure from 1470*. Urbana: University of Illinois Press, 1947.

Barton, Anne. Introduction. *Riverside Shakespeare*. 2nd ed. Ed. G. Blakemore Evans. Boston: Houghton Mifflin, 1997. 208–212.

Binns, J.W. "Shakespeare's Latin Citations: The Editorial Problem." *Shakespeare Survey* 45 (1987): 119–128.

Bland, Desmond, ed. *Gesta Grayorum, or the History of the High and Mighty Prince Henry Prince of Purpoole*. English Reprint Series, #22. Liverpool: Liverpool University Press, 1923.

Bullough, Geoffrey. *Narrative and Dramatic Sources of Shakespeare*. Vol. 1. London: Routledge, 1957.

Dash, Irene G. *Wooing, Wedding, and Power: Women in Shakespeare's Plays*. New York: Columbia University Press, 1981.

David, Richard W., ed. *Love's Labour's Lost*. Arden Shakespeare. 2nd series. London: Routledge, 1994.

Gray, Henry David. *The Original Version of Love's Labour's Lost, with A Conjecture as to Love's Labour's Won*. Stanford: Leland Stanford Junior University Publications, Stanford University, 1918.

Greenblatt, Stephen, gen. ed. *The Norton Shakespeare*. New York: W.W. Norton and Company, 1997.

Greg, Walter. *The Editorial Problem in Shakespeare*. Oxford: Oxford University Press, 1942.

——— *The Shakespeare First Folio*. Oxford: Oxford University Press, 1954.

Hamilton, A.C. "The Early Comedies: *Love's Labour's Lost*." *The Early Shakespeare*. San Marino: The Huntington Library, 1967.

Harbage, Alfred. "*Love's Labor's Lost* and the Early Shakespeare." *Philological Quarterly* 41 (1962): 18–36.

Hart, H.C., ed. *Love's Labour's Lost*. The Arden Shakespeare. 1st series. London: Methuen, 1930.

Hibbard, G.R., ed. *Love's Labour's Lost*. The Oxford Shakespeare. Oxford: Clarendon Press, 1990.

Johnson, Samuel. *Samuel Johnson on Shakespeare*. Ed. H.R. Woudhuysen. London: Penguin, 1989.

Mowat, Barbara, and Paul Werstine, ed. *Love's Labor's Lost*. The New Folger Shakespeare Library. New York: Washington Square Press, 1996.

Strathman, E.A. "The Textual Evidence for 'The School of the Night.' " *Modern Language Notes* 56 (1941): 176–86.

Swandler, Homer. "*Love's Labor's Lost*: Burn the Parasols, Play the Quarto!" *Shakespeare's Sweet Thunder*. Ed. Michael J. Collins. Newark: University of Delaware Press, 1997.

Taylor, Rupert. *The Date of Love's Labour's Lost*. New York: AMS Press, 1966.

Wells, Stanley. "The Copy for the Folio Text of *Love's Labour's Lost*." *The Review of English Studies* 33 (1982): 137–147.

Werstine, Paul. "Variants in the First Quarto of *Love's Labour's Lost*." *Shakespeare Studies* 12 (1979): 35–47.

Wilson, John Dover, and Arthur Quiller-Couch, eds. *Love's Labour's Lost*. New Shakespeare. Cambridge: Cambridge University Press, 1923.

Woudhuysen, H.R., ed. *Love's Labour's Lost*. Arden Shakespeare. 3rd series. Walton-on-Thames: Thomas Nelson and Sons, 1998.

2

CONTEXTS AND SOURCES

Love's Labour's Lost is one of three Shakespeare plays with no known source, joining *A Midsummer Night's Dream (MND)* and *The Tempest*. These three plays give us an opportunity to consider Shakespeare's composition methods in ways that other plays do not. How, for example, did Shakespeare conceive of plot? When left on his own to develop motives and actions for his characters, what did he do? One thing that all three plays have in common is a reliance on artifice and artistry as a major theme: in *The Tempest* it resides most clearly in Prospero's books ("But this rough magic/I here adjure") (V.i.50–51) and in *MND* in the play of the rude mechanicals. When Berowne says at the end of *LLL* that "Our wooing does not end like an old play," Shakespeare seems to be self-conscious of the limitations of his art. Likewise, *LLL* shares with the two plays a fascination with imagination and fancy. Chronologically, *LLL* probably comes right before *MND*, which explains the particularly close affinity between the two plays. Most important, all three plays have "local" influences, that is, sources for particular scenes or characters, but none have a basic source for the plot; in all three, Shakespeare is solely responsible for the main story line. According to Stanley Wells, there are other telling resemblances between the three plays, all of which center around comparisons with *MND* (60). For example, in *MND* Shakespeare arranges his characters in groups, such as a series of romantic couples and lower-class characters whose lives and actions parallel those of the upper class, just as he does in *LLL*. Finally, the last act in both *LLL* and *MND* is given over to a play-within-a-play, while the masque in *The Tempest* occurs late in the play, in Act IV. In all three plays, the action is commented on by the characters, and courtesy, proper behavior and social roles are emphasized by the responses of the audiences to the play (although Stanley Wells notes, as do others, that in *MND* the characters are more polite in their criticism of the play [62]). The masques in *MND, LLL*, and *The Tempest* are all interrupted; in *The Tempest* it is interrupted by Prospero's remembrance of Caliban, while in *LLL*, Marcade, like Caliban, a servant character not in the masque, interrupts with serious news.

Like *LLL, The Tempest* also has a "highly schematic structure" (64), and is less episodic than the other romances and more like *MND* and *LLL*. All three plays take place in "a place apart" (Wells 68) where the characters are free to let their imaginations go. This last characteristic, however, is common in many plays that do have a clear source, especially the comedies *Twelfth Night* and *As You Like It*, and should not be seen as a characteristic of Shakespeare's plot development. Finally, all three plays represent a "preoccupation on the part of the dramatist with his own art" (69).

"The resemblances among these three plays may suggest that, left to his own inventive powers, Shakespeare was apt to confine himself to a comparatively narrow range of techniques and themes" (Wells 72). Finally, the three plays, quoting Johnson, "repose in a mode of thinking congenial to his nature," for they "reveal something of his personal concerns, especially in relation to his art" (Johnson 74). Johnson is typically insightful here, for as we will see, much of the criticism of the play has centered around what the play reveals about the historical man Shakespeare. It is ironic that the language and artistry of the play, two components of Shakespeare's art that need the least explanation in terms of source, are for many of the critics of the play the main focus of debate.

R.W. David disagrees with the accepted opinion that there is no source for the plot and notes that there is some reason to think that a source for the play did exist but is now lost (David xxviii). He reasons that the 1598 quarto's title page describes the play as "newly corrected and augmented," which could suggest either the existence of an earlier version of the play by Shakespeare, or an unlicensed and now lost separate play. However, that source has never been found, so, predictably, critics often turn to contemporary events and personages in their search for possible sources. In many ways, such attributions often create more problems than solutions, especially when attempts are made to trace the author's imaginative threads back to precise biographical persons. However, such attempts are not without merit, since all this critical speculation reminds us that what is most interesting about the play's various "sources" is that they all point to the cultural and societal fabric of Shakespeare's time and the play's uniquely close relationship to it.

TOPICAL SOURCES

As Johnson reminds us, there is no doubt that *LLL* is Shakespeare's most "contemporary" play in the sense that it reveals a great deal about the attitudes and habits of Shakespeare's England. Most of these attitudes are centered around the pedagogical and linguistic habits of Shakespeare's contemporaries. Nonetheless, a great deal of the play's reputation is still based on problematic opinions about who or what Shakespeare was cryptically referring to in the play. Rather than acknowledging that the play is valuable enough for what it suggests about Shakespeare's poetic sensibilities, many readers want to find evidence in the play for what often seems like a literary conspiracy theory—surely the play's now elusive qualities are a result of then cryptic references, and the whole play suggests a playwright "in the know" and secretly sharing his knowledge and opinion with an initiated coterie. There are obvious flaws with this logic, the least of which is that Shakespeare did not adopt this type of referencing in any other work, and no strong evidence exists that he had a reason to do so here. In discussing these topical allusions, it is important to heed the warning of E.A. Strathman:

> The endless game of finding topical allusions in Elizabethan literature, when it is not played in open rebellion against the rules of common sense, requires that the suggestion of secondary meanings rests upon something more than coincidence between the poet's fiction and the historian's fact. The harmony, real or fancied, between the incidents of a tale and events contemporaneous with the telling can produce a host of rival and mutually contradictory "interpretations" of a single work. What is needed is a link between the story and event, some evidence, internal or external, that the writer intended the application proposed by his interpreter. (176)

In addition, I would add, what is necessary is a rudimentary understanding of how the artistic mind works and how it processes information and turns it into influence, and in turn how influence is turned into art. This three-stage process is impossible to fully understand, but I would argue against those critics who attempt to do so that it is also equally impossible to trace, especially through the narrow lens of history. However, it is probable that contemporary persons are reflected, in varying degrees, in the characters and events of the play, but this suggests only that these persons or events were types of characters whom his audience would find funny, not unlike a modern playwright taking a well-known political figure, for example, and creating a character who resembled that historical person in certain broadly defined features, but who was not meant as a direct parody. In other words, it is important to treat topical references in the same way we treat literary ones, as influences on the writer's imagination. If we do so, we avoid many of the problems inherent in the following theories—namely, that of consistency.

Often real historical events do not parallel the characters or events in the play. We see this problem most clearly when we simply try to align the characters with their "real" historical predecessors. The most obvious historical allusion in the play is to the real King of Navarre, a well-known figure in Elizabethan society. His real name was Henri, not Ferdinand, and he had two supporters, the Duc de Biron and the Duc de Longueville, who obviously provided Shakespeare with names for two of the young men. From October 1589 to August 1591, Henri was very popular in England, having challenged, along with some British help, the Catholic League in his claim to the throne of France. In August 1591, Henri converted to Catholicism, after which he would have been much less sympathetic to English audiences. As R.W. David notes, a playwright would be more likely to present Navarre as a sympathetic character in 1591–93, and thus this is often used by some as evidence for dating the work earlier than is now generally accepted. However, if we cannot accept this early date for the play, then the historical persons lose some of their urgency and familiarity and, thus, they no longer can serve so easily as identifiable characters.

But this is not the least of the problem. The play is not about the historical events, or any historical event, with which the real Navarre was associated. The play is not a debate on statehood or war or religious conversion. One could argue that the initial mission of the young ladies, to receive lands taken from France, is political, but it serves no real purpose in the play other than to bring the potential lovers together and isn't really mentioned after Act II, scene i. Albert Tricomi sees the use of historical names as a specific example of "anti-topicality"—Shakespeare intended to use the names to spark recognition in his viewer's minds, but then to contrast the historical reality with the pastoral and leisurely tone of the play. What this anti-topicality suggests is that characters are not really the historical figures, but mock representations of them.

Perhaps the most thorough study of historical allusions in the play is Frances Yates' *A Study of Love's Labor's Lost*. Yates suggests a number of sources for the play's emphasis on style and wit and argues that a major source for the play is the debate between Gabriel Harvey and Thomas Nashe. Gabriel Harvey, a nephew of Sir Philip Sidney, wrote a lampoon on the pretentious Earl of Oxford and his Italianate habits and questionable political and religious affiliations. It was the playwright John Lyly, discussed later as another possible influence on Shakespeare, who brought Harvey's lampoon to the attention of Oxford. As a result, the debate escalated to eventually include the playwrights Robert Greene and Thomas Nashe, the former having published a scathing attack on Harvey in 1592 in which he made fun of Harvey's modest family origins. From here ensued the infamous "pamphlet wars," a series of publications, mostly by Nashe and Harvey, in which the two traded insults, apologies, and retractions of apologies until 1596; some of the pamphlets included Nashe's *Pierce Penilesse his Supplication to the Divell* and *Pierce's Supererogation*, and Harvey's *Foure Letters* (which eventually included a sermon against Nashe) and *Christ's Teares*. Yates sees a reference to the pamphlet war in the following exchange:

> *Hol.* Master Person, *quasi* pierce-one. And if one should be pierced, which is the one?
>
> *Cost.* Marry, master schoolmaster, he that is likest to a hogshead.
>
> *Hol.* Of piercing a hogshead! a good lustre of conceit in a turf of earth; fire enough for a flint, pearl enough for a swine: 'tis pretty; it is well. (IV.ii. 80–86)

Specifically, Yates sees a parallel to this in Gabriel Harvey's *Pierce's Supererogation*, in which he refers to a gentlewoman's opinion of Nashe's *Pierce Penilesse*: "She knew what she said that entitled Pierce, the hoggeshead of witt: Penniles, the tosspot of eloquence: & Nashe the very inventor of Asses. She it is that must broach the barrel of thy frisking conceit, and canonize thee Patriarke of new writers" (quoted in David 80). The gentlewoman's opinion about Nashe's conceited wit and eloquence certainly suggests similar interests in deflating overly pretentious and egotistical writers.

The fact that in Shakespeare's play Holoferenes is a schoolmaster and a laughable character makes the comparison tempting, but the problem lies in the fact that the word "hogshead" is not that rare in Renaissance literature. The reference could be to "piercing a hogshead," which was contemporary slang for getting drunk. R.W. David argues in a footnote to this passage that "Hogshead" was also commonly applied to a thick-witted person. Neither of these additional meanings preclude a reference to Harvey, but Yates writes: "There is no doubt that Harvey and Nashe lurk behind these lines, for the play on 'pierce' and 'person' proves this. Harvey's *Pierce Supererogation* was a reply to Nashes's *Pierce Penilesse* . . . [and therefore it] unmistakably refers to Nashe and to his quarrel with Harvey" (4). This is Yates's most convincing example to support such an allusion, but it is still far from conclusive since Shakespeare could have had any number of other references in mind. In another possible allusion to the pamphlet wars, Shakespeare has Armado call Moth "my tender juvenal" (I.ii.8). In 1598, Francis Meres in *Palladis Tamia* referred to Nashe as a "gallant young juvenal." The year 1598 is relatively late for Shakespeare to have borrowed directly from the published source, and relying on unpublished manuscripts as a form of influence is always highly speculative. In addition, Yates reminds us that any topical allusions to be found in the play usually reside in the various puns and word play found in *LLL*, and that this word play remains its defining aspect, and this is where the specific attributions face the most resistance since punning and word play were not limited to the Harvey/Nashe debates any more than, for example, modern political doublespeak is limited to any one candidate—Shakespeare is likely tapping into the same cultural references that Harvey and Nashe, and their detractors, did.

What is debated by the characters, whether or not Shakespeare intended them to be allusions to Harvey and Nashe, is the "controversy between the rival virtues of rhetoric and plain speaking, one of the issues in the feud between Nashe and Gabriel Harvey" (Wilders 23). However, the dramatist in Shakespeare effectively wiped out the specific personalities of Nashe and Harvey in favor of more lively comic characters, and the issues at stake in the Harvey/Nashe debates are too universal and important to Elizabethan culture to serve merely as topical allusions. In short, "Shakespeare sees beyond the purely contemporary debates to the conflicting impulses within the human personality itself" (33).

Another often noted topical reference has to do with the so-called "School of the Night" centered around Sir Walter Raleigh. Yates considers "the whole pretentious plan" of Navarre's to be a possible reference and attack on Raleigh's "School of Night" (8). In 1594, George

Chapman published *The Shadow of Night*, a poem that extolled night and dark, possibly in a manner that suggested the kind of astronomical investigation Raleigh's group was reportedly involved in. Yates quotes the following from *The Shadow of Night* to support this assertion:

> Since Night brings terror to our frailties still.
> And shameless Day doth marble us in ill;
> As you posseed with indepressed spritits,
> Endued with nible an aspiring wits,
> Come consecrate with me to sacred Night
> Your whole endeavours, and detest the light.

For Yates the "play becomes an expression of the spirit of aristocratic faction" (9). Yates's evidence for this connection is thin, however; Yates notes, for example, that Raleigh's faction was interested in numbers and followed Pythagereans in the fascination with odd and even numbers. She then quotes *LLL*, III.i.94–97 ("Staying the odds by adding four") and suggests that "there is probably a memory of some jargon familiar to 'the School of Night' in this and other passages hinting at number" (99). This is a very problematic assertion since the existence of the School of the Night was itself based on rumor, anti-Catholic propaganda, and insinuation. The fact that there were rumors to its existence does suggest that Shakespeare had possibly heard of them, but the reference is so brief in the play that it is questionable Shakespeare meant anything more by it than a figurative description. E.A. Strathman in "The Textual Evidence for 'The School of the Night,'" concludes that there is no evidence that "School of the Night" refers to Raleigh (186). Besides, as G.R. Hibbard notes, how could an audience glean all of the connotations and history from a single passing mention (Oxford 56)?

How Shakespeare became immersed in this school, if it even existed, and what he had to gain by parodying it in the play, are arguments I will leave to Yates's discussion for those so interested, but to rely too much on possible connections based on the slightest linguistic suggestions is to oversimplify the artistic method. Shakespeare could, and undoubtedly does, make fun of pretentiousness and breeding without narrowing his parody to one specific target. There is no internal or external evidence to suggest that this play was written solely for a courtly audience; likewise, there is no play as we currently know it that was written solely and ultimately for such a narrow audience. However, Yates's desire to find a precise cultural referent for Shakespeare's satire

is well intended and serves to remind us that this play is one of his most
contemporary. For example, Yates further argues that the Italian teacher
John Florio was a source for Holofernes (13). Yates quotes William
Warburton who in 1747 wrote that "by Holofernes is designed a particular character, a pedant and schoolmaster of our author's time, one John
Florio, a teacher of the Italian tongue in London, who has given us a
small dictionary of that language under the title of *World of words*" (from
*The Works of Shakespear... collated... corrected and emended...
by Mr. Pope and Mr. Warburton*, 1747, vol. II, pp. 227–228; quoted in
Yates 13). As Yates states, any obvious connection is unsupported by
evidence (15). That Florio had a reputation similar to Holofernes is evidence simply that Shakespeare had a type in mind when he created
Holofernes. More important, it reminds us that one of the major themes
of the play is education—more specifically, the social role language
plays in terms of formal education and preparedness for entrance into
adulthood. Such a theme was probably important to Shakespeare when
he created a schoolmaster whose rhetorical style was a joke, but it is just
as likely that Shakespeare's interest in Florio ended there. Florio represented to Shakespeare an example of his own society's preoccupation
with style and ornament; it is still possible that Shakespeare's attempt to
"recreate" Florio also ended there.

Yates sees a comparison between Holofernes's verbal style and the
style of Florio, who used proverbs, synonyms, and Italinate and Spanish
devices in his own writing. Yates notes that he used long words, parodied
in Costard's "honorificabilitudinitatibus" in his own work (38). According to Yates, Florio complained of the difficulty of pronouncing English
words because not all the letters in the words were sounded, as they were
in Italian (38). Florio's complaint is one reflected in the play; for example, Holofernes complains about the lack of consistency in English
pronunciation:

> He draweth out the thread of his verbosity finer than the staple of
> his argument. I adhor such fanatical phantasimes, such insociable
> and point-devise companions; such rackers of orthography, as to
> speak dout, fine, when he should say doubt; det, when he should
> pronounce debt, d, e, b, t, not d, e, t; he clepeth a calf, cauf; half,
> hauf; neighbour vocatur nebour; neigh abbreviated ne. This is ad-
> hominable, which he would adominble, it insinuateth me of insanie:
> *ne intelligis domine*? to make frantic, lunatic. (V.i.16–25)

Likewise, a word such as "honorificabilitudinitatibus" reflects a pedantic view of language—the word is potentially a word by the rules of Latin, but it is far from a useful word. However, this issue is characteristic of the age and impossible to attribute to any one source. For example, Richard Carew, a scholarly antiquary and friend of Sir Philip Sidney, wrote a letter entitled "The Excellency of the English Tongue" in 1605 on the superiority of the English language:

> For easye learning of other Languages by ours, let these serve as proofs; there are many Italian wordes which the Frenchmen cannot pronounce, as *accio*, for which he says *ashio*; many of the French which the Italian can hardly come away with [at] all, as bayller, chagrin, postillon; many in ours which neither of them can utter, as Hedge, Water. So that a stranger though never so long conversant amongst us carryeth evermore a watch word upon his tongue to descrye him by, but turn an Englishman at any time of his age into what country soever, allowing him due respite, and you shall see him perfitt so well that the Imitation of his utterance will in nothing differ from the pattern of that native Language: the want of which towardnes cost the Ephramites their skins. Neither doth this cross my former assertion of others easy learning our Language, for I mean of the sense of words and not touching the pronunciation.

We see reflected in this passage two important comic attributes found in Holofernes, Nathaniel, and Armado—namely, that there is a correct way of pronouncing words in English, and that when the English attempt to use the words of others, which ideally they should be able to incorporate into the "pattern of that native Language," what really happens, often, is that speakers attempting to use foreign words mess them up. *Love's Labour's Lost* shares with many of the writers cited by Yates as potential sources for the themes of the play not so much specific words or phrases but a general cultural concern with the role of language in everyday life.

Despite Yates's overreliance on this one issue, there is undoubtedly one reference to Florio, however, that is important: in Florio's *First Fruits* (1578) he writes that "we need not speak so much of love, al books are ful of love, with so many authours, that it were labour lost to speake of Love" (quoted in Yates 34). It is possible that this sentence is Shakespeare's source for the title; the combination of loss of love with "many authors" reflects Shakespeare's emphasis on the bookishness of love and the resulting loss of it. The question whether Holofernes is Florio, as Yates acknowledges, is ultimately not as important as Shakespeare's achievement in creating Holofernes: in Yates's words, "Holofernes is—Holofernes" (49).

Samuel Johnson expressed some hesitancy at making too specific attributions to contemporary persons. For example, in Act IV, scene ii, Johnson glossed: "Enter Holofernes, Nathaniel, and Dull."

> I am not of the learned commentator's [Warburton's] opinion that the satire of Shakespeare is so seldom personal. It is of the nature of personal invective to be soon unintelligible; and the author that gratifies private mailic, *animam in vulnere ponit*, destroys the future efficacy of his own writings and sacrifices the esteem of succeeding times to the laughter of the day. . . . Yet whether the character of Holofernes was pointed at any particular man I am, notwithstanding the plausibility of Dr. Warburton's conjecture, inclined to doubt . . . . Before I read this note I considered the character of Holofernes as borrowed from the Rhombus of Sir Philip Sidney who, in a kind of pastoral entertainment exhibited to Queen Elizabeth, has introduced a schoolmaster so called, speaking 'a leash of languages at once' and puzzling himself and his auditors with a jargon like that of Holofernes in the present play. (Johnson 181)

Johnson illustrates what in Rhombus's character is similar to Shakespeare's Holofernes. The fact that *The Lady of May* did not appear in print until 1598 (Woudhuysen 2) makes a direct influence questionable, and the presence of a Latin teacher named Holofernes in Rabelais's *Gargantua and Pantagruel* (I.14 and 19) suggests that Holofernes and Rhombus were comic types and as such no specific source is necessary for appreciating Shakespeare's creation. In Sidney's *A Defense of Poetry*, he describes a type of "self-wise-seeming schoolmaster; an awry-transformed traveller" who, if we "saw walk in stage names, which we play naturally" would lead to "delightful laughter" (quoted in Woudhuysen 3). Clearly, for Sidney, the type was so well known that it served as an automatic source of delight and laughter.

Beyond biographical references, the play may contain references to contemporary events. The notorious Gray's Inn revels, described in *Gesta Grayorum: or The History of the High and Mighty Prince Henry, Prince of Purpoole*, an anonymous account of the Inns of Court festivities, was a celebration by the members of the Gray's Inn, led by an elected Lord of Misrule, celebrated in the Christmas season of 1594 and in the new year of 1595. The *Comedy of Errors* was performed on December 28, and the day was known afterward as the "Night of Errors" due to the rowdiness of the spectators. One of the mock "rules" the knights were to observe was that "No Knight of this Order shall, in point of honour, resort to any Grammar-rules out of the Books *De Dullo*, or such like." Further, the knights were encouraged to "endeavour to add Conference and Experience by Reading; and therefore shall not only read and peruse *Guizo*, the *French* Academy . . . but also frequent the Theatre, and such like places of Experience"(154). The knights were equating life experience with the theater and reading, a connection not unlike that called for in the academe and a mistake made by the young men throughout the play. In other words, the pageant follows the same basic movement of the play.

In the *Gesta Grayorum* six councilors give advice to the Prince of Purpoole, the Lord of Misrule. The first urges him to seek fame in war, the third suggests he erect monuments and buildings, the second, however, suggests he study philosophy, so "that you bend the Excellency of your Spirits to the searching out, inventing and discovering of all whatsoever is hid in secret in the World, that your Excellency be not as a Lamp that shineth to others, and yet seeth not itself; but as the Eye of the World, that both carrieth and useth Light." These last two are of particular interest to *LLL* as they suggest that the search for fame and fortune through knowledge leads to the downfall of the lords. The sixth councillor, like Berowne, contradicts the others and suggests that his time is best spent in pleasurable activities: "What! . . .Nothing but tasks, nothing but Working-days? No Feasting, no Musick, no Dancing, no Triumphs, no Comedies, no Love, no Ladies?" (quoted in Yates 154–155). The next day the princes are visited by "mock ambassadors from Russia." This last event particularly has long been seen as a source for the final act of the play. The *Gesta Grayorum* reads:

> First, there came six Knights of the Helmet, with three that they led as Prisoners and were attired like Monsters and Miscreants. The Knights gave the Prince to understand, that as they were returning from their Adventures out of Russia, wherein they aided the Emperor of Russia, against the Tartars, they surprised these three Persons, which were conspiring against His Highness and Dignity . . . Which being done, the Trumpets were commanded to sound, and then the King at Arms came in before the Prince, and told His Honour, that there was arrived an Ambassador from the mighty Emperor of Russia and Muscovy, that some Matters of Weight to make known to His Higness. So the Prince willed that he should be ad-

mitted into his Presence; who came in Attire of Russia, accompanied
with two of his own County, in like Habit. (Bullough 439–440)

These various excerpts from the festivities show a juxtaposition of fame,
philosophical study, and the pursuit of fun and romance, all spoken about
tongue-in-cheek, which strongly suggests a significant influence or inspiration, if not actually a source, for Shakespeare's play.

There are two other possible historical sources for the Muscovites
scene. According to R.W. David, the voyages of Richard Chancellor had
opened up trade with Russia and the Company of Muscovy Merchants
that was formed in 1594. There was also an exchange of ambassadors
between England and Russia and in 1583 an envoy from Czar Ivan the
Terrible was sent to England (xxvii). Similarly, there were also other
Muscovite maskers and blackamoor in a court masque of 1510 that was
described in *Holinshed's Chronicles* in 1587. Any one of these events
could have been the source for Shakespeare's masque, but more likely
it was the general cultural fascination with Russia that is reflected in *LLL*
and in the various news reports of Russians.

Most arguments about the source of the play are dependent on the
notion that the play is more "aristocratic" than other Shakespeare plays
and that it was written for a courtly audience. Mary Ellen Lamb, in "The
Nature of Topicality in 'Love's Labour's Lost' " questions that assumption, noting that to focus too much on the mannered quality of the play
is to miss "its truly broad and sometimes gross humour, not beyond the
reach of most twelve-year-olds, Renaissance or modern" (50). Therefore,
there is no reason to assume that the play is necessarily more topical
than any other play. Critics arguing for an audience made up of fashionable and in-the-know aristocrats ignore the fact that much of the contemporary criticism of the play condemned it as childish. For example,
Samuel Johnson complained of the "vulgar passages" that should not
have been presented to a maiden queen. When Burbage recommended
the play for Queen Anne, he did so because the play contained "mirth"
and "wit," and because she had not yet seen it (51), possibly suggesting
that the play was not that fashionable after all. Robert Tofte's comments
about the play focused on its humor: "To every one (saue me) twas
Comicall," suggesting that the play had wide appeal but was not seen
by at least one contemporary audience as a work to be taken seriously.

Instead of treating any topical references in the play as unique and
precise allusions, and thus turning the play into a contemporary satire,

which it is not, Lamb argues for treating the topical allusions the same way we treat literary ones:

> We must invest the play, not the sources, with meaning. Perhaps the problem lies in treating topical sources too differently from literary ones. We seldom fall into the same error with literary sources. We do not locate the meaning of *The Winters Tale*, for example, in its similarities or differences from *Pandosto*. We do not expect its audience to smile in bemused delight when Leontes does not commit suicide as did his literary counterpart. . . . Similarly, identifying the topical sources underlying *Love's Labour's Lost* is not necessary to an understanding of the play for the average theatre-goer. (54)

Lamb provides an excellent discussion of what she labels as the three stages of topical criticism of the play, starting with the first stage, which was "marked by impressive historical knowledge and balanced good sense" (52). However, these readings were often discounted by the need, for the sake of consistency, for a very early date. These critics did not attempt to see the play as a topical one, rather, they were simply looking for historical sources for the actions and characters. It was the second stage of critics, which included Frances Yates, who began looking at the biographical persons behind the characters in very narrow and precise terms, no longer relying on a general audience's knowledge. Instead they turned to precise persons and debates known to a smaller, elite coterie. Hence, the play became an allegory of the School of the Night and/or the Harvey/Nashe debate (53). With the exhaustion of the second wave, which collapsed under the sheer demands of its own intricate arguments, came the third wave, which no longer assumed close consistency between characters and historical persons. For example, Albert Tricomi sees the play as escapist: the characters only shared names with famous persons, but the frivolity of the play made for humor and served as a contrast to the real-world problems represented by the names (54). For Tricomi, the historically accurate names are "charmingly transmuted from the French civil war into the fairy-tale world of Nerac" (Tricomi 29). Rather than fighting a war of profound political and religious importance, Shakespeare's men are fashionable, "leisured, studious," and in love. In Tricomi's reading, it is possible that the names of the lords were added as an afterthought, and carry no real relationship to the historical events from which they are taken. In the end, both Tricomi and

Lamb are correct to question all these trends as investing too much into what ultimately serves, at best, as a source for the play, not a blueprint.

STYLISTIC INFLUENCES

Love's Labour's Lost suffers most from topical criticism because such criticism subordinates the play's wonderful dramatic qualities to some of the play's lesser themes. For example, the play is definitely not about religious issues or contemporary political intrigue. Analyzing Shakespeare's stylistic influences, on the other hand, is more productive for revealing Shakespeare's intentions. Although Shakespeare's comic influences are as varied as his tragic influences, one playwright in particular, John Lyly, stands out as a major influence on Shakespeare's comic sensibilities. Lyly (1554?–1606) was one of the first writers of English comedies, and his plays were very popular in the early years of Shakespeare's apprenticeship in the theater. His plays were mostly in prose, written in a style that came to be called "Euphuistic" after his prose romance *Euphues: The Anatomy of Wit*, published in 1578, a style of writing that was highly patterned, self-consciously ornate, and which put a great deal of emphasis on mythological references.

There is little doubt that Shakespeare saw, and perhaps acted in, at least a couple of Lyly's plays. Oscar Campbell summarizes the dramatic lessons Shakespeare learned from Lyly:

1. How to present the intercourse of refined persons whose talent for "verbal ingenuity" is the major form of social delight.

2. How to write dialogue, a majority of it in prose, which fits such a group: witty, brisk, fanciful, and learned.

3. How to make love the major focus of these conversations, and to have those conversations guided by women, who often treat their suitors in a "flippant" manner.

4. How to subordinate plot and characterization to dialogue.

5. How to introduce numerous songs. (95)

All of these aspects influenced the structure of *LLL*, but, more deeply, the influence of Lyly's "exquisite" style can be felt in almost every line of *LLL*. In an important study of Lyly's drama, G.K. Hunter summarizes one of the most important lessons Shakespeare would have learned from Lyly, namely, that "exquisiteness of form in Lyly, Spenser or Sidney is no more an argument for superficiality of treatment than are love-locks and silk stockings of the courtiers a sign of effeminateness" (8). In other words, Shakespeare could foreground artifice and decorum without sacrificing depth of thought. Further, Shakespeare would have found in Lyly the basis for his treatment of wit as a theme and of courtly wit as a dramatic subject for a comedy. Hunter reminds us that the "real" court, like the court in *LLL*, was "neither natural nor free" (7). Wit, especially courtly wit, is of the courtly world and can be defined as the use of eloquence to produce a human, rather than theoretical, order (6). It is, thus, rhetorical and dramatic. Hunter notes that popular drama of the time shared with courtly drama an emphasis on art and wit, but the popular theater did so somewhat less obviously. Popular art, such as represented by Shakespeare, was usually concerned with seeming more natural than courtly. It is for this reason that many critics have found *LLL* problematic: it is the play most inspired by Lyly's dramatic appropriation of courtly artifice. However, Hunter notes that Lyly's aim was to "create a mode of life which is so witty, so poised, so brilliant that we are flattered by being thought refined enough to forget real life and enjoy its ideals of love and honor" (12). This sounds a lot like the world of *LLL*, and represents the central tension in that play between idealization and "real" life.

It would be too simplistic to assume that Shakespeare was primarily concerned with acting out the contrast between the courtly world and the "real" world; rather, Shakespeare seems to suggest that both worlds are dependent on each other. Shakespeare was a secular writer interested in the world, and *LLL* is a particularly secular play, and many of the critics who have attempted to read the play as a commentary on courtly life and characters have missed the true parodic nature of Shakespeare's appropriation of Lyly's style. Furthermore, Lyly's dramas were "baroque" since they juxtaposed parody of a subject with a serious statement about the subject. Hunter notes as examples *The Second Shepherd's Play* or a gothic cathedral in which a single visual impression of the whole structure is impossible. "Recognizable unity" (138), in the plays of Lyly, and by extension *LLL*, is subordinate to idea. Separate sections of a play, sermon, or cathedral may rely on humor, horror, or reason; however, in the end the different parts point to a unified action. *Love's Labour's Lost* is similarly an aggregation of diverse sources, moods, and genres that nonetheless result in a unified whole. When critics question the entrance of Marcade, for example, they neglect that Marcade is only one manifestation of an important theme in the play—death and the intrusion of an "outside" world on the court—and that dramatically the play allows for what might seem like disparate parts.

Shakespeare's ability to contrast levels of acceptable behavior and to play them off one another is a skill perfected earlier by Lyly. "While Lyly keeps his parallel episodes in separation from one another, and stresses their similarity, Shakespeare interlaces his episodes and stresses the *different* responses which make up a unified though wide-ranging social scene" (Hunter 317). These episodes are centered around groups of characters. At the top of the social scale are the king and his attendants, who are matched with the princess and her ladies. Next comes Armado and his page, Moth, and then those who are learned but not courtly, Holofernes and Nathaniel (332). At the bottom, those who are neither learned nor courtly, are Costard, Jaquenetta, and Constable Dull. Although Shakespeare similarly uses groups of characters in opposition to each other in *MND*, in *LLL* he does so not to reveal a plot, but to "build up a range of affectations" (332). The purpose of these levels is to cause us to judge all the characters and to make psychological judgments about them based on their affectations. In other words, it reflects the movement inherent in Shakespeare's poetic and dramatic development of putting more and more emphasis on character rather than plot. For example, Hunter notes that Shakespeare adopted from Lyly a concept of courtship as a game, one in which the lady "holds the gentleman at bay" with her wit (302). This is an important theme not only in *LLL*, but in many of the middle and later comedies. Shakespeare surpasses Lyly in his ability to give these women real personalities and to make the men more lifelike despite their reliance on fashionable paradigms.

John Lyly's *Gallathea* reveals the extent to which Lyly was an influence on Shakespeare's drama. In the following exchange between Diana, the goddess of the hunt, her nymph Telusa, and Gallathea, who is disguised as a boy, we see a possible precursor to the young women in *LLL*, especially the princess who similarly uses her wit to distance a would-be wooer:

> *Tel:* Saw you not a deer come this way? He flew down the wind, and I believe you have blanched him.
>
> *Gall:* Whose deer was it, lady?
>
> *Tel:* Diana's deer.
>
> *Gall:* I saw none but mine own dear.
>
> *Tel:* This wag is wanton or a fool. Ask the other, Diana.

Gall: [aside] I know not how it cometh to pass, but yonder boy is
in mine eye too beautiful. I pray gods the ladies think him
not their dear.

Although the dear/deer pun is common throughout the Renaissance, that, combined with the theme of love at first sight, classical allusions, and the extended pun within the specific context of wooing and exchange of wit, makes it a safe assumption that Lyly reflected a trend that would eventually influence Shakespeare. *Gallathea* centers around a group of women, Diana and her nymphs, who reluctantly fall in love despite constant warnings against it. Likewise, the play was written for a well-educated audience; whether *LLL* was originally planned for such an audience is open for debate, but the play still contains many allusions aimed at a well-educated audience.

Shakespeare also learned from Lyly the art of creating complex and harmonious relationships between clowns and other lower-class and upper-class characters. Rafe in *Gallathea* could clearly be seen as the source for Moth and other lower-class characters who find themselves surrounded by affectation and highbrow, cultured people. Rafe and a young apprentice, Pete, illustrate that like Moth and Costard in *LLL*, they are fascinated by "big" words and that big words can be their bridge to higher class standing:

Pete: What a life do I lead with my master! Nothing but blowing
of bellows, beating of spirits, and scraping of crosslets! It is
a very secret science, for none almost can understand the language of it: sublimation, almigation, calcination, rubinfication,
incorporation, circination, cementation, albification, and fre-
mentation, with as many terms unpossible to be uttered as the
art to be compassed.

Rafe: Let me cross myself. I never heard so many great devils in a
little monkey's mouth.

Pete and Rafe's fascination with the language of others—namely, the educated upper class—compares with Costard's fascination with "remuneration" at III.i and his marveling that they have not eaten "at a great feast of languages" (V.i.35–36).

Finally, Shakespeare learned from Lyly but in many ways surpassed him, especially in terms of humanizing his characters. Whereas Lily cleverly found ways to oppose characters in a dramatized debate, his plays were most noteworthy for their structure and dramatic grouping of characters. Shakespeare, on the other hand, humanized the debate structure of Lyly by putting the debate into the hands of "real" people, even if the original archetypes are still visible through the masks.

Another example of how Shakespeare humanizes his characters is represented by the character of Don Armado. Oscar Campbell was the first critic to see Don Armado as resembling the stock braggart of Italian popular comedies of the time. Often the Italian comedies presented the braggart, or *capitano*, as a Spaniard (Campbell 98). This character, like Armado, was too proud and boastful of his military experience and overly fond of high-sounding phrases and words. As Campbell notes, Shakespeare often poured his dramatic creations "into dramatic molds already cast" (98). After citing evidence that Shakespeare would have had plenty of opportunities to see Italian companies in England, Campbell notes that other stock characters, such as the sidekick Moth and the pedant Holofernes, were also popular stock characters (102–104). It is likely that Shakespeare discovered "dramatic suggestions" for his own inspiration and rekindled many "smouldering fires" (110).

In addition to the archetypal character traits borrowed from the Italian comedies, Shakespeare borrowed certain plot incidents as well: for example, the confusion and mistaken exchange of letters is a common occurrence in the commedia dell'arte. However, certain important differences are evident on closer inspection: unlike his Italian cousin, Armado undergoes no amorous delusion or any cuckolding (Boughner 203). Another important difference lies in the handling of rhetorical figures: those characters who influenced Shakespeare, like Lyly's, were often truly masters of rhetorical invention and were both elegant and heroic, even if they liked a little too much to show off their skills. Shakespeare's Armado, however, never appears eloquent since he always adheres to an elevated diction (212–213). Again, the result is the same: Shakespeare has succeeded in making his *capitano* more real and human.

RENAISSANCE EDUCATION

The best way to understand the sources and influences that prevailed on Shakespeare in the writing of *LLL* is to look beyond the specific allusions to the broader cultural trends that influenced both Shakespeare and his contemporaries. The most important influences on Shakespeare were linguistic: Renaissance England experienced rapidly changing concepts of both literary and everyday language. The lower-class characters in the play, for example, see language as a practical commodity; words like "remuneration" or "guerdon" become actual coins with a specific exchange value. The upper-class characters are also fascinated with language's ability to create meaning and establish reputations, hence the ongoing fascination with etymology and poetic discourse. Throughout the play various controversies regarding language that were germane to the sixteenth century (e.g., pronunciation, spelling, language acquisition, classical versus vernacular language, wit through verbal dexterity, poetic sensibility etc.) are also issues that divide the classes and hinder communication between the characters. One of the most contentious aspects to be debated at the time had to do with the relationship between the vernacular and foreign languages. As Keir Elam notes, "The hectic lexical spinning, borrowing, coining and joining that goes on in *LLL* re-enacts the whole history of the grammatical-rhetorical Tudor debate on the subject" (266). At IV.i.70, Armado, in his letter to Jaquenetta, calls the vernacular English the "base and obscure vulgar," suggesting that for him English is a secondary language to Latin, even though the vernacular English is the only language spoken by Jaquenetta.

Sir Thomas Chaloner, the sixteenth-century translator of Erasmus, wrote: "[Rhetoricians] plainly think themselves demi-gods, if . . . they can show two tongues, I mean to mingle their writings with words sought out of strange languages . . . to powder their books with inkehorne terms" (quoted in Elam 265). "Inkhorn terms" are those words that are pedantic or borrowed only for the sake of decorating or embellishing the vernacular. This could serve as a perfect description of the pedants in the play, Holofernes and Nathaniel, as well as Armado. Chaloner highlights what must have been an apt description of at least some pedagogues of the time who took great delight in their ability to "mingle" different languages together and who, like Holofernes and Nathaniel, make prideful show of their abilities at the expense of actual worth. The fact that the play contains two pedagogues serves as a reminder of how important the teaching of vernacular and foreign languages was. The Renaissance education theorist Richard Mulcaster wrote in *The Elementarie* that foreign words needed to "become English to serve our need, as their people are to thank our tongue, for returning the like help, in cases of like need, though their occasions to use ours be nothing so often, as ours to use theirs" (157). In describing this process, Mulcaster used a word found frequently in *LLL*—"enfranchisement." As it does in the play, the word suggests an economic as well as linguistic freedom. By using the word, Mulcaster meant that foreign words "become bond to the rules of our writing, which I have named before, as the stranger denisons to the laws of our country" (174). We see enfranchisement throughout the play, especially in the lower-class characters' attempts to parrot what they hear: for example, Costard "enfranchises" the word "remuneration," which is Latin for payment, and which he has just heard from another character:

> Now will I look to his remuneration. Remuneration! O that's the Latin word for three farthings: three farthings, remuneration. 'What's the price of this inkle?' 'One penny': 'No, I'll give you a remuneration': why, it carries it. Remuneration! why it is a fairer name than French crown. I will never buy and sell out of this word. (III.i.132–138)

Later Costard will use the word himself in its new meaning, as an English word:

> *Cost:* Pray you, sir, how much carnation ribbon may a man buy for a remuneration?
>
> *Ber:* O what is a remuneration?
>
> *Cost:* Marry, sir, halfpenny farthing.
>
> *Ber:* O! why then, three farthing worth of silk.

Costard, a little earlier in the play, did the same thing with the word "enfranchise": "O! marry me to one Frances—I smell some l'envoy, some goose in this" (III.i.118–120). Costard is consistently taking "inkhorn terms" and enfranchising them to his native English, mirroring in a comedic way the manner in which words do actually become enfranchised to English due to the constant exchange of words across linguistic boundaries. Costard is mimicking what the upper-class characters do unreflexively—namely, seasoning their English with foreign words, sometimes nonsensically. If we can assume that Mulcaster's (and other Renaissance theorists') concerns reflect a real cultural trend, then Shakespeare was satirizing the linguistic habits of the middle and upper classes.

Mulcaster's famous remark that "I love Rome, but London better, I favor Italie, but England more, I honor the Latin, but I worship the English" (269) can serve as a description of how the characters use the various foreign tongues, Latin most importantly: throughout the play characters such as Costard and Moth honor Latin through their mystification and misuse of it, while they show the worship and love they have for English by enfranchising the Latin to it. In this way Latin is by far the most important foreign language in the play, as it was throughout the Renaissance. As T.W. Baldwin and Sister Miriam Joseph have examined in their respective studies of Shakespeare's education, the study of Latin and rhetoric were foundational facets of Renaissance schooling. In fact, Latin education was so important that as early as the reign of Henry VIII there was a move to regularize the teaching of Latin in all of the English schools. This movement began about 1540 when a new text, based on a Latin grammar by William Lily, was published with the following preface:

> Henry the VIII . . . to all schoolmasters and teachers of grammar within this his realm greeting . . . to the intent that hereafter they [English children] may the more readily and easily attain the rudiments of the Latin tongue, without the great hindrance, which heretofore hath been, *through the diversity of grammars and teachings*: we will and command, and streightly charge al you schoolmasters and teachers of grammar within this our realm, and other our dominions, as ye intend to avoid our displeasure, and have our favor, to teach and learn your scholars this English introduction here ensuing, and the Latin grammar annexed to the same, and none other, which we have caused for your ease, and your scholars speedy preferment briefly and plainly to be compiled and set forth. Fail not to apply your scholars in learning and godly education. [quoted in Flynn 22; italics mine]

Latin had become so important to the cultural well-being of the English that it needed to be centralized and "domesticated." Lily's grammar remained the preferred text well into the late seventeenth century. Foster Watson notes that 10,000 copies were allowed to be printed annually, when 1,250 copies of a book were considered an ordinary edition (Flynn 29).

What was so special about Lily's grammar and why was it chosen to be the text taught to all English schoolchildren, including Shakespeare (see Photo 2)? One reason could be the manner in which Lily situated Latin in relation to English. Lily's grammar began with the statement, "Whan I have an englysshe to be tourned into Latin I shal reherse it twyes or thries and loke out the verbe." By turning from English to Latin, Lily suggested that English and Latin were in many ways equal, and could be enfranchised to each other (as opposed to a more traditional humanistic practice that treated Latin as prior, and therefore more important, than English). The English pride in their language is emphasized throughout Renaissance pedagogical texts, but often in relation to the

DE OCTO
ORATIONIS PAR-
TIVM CONSTRVCTIONE
libellus perelegans, authore Deside=
rio ERASMO ROTERODAMO,
Scholijs Henrici Primæi apud
Monasterienses gymna=
siarchæ illustratus.

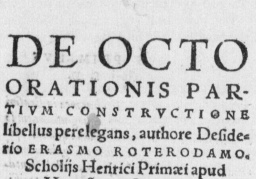

TIGVRI

Excudebat Christophorus Froschouerus,
Anno M. D. LXVIII.

Photo 2. Title Page for Lily's Grammar.

practical importance of Latin, as it is in the following from the intro-duction to Lily's grammar:

> When these Concords be well known unto them, an easy and a pleasant pain, if the foregrounds be well and throughly beaten in, let them not continue in learning of their rules orderly all as they lie in their Syntax, but rather learn some preatty book, wherin is contained not only the eloquence of the tongue, but also a good plain lesson of honesty and godliness, and thereof take some little sentence as it lieth, and learn to make the same Art Out of English into Latin.

As Lily makes clear, eloquence is based on the ability to turn from one language to another, to find a verbal equivalent of an idea in *two* lan-guages (or "show two tongues"). Clearly the main purpose of learning Latin was not virtue, for virtue may lie in English texts. A "pretty book" in English was just as likely to express virtue as a Latin book. Many of the examples previously noted from *LLL* likewise show a pride in En-glish in relation to Latin (and other foreign languages). Similarly, the ironic inversion of student over teacher, seen so often with Moth and Costard in opposition to Holofernes and Armado, could be traced back to the same cultural tension that produced Lily's grammar.

Shakespeare seems to be parodying not only Lily's grammar and its emphasis on a "vernacularized" Latin, but those texts that warned against the overuse of foreign languages. Thomas Wilson, in his 1553 *Arte of Rhetorique*, warns readers against using "strange inkhorn terms, but to speake as commonly received" (183). He compares those who bring for-eign words home (i.e., to England) to those who wear foreign apparel after they return from a trip abroad. "He that cometh lately out of France will talk French English, and never blush at the matter. Another chops in with Anglo-Italian." Wilson cites many other examples, finally noting that these pretentious persons will turn to Latin so "that the simple cannot but wonder at their talk, and think surely they speak from some Reve-lation" (185), which is essentially Costard's response to "remuneration": for him the word becomes incantational and represents a strange, magical language.

A similar condemnation of European tastes and fashion, in similar language, appears in Shakespeare's *Henry VIII* when the Lord Cham-berlain and Sir Thomas Lovell are complaining about the ubiquitous nature of French fashion in the court:

> *Lov:* They must either
> (For so run the conditions) leave those remnants
> Of fool and feather that they got in France,
> With all their honorable points of ignorance
> Pertaining thereunto, as fights and fireworks,
> Abusing better men than they can be
> Out of a foreign wisdom, renouncing clean
> The faith they have in tennis and tall stockings,
> Short blist'red breeches, and those types of travel,
> And understand again like honest men,
> Or pack to their old playfellows. (I.iii.23–33)

Armado is described as a "fashionable Spaniard," and he best represents a vice all the characters could be accused of, namely, the overemphasis they put on fashion, especially linguistic fashion, such as the use of foreign terms and witty exchanges. What the play reminds us is that with England's emerging presence as a world power, as well as the new international economic system, there was an ever-increasing tension between cultures and languages. Armado is, after all, likely named after the Spanish Armada and as such represents a clash of cultures, and his characterization as a fool primarily because of his linguistic exuberance serves to highlight one of the main ways this tension was played out on the Elizabethan stage. Wilson would have Latin used only when fitting, and Latin and Greek "further our meaning in the English tongue, either for lack of some, or else because we would enrich the language" (Wilson 183). This is exactly what Armado, Holofernes, and Nathaniel do not do and why, hence, they are comic. Despite his distrust of Latin and other foreign tongues, Wilson comes to a conclusion similar to that of Mulcaster and many of their contemporaries—namely, that Latin, although far from a better language, can benefit English. Again, Armado and Holofernes are comic characters because they neatly fit into Wilson's paradigmatic fashionable traveler. This comic stereotype reflects real cultural tension about the role of the vernaculars in national identity.

This tension is also clearly seen in Richard Carew's *The Excellency of the English Tonque*:

> For our own partes, we employ the borrowed ware[s] so far to our advantage that we raise a profit of new words from the same stock, which yet in their own country are not merchantable; for example, we deduce diverse words from the Latin which in the Latin self cannot be yielded, as the verbs To Aire, beard, cross, flame, and

their derivations "airing, aired, bearder, bearding, bearded, . . . , as also closer, closely, closeness, glossingly, hourly, majestical, majestically. In like sort we graft upon French words those buds to which that soil . . . "

This is perhaps the best example of how Elizabethans saw the changing linguistic nature of their modern Europe—languages were a commodity to be traded, bought, and spent. Although the knowledge of Latin was a cultural sign of education and good birth, the Costards and Moths of the world were able, under the right circumstances, to also learn Latin and Greek as well as other European vernaculars. In short, the medieval economic and cultural stratification was no longer in place, and through *LLL* Shakespeare was presenting his audience with what that new world was beginning to look like.

WORKS CITED

Boughner, Daniel C. "Don Armado and the Commedia dell'Arte." *Studies in Philology* 37 (1940): 201–224.

Bullough, Geoffrey. *Narrative and Dramatic Sources of Shakespeare*. Vol 1. London: Routledge, 1957.

Campbell, Oscar. "*Love's Labor's Lost* Restudied." *Studies in Shakespeare, Milton, and Donne. University of Michigan Publications in Language and Literature.* 1 (1925): 3–45.

Carew, Richard. *The Excellency of the English Tongue*. British Library MS Cott. F. xi, f. 265.

David, Richard W., ed. *Love's Labour's Lost*. Arden Shakespeare. 2nd series. London: Routledge, 1994.

Elam, Keir. *Shakespeare's Universe of Discourse: Language-Games in the Comedies*. Cambridge: Cambridge University Press, 1984.

Flynn, Vincent Joseph. "The Grammatical Writings of William Lily, ?1468–?1523." *Bibliographical Society of America* 37 (1943): 27–42.

Hibbard, G.R., ed. *Love's Labour's Lost*. The Oxford Shakespeare. Oxford: Clarendon Press, 1990.

Hunter, G.K. *John Lyly, The Humanist as Courtier*. Cambridge, MA: Harvard University Press, 1962.

Johnson, Samuel. *Samuel Johnson on Shakespeare*. Ed. H.R. Woudhuysen. London: Penguin, 1989.

Lamb, Mary Ellen. "The Nature of Topicality in *Love's Labour's Lost*." *Shakespeare Survey* 38 (1985): 49–59.

Lyly, John. *Gallathea. Drama of the English Renaissance I: The Tudor Period.* Ed. Russell A. Fraser and Norman Rabkin. New York: Macmillan, 1976.

Mulcaster, Richard. *The Elementarie*. Ed. E.T. Campagnac. Oxford: Clarendon Press. 1945.

Strathman, E.A. "The Textual Evidence for 'The School of the Night.' " *Modern Language Notes* 56 (1941): 176–186.

Tricomi, Albert H. "The Witty Idealization of the French Court in *Love's Labour's Lost.*" *Shakespeare Studies* 12 (1979): 25–33.

Wells, Stanley. "Shakespeare Without Sources." In *Shakespearian Comedy*. Ed. D.J. Palmer and Malcolm Bradbury. Stratford-upon-Avon Studies 14. London: Arnold, 1972. 58–74.

Wilders, John. "The Unresolved Conflicts of *Love's Labour's Lost.*" *Essays in Criticism* (1977): 20–33.

Woudhuysen, H.R., ed. *Love's Labour's Lost*. Arden Shakespeare. 3rd series. Walton-on-Thames: Thomas Nelson and Sons, 1998.

Yates, Francis A. *A Study of "Love's Labour's Lost."* London: Cambridge University Press, 1936.

3

DRAMATIC STRUCTURE

Love's Labour's Lost is Shakespeare's most untraditional comedy. This assertion, however, must be made in light of the body of criticism that also designates it as the most representative of Shakespeare's time and one of his most self-reflective works. The play is unusual primarily due to its dramatic structure—that is, the movement of its action and the resolution of the character's conflicts. As we noted in Chapter 3, the play is noteworthy for having very little in the way of a formal plot or connective action: the play is made up primarily of a series of independent scenes with most of the "action" consisting of the verbal exchanges between characters. However, what tension it does have is suggestive of a "typical" comedy (and I will discuss what that entails later), but in the final act and scene of the play most of those expectations are thrown out, leaving an ending that seems to resist the conventional resolutions of Elizabethan comedy.

The plot, basic as it is, is as follows. King Ferdinand and three young friends, Longaville, Dumain, and Berowne, have come together to create an academe where they will be able to study free of the world's cares. They swear an oath to devote three years to this study and during that time to fast, sleep only three hours a night, and, most important, to speak to no women and to allow no women to enter their community. This plan is immediately hampered with the arrival of the princess of France and her three ladies, Rosaline, Maria, and Katherine, who have come to Navarre on a diplomatic mission. The proclamation is also immediately broken by a clown, Costard, who is in turn sentenced to imprisonment for a week having been caught speaking to a country wench, Jaquenetta.

In Act II, the arrival of the princess and her young ladies forces Ferdinand to refuse admittance to them and, therefore, to restrict them to camping outside his gates. In the exchanges that follow, the four young men reveal their attraction to the four young women, thus breaking their oaths. In the next act Armado, a "fantastical Spaniard" who has been charged with watching over Costard, frees him so that he might take a letter to his beloved, Jaquenetta, the same wench with whom Costard was so taken by in Act I. Berowne also enlists Costard with taking a letter to his beloved, Rosaline. Act IV opens with Costard mistakenly giving Armado's letter to Rosaline, who takes great amusement at its style, and then giving Berowne's letter to Jaquenetta, who cannot understand it. Holofernes, once he discovers the true writer of the letter, vows to give it to the king. In the next scene, Berowne, hiding in a tree, overhears Ferdinand composing love poetry to the princess, and then the king overhears Longaville composing love poetry to Maria, and finally, the three of them overhear Dumain sighing about his love, Kate. Berowne takes this opportunity to make sport of his companions for their lack of honesty and for failing to keep their oaths, only to be exposed himself with the delivery of his missent letter to Rosaline. With this revelation, the men resolve to study love and pursue the young women and the act ends with the men planning a masque for the entertainment of the young women.

In Act V, the men enter disguised as Russians and dance with the ladies, who, knowing in advance the young men's plans, have disguised themselves to confuse their suitors. Once this confusion is settled, the couples watch the masque of the Nine Worthies, presented by Armado, Costard, Nathaniel, Holofernes, and Moth. The masque is interrupted by the news of the death of the princess's father. Since the princess and her ladies must return home, Ferdinand asks directly for the princess's hand in marriage, as do his attendant for the hands of her three ladies; they refuse, first requiring the young men to forswear wit and to mourn for a period of one year, at which point they will reconsider the offers.

Although on the surface the plot seems to offer plenty of opportunities for intrigue (e.g., the political machinations of the princess, the missent letters, the four pairs of wooing couples, and the possibility of jealous competition between Costard and Armado), Shakespeare instead focuses on spectacle and verbal acrobatics rather than elaborate plot twists or development. One critic noted that "one is forced to conclude that either the playwright was not concerned with constructing a complex but integrated plot or that he had not yet found the formula which would permit the synchronizing of disparate stories into a unified plot structure"

(Bonazza 72). The same critic goes on to compare *LLL* negatively to *MND* in which Shakespeare does show a command of plot and structure. A close examination of the plot will reveal that Shakespeare did not intend to create a complex plot; moreover, the plot he did create brilliantly serves his comic intentions. As a result, the structure, if not the plot, of the play is very complex.

The most general structural shape of Renaissance comedies is the movement from restriction and chaos to festivity, freedom, and the restoration of social order. *Love's Labour's Lost* moves against this movement in the simple fact that "Jack hath not Jill"; however, by play's end Jack has Jill more than he did at the beginning of the play. Nonetheless, the play overtly denies the typical marriage one associates with a Renaissance romantic comedy. In fact, the play is so self-consciously deliberate in its modification of the basic structure of comedy (even the title betrays this modification in the fact that the labor of love, the usual subject of comedies, is lost, a conclusion most often associated in tragedies), without losing sight on it altogether, that a reader could safely conclude that Shakespeare intended the play to be a commentary on the genre. Unlike *The Taming of the Shrew* and *The Two Gentlemen of Verona*, two plays that force a "happy" marriage resolution onto otherwise seemingly imperfect and potentially disastrous relationships (to modern audiences, at least), and unlike *MND*, which effortlessly harmonizes all chaos in a flurry of music and courtship, *LLL* does not resolve in a contrived marriage conclusion. Rather, we are reminded that the play is a play, but a new type of play:

> Our wooing doth not end like an old play;
> Jack hath not Jill: these ladies' courtesy
> Might well have made our sport a comedy. (V.ii.866–868)

Berowne acknowledges that there are "old" plays (i.e., those of Lyly, perhaps) and there are "new" plays. After all, the play will end, in the king's words, "a twelvemonth an' a day," which is "too long for a play," again in Berowne's commonsensical view. This exchange, at V.ii.862–866, serves to illustrate the extent to which Shakespeare wrote *LLL* to recast the accepted "form" of romantic comedy.

Love's Labour's Lost does not reveal what happens outside the action of the play; we do not know for certain that the young couples will marry. The satisfaction that comes from an unambiguous conclusion is denied readers or viewers of the play. However, it could be argued that the choice to end *LLL* in this manner was a deliberate gesture toward realism: "the lack of finality is much more like life than the neatly tailored conclusions of most works of art" (Woudhuysen 9). Was Shakespeare consciously taking his art to a new level of representation by making it "realistic"? A close reading of the play suggests that the answer is yes, but one must be careful of considering the play realistic given the number of of stock characters whose presence deliberately calls to mind more traditional comedies. Second, to what extent is the conclusion unknown or denied? The title is somewhat deceptive—the "labour" of "love" is not completely "lost"; after all, the couples have paired up, offers of marriage have been made, and, arguably, accepted pending the modification of behavior. In other words, the action is not really terminated at the end of the play, but "suspended" (Heninger 25). Another way to think about the structure of the play is that the action of it is too big for "a play" to contain. It is not that the plot is so slight as to be insignificant, rather, the action is too large to be contained by a play.

Before examining where *LLL* differs from the other Renaissance comedies, it is useful to consider how it is similar in form to more traditional comedies. C.L. Barber, in *Shakespeare's Festive Comedy: A Study of Dramatic Form and its Relation to Social Custom*, notes that the basic structure of *LLL* is one in which "resistance" to festivity is "swept away" (88). The basic structure of Shakespeare's comedies, the movement toward "release" and festivity, reflects the spirit of "Merry England" and its many public festivities: public holidays and celebrations, such as May Day, Midsummer Eves, and Twelfth Night, all of which are centered around a "release" from everyday life and constrictions and a new appreciation for vitality and nature's power for renewal. In particular, Barber argues that in *LLL* Shakespeare is "making up action on the model of games and pastimes." The opening speech in *LLL* is a deliberate statement against festivity: the "brave conquerors" are to "make war" against their "own affections." The comic movement is further acted out when Berowne, just a few lines later, suggests that such a vow will not hold up. From there the play progresses to undermine the vow, to illustrate that comedy is, in Barber's words, a sweeping away of resistance. Festivity is manifested in comedies through the harmonizing of characters and through the reconciliation of differences. "The evolutions in *Love's Labour's Lost* express the Elizabethan feeling for the harmony of a group acting in ceremonious consort" (89). The spring and winter songs in Act V express the celebration of nature in which so many of Shakespeare's comedies are rooted. The games and pastimes are what give the play much of its movement and plot; these serious young men (and slightly less serious young women) are shown at leisurely and bourgeois play; whether it be by hunting, sonnet writing, or acting in a masque, the characters are basking in their "own affections" rather than warring against them. However, despite the emphasis on festivity, the play does deny the usual procreative marriage. This is one of the defining structural aspects of the play: a play so full of leisure and festivities in the end denies the ultimate comic festivity, a marriage. So much of the day has been taken with frivolous festivities that in the end there is literally no time for marriage.

THE ROOTS OF SHAKESPEARE'S COMIC STRUCTURE

T.W. Baldwin, in *Shakespeare's Five-Act Structure: Shakespeare's Early Plays on the Background of Renaissance Theories of Five-Act Structure from 1470*, argues for *LLL* as Shakespeare's earliest surviving play, a notion already dealt with in Chapter 2, and his evidence reveals a great deal about the structure of the play. The "backbone idea" of the play is that study can win fame and conquer all (586). However, the plot of the play rests on putting that idea to a test. Baldwin cites Vives, who in his *On Education* wrote that an academe should be "far . . . from the neighborhood of girls . . . [who] by their beauty allure the student at a time of life exposed to that attractive form of evil" (Baldwin 588). As the young men are quick to note, such truisms are not for them, and thus the overall structure becomes a morality play in reverse (588)—the young men must move away from idealized behavior and toward merrymaking and life. Thus, they move toward the world of festivity that marks Renaissance comedies.

In this way, the action of the play is reminiscent of the morality plays that Shakespeare would have seen as a young man. Like these morality plays, *LLL* develops around a single central moral theme, which J.J. Anderson summarizes as being "responsibly human" (54). The various scenes of the play are linked more by this theme than any overarching plot. Although the characters are not as flat as those found in morality plays, the characters in *LLL*, like those allegorical characters, are often developed around one, or at best two, character traits that relate to the play's overall thematic focus. Armado, for example, serves no real purpose beyond his constant misuse of language and representation of the vice of vanity. Although certain characters, most notably Berowne, rise above such simple development, most of the characters exist to illustrate some human folly. Even Berowne, in the words of Anderson, "cannot resist the lure of the intellect. Fine words are the men's delight and downfall, Berowne's most of all" (56). Berowne, who seems to have a depth not allowed your average allegorical personification, can be more self-righteous than most of the other characters. The Pageant of the Nine Worthies further illustrates the play's similarity to morality plays: the traditional Nine Worthies represented various human virtues. In addition, the Nine Worthies traditionally served as a moral and allegorical warning against excess pride and arrogance on the part of mere mortals. Shakespeare reverses this moral by making fun of such high-minded seriousness, but the play's final inclusion of Marcade suggests that the wit and intellegence of the young men are not enough; in the end, like Everyman, we are accountable for our actions and spiritual well-being, not any fame we might have acquired while on earth.

At the center of a young Renaissance man's education was the study of the Roman playwright Terence. Baldwin argues that it is from Terence that Shakespeare would have first learned about the basic five act structure of the "old plays" referred to at line 862 of the final scene of *LLL*. In the five-act structure, the first act serves primarily as exposition or background, and the second act starts the action proper. The third act introduces hostility or complication that influences the rest of the play. The fourth act begins the move toward a solution or unity, but that attempt either fails or must be delayed until the final act, at which point harmony prevails. In *LLL*, the first act certainly serves to establish the major themes and dramatic situations of the play, while Act II introduces the young ladies for the first time and presents the young men as falling in love. Act III does not so much complicate the action of the plot as complicate the relationships between several main characters; Act III is primarily a long battle of wits between Armado, Moth, Costard, and later, Berowne. Certainly the fourth act, with the letters arriving at the wrong destination and the sonnet-reading scene, complicates the various relationships between the couples and between friends. The most obvious departure from Terence and the "old plays" is that Act V does not present a perfectly harmonious ending, although there is more harmony that at any other point in the play.

Terence's plays were available in a wide variety of editions, as were writers such as Nicholas Udall, who wrote his own compendium on Terence entitled *Floures for Latine Spekyng Selected and Gathered out of Terence, and the same translated in to Englishe*, and the play that Baldwin cites as the first regular English comedy, *Ralph Roister Doister*.

The average Elizabethan schoolboy began memorizing Terence at the age of nine. From the earliest stages of his education Shakespeare would have become aware of the structure of classical comedy and in turn would likely have viewed the morality plays that were common at the time. The young Shakespeare would have experienced exactly the mixture of low-brow comedy and paradigmatic structure of Terence and the high-minded yet simplistic didacticism of the morality plays that is evident in *LLL*. Later in his education, Shakespeare would likely have investigated the theory behind this aesthetic. As Baldwin notes, Renaissance theorists insisted upon the examination of the structure and principles behind that structure (544). At this point in his life Shakespeare could have seen the newest stage fashion, the new comedies of John Lyly that were overtly built around the five-act structure. "Thus the thought structure of the play itself makes it clear that *LLL* was constructed in five stages or acts in accord with the five-act formula . . . . [T]he relation of *LLL* to two of Lyly's plays also makes it clear that *LLL* uses the five-act formula, and raises the question of whether Shakespeare might not have attained this structure by adapting Lyly" (617). As we have already noted, the general plan of the play is borrowed from Lyly's *Endimion* (618), but the "new wine of comic additions has burst the old bottle of balanced form" (622).

However, it is John Lyly who makes the five-act structure all but standard in England, and it is from Lyly that, Baldwin argues, Shakespeare learned about the structure of comedy. Shakespeare's reliance on Lyly for the basic structure of the play is revealing for other reasons. Blaze Odell Bonazza, in *Shakespeare's Early Comedies: A Structural Analysis*, also uses the structure of the play to give it an early date, but further argues that the play can be broken down into three plots, labeled A, B, C. The A and B plots (the lord's misguided plan and the romantic machinations, respectively) are wholly borrowed from Lyly. The C plot (the parallel subplot involving the lower-class characters), however, is a clear example of later revision: Holofernes and Nathaniel appear to belong to the C plot yet do not completely fit into it. It is the sudden appearance of Nathaniel and Holofernes that suggests that Shakespeare owes his plot to Lyly since only Holofernes and his crew are not found in the basic structure of *Endimion* and therefore they may not have been in the original play but were added to the newly augmented edition of

1598 (49–50). The most important borrowing is the arrangement of characters into symmetrical groups. The parodic subplot is another borrowing from Lily.

Bonazza, however, is very critical of the play, primarily due to its slight plot. Bonazza notes, for example, that Act III is weak. There is not enough action and too many witty exchanges which do not complicate the B or C plots. "Throughout this central portion of the play, which should contain a series of rapidly occurring incidents leading to a climax, the playwright relies heavily on language as a structural device to create the atmosphere of affectation versus nature instead of using action to create suspense" (68). Why a play entitled *Love's Labour's Lost* would need suspense is not clear, nor is the reliance upon verbal exchanges now taken by most critics as a sign of weakness. In fact, if we acknowledge that Shakespeare intended this play as a commentary on comic plays, then these exchanges are the heart and soul of the play. Bonazza makes the common mistake of assuming that difference or experimentation is easily equitable with amateurism. Additionally, is it necessary to date the play early just because it was most directly influenced by Lyly? Or did the nature of the play conjure for Shakespeare a desire to return to an "academic" structure? Could he have been experimenting, as the play strongly suggests, or could his audience (assuming a courtly performance) have shown a preference for "traditional" plays? Assuming simply that because the play directly reflects his early influences Shakespeare must have written it early in his career seems mistaken and overly simplistic—Shakespeare the artist was undoubtedly more complicated than that.

CHARACTERS

It is pertinent to discuss character in a chapter dedicated to plot and dramatic structure since character and character interaction are the plot of this play. More specifically, the "wit" of each character is defined against the wit, or witlessness, of other characters. The most comic characters spout witticisms seemingly straight out of textbooks and what they produce is neither artful nor beautiful. But Shakespeare contrasts this artlessness to great effect by having other characters, most notably Berowne, make beautiful poetry often using the very same conceits. For example, at III.i.181–190, Berowne uses images of war and his desire to be Cupid's "soldier," while throughout the play Armado uses the same image only to sound foolish and inappropriate. This creates a counterpoint throughout the play, a building up of tones not unlike a symphony. A careful reader of the play, or better, a careful viewer, must be aware of these sometimes very subtle tonal distinctions to fully appreciate the "story" of the characters.

Many of the characters are pre-cast types whose attributes dictate their behavior. Late in the play Berowne refers to the familiar stock types from the commedia dell'arte: "The pedant, the braggart, the hedge-priest, the fool, and the boy" (V.ii.536–537). The commedia dell'arte tradition dates to sixteenth-century Italy and was a type of theater utilizing professional actors who often improvised using stock characters. Many of the companies traveled to England and in turn influenced much of Renaissance drama, especially in the use of many of the stock character types. We can briefly examine each of the these types to better understand how Shakespeare's audience would have reacted to them. As Shakespeare's audience would have probably noted, many of the characters come to the play already assembled with their stereotypical traits in place. A brief examination of each will note not only their comic role in the play but their unique dramatic purpose to the commedia dell'arte tradition.

In a play about education, it is not by accident that the most humorous character is a "pedant," Holofernes. It is likely that Shakespeare originally found the name in Rabelais's *Gargantua and Pantagruel*, I. 14, where the name is used by a sophistic teacher of Latin. Despite his learning, Shakespeare's Holofernes shows very little true "wit"; his preferred method of communication is the synonym, as exemplified at IV.ii.13–17: "yet a kind of insinuation, as it were in via, in way of explication, to show, as it were replication, or, rather, *ostentare*, to show, as it were, his inclination,—after his undressed, unpolished, uneducated." Because of his peculiar speech habits, he is the best example of Shakespeare's distinction between wit and education: although Holofernes is undoubtedly well educated, that education does not translate into eloquence. For example, at IV.ii.92–193 he is able to quote Mantuan's first eclogue, a common school text that the character should know (and which most of the educated theatergoers would know). The line should read: *"Facile precor gelida quando pecus omne sub umbra Ruminat"* ("since your entire flock is resting in the cool shade, I say . . ."), but he makes a telling mistake, saying instead, *"Facile precor gelida quando peccas omnia sub umbra. Ruminat"* ("Easily, I say, you are making a mess of everything under the shade; it ruminates"). As R.W. David notes in his edition of the play, "A line so well known and so recently notorious

could hardly be misquoted by Shakespeare. Surely the blunder is Holofernes's" (81). The line was notorious for it had been bantered back
and forth in the Harvey Nashe pamphlet wars. Holofernes makes the
mistake even more damning by commenting that "who understandeth
thee not, loves thee not" (95–96). (In all fairness to Holofernes, some
editors argue that this is not a dramatic mistake but a printing error; for
a full treatment of the issues see the 2nd Arden edition, p. 81.) Despite
this possible mistake, and his general lack of true wit, he is the self-
appointed arbitrator of correctness. For example, it is Holofernes who
insists upon a "correct" pronunciation of "debt" at V.i.18–24. Yet, when
he speaks, it is very clear that he has no concept of "correctness" in the
sense of appropriateness. Also, his propensity for synonyms and ety-
mologies suggests that for Holoferenes, language is dead or uncreative,
and that alone, in a play in which characters display their integrity
through their creative and appropriate use of language, makes him a
lifeless and foolish character.

We are first introduced to Aramado, the "braggart," in the words of
another character, the king, who tells us in the first scene that he is "a
refined traveller of Spain" (I.i.161). We are also told he is "in all the
world's new fashion planted," that he is full of "complements" and that
he is a soldier. The name Armado inevitably suggests his Spanish roots
and the allusion to the Spanish Armada undermines his claims to glory.
Thus, Shakespeare's audience is set up to expect a humorous character
from the very beginning. He does not let us down; in the course of the
play he is the character who most represents the distinction between
role playing and true personality, thus, he is the "braggart." His role in
the play is to serve as a court jester, except that unlike a true jester, he
does not know he is being made fun of. After being introduced as a
traveler, he is noted as having "a mint of phrases in his brain;/One who
the music of his own vain tongue/Doth ravish like enchanting harmony."
He is entertaining because his "vain tongue" constantly "provokes" the
audience to "ridiculous smiling" and the "heaving" of lungs (III.i.74), to
use his own words.

It is fitting that we hear about Armado before we see him. In fact, in
addition to hearing about him, we hear from him, in the form of a letter
written charging Costard with breaking the king's edict. At line 215, we
are first introduced to Armado's style of writing: "Great Deputy, the
welkin's vicegerent, and sole dominator of Navarre, my soul's earth's
god and body's fostering patron." Through Armado's own words Shakespeare sets up the audience for his arrival, and he does not disappoint,
for when he does make his entrance, in the opening of scene ii, he is

quizzing Moth on great men who have been melancholy. However, in a reversal typical of the play, Moth gets the best of Armado, who cannot follow the young man's puns and commonsense witticisms. As his letters and interaction with other characters suggests, he is the village explainer, as he is in I.i.253 when he refers to Jaquenetta as "a child of our grandmother Eve, a female." His attempts at linguistic precision and clarity render him one of the least creative and witty characters. Armado is generally an ineffectual character in all his pursuits, but this is clearest when he is put in charge of Costard. His role as a figure of authority is constantly undermined both by Armado's own foolish conduct with Jaquenetta and because other characters refuse to acknowledge him as anything other than a clown. Shakespeare is continuing a long tradition of the braggart as the object as well as source of laughter. Braggarts are funny because they think of themselves as complete and self-sufficient, but comedies generally emphasize community and exchange and, as we will note, the lower-class characters, who often act just as foolish, are laughed with rather than at. Throughout the play, the dominant way in which this is illustrated is through language and its misuse.

Nathaniel, Costard's "hedge-priest," exists primarily as the parasite to Holoferenes and it is his role to consistently praise his host. When the two characters enter the play at IV.ii., Nathaniel speaks first, praising his companion for a previous offstage comment: "Very reverend sport, truly: and done in the testimony of a good conscience." Like Holofernes, he uses Latinate language solely for the sake of doing so, not because it is appropriate or suitable. It is Nathaniel who condemns Dull for a lack of eloquence and formal learning: "Sir, he hath never fed of the dainties that are bred in a book/He hath not eat paper, as it were; he hath not drunk/ink: his intellect is not replenished; he is only an/animal, only sensible in the duller parts" (IV.ii.23–26). Although he is right that Dull is unlearned, he misses the punning that Dull creates in the exchange that precedes his comments. More important, his praise for Holoferenes is clearly out of line with what the audience has already come to think of Holofernes. Like Holofernes and Armado, he serves to anchor the theme of education and linguistic acrobatics; unlike the less educated characters, these typical stock characters are laughed at rather than with.

Of the lower-class characters, Costard, the "fool," is the most representative of the class distinctions Shakespeare uses to define his characters. He is on stage more than any other character, appearing in every scene except II.i. As Carroll notes, he almost always enters after the scene has begun and the basic situation has been set up. This is his central role—he is a provocateur, a deflater, which is the traditional role of the clown. It is Costard who summarizes the play so nicely at V.i.36–40: "O, they have lived long on the almsbasket of words! I marvel thy master hath not eaten thee for a word, for thou art not so long by a head as *honorificabilitudinitatibus.*" Costard beats pedants at their own game, creating (or parroting) the type of artificial Latin that distinguishes them. At the risk of overgeneralizing Shakespeare's audience, it is possible Costard best represented the commoners in the audience—occasionally making malapropisms, and thus being laughed at by the better educated, Costard is also capable of puns and true insights, as in I.i.215, "Such is the simplicitie of man to hearken after the flesh," a fitting aphorism for the play. Costard plays a role in three of the play's most interesting and complex verbal exchanges, and in each he is responsible for a major pun on a Latin term used by another character but appropriated by him for the sake of laughter: at III.i.69 he translates "enigma" as "egma"; at III.i.118 "enfranchise" becomes "one Frances" and finally, "remuneration" at III.i.134–140 becomes for him a new unit of currency. All these examples suggest that Costard is the best exemplar of Shakespeare's attitude toward language: Costard is truly creative as opposed to merely learned. This assessment must be made in the dramatic context of the play—although Costard is not always aware of what he is saying, his creativity and linguistic energy that highlight the central theme of language and its relation to personality and social roles.

"The boy" is Moth, our final stock commedia dell'arte character. It is fitting to end with Moth, the young boy page, since his name is itself a pun: "moth" is reminiscent of both *mote*, meaning "fly" or "moth," and on "note-ing," as in *Much Ado About Nothing*—that is, nothing. Moth is surprisingly quick-witted and usually holds his own against the other characters, as he does in the following from I.ii.7–23:

> *Armado:* How canst thou part sadness and melancholy, my tender juvenal?
>
> *Moth:* By a familiar demonstration of the working, my tough senior.
>
> *Armado:* Why tough senior? why tough senior?
>
> *Moth:* Why tender juvenal? why tender juvenal?
>
> *Armado:* I spoke it, tender juvenal, as a congruent epitheton appertaining to thy young days, which we may nominate tender.

Moth:	And I, tough senior, as an appertinent title to your old time, which we may name tough.
Armado:	Pretty and apt.
Moth:	How mean you, sir? I pretty, and my saying apt? or I apt, and my saying pretty?
Armado:	Thou pretty, because little.
Moth:	Little pretty, because little. Wherefore apt?
Armado:	And therefore apt, because quick.

In this exchange, Moth not only holds his own against the much older and better educated Armado, he leads the conversation by questioning Armado's tendency toward pretentious Latinate words and sentence structure, a tendency suggested by the pun on "Juvenal," the name of the Roman satirist. Like Costard, he depends on the words of others to make his puns; thus, he is constantly entangled in the words of others, which is the main impetus for forwarding the action of the play. Like Costard, Moth summarizes the dominant theme of the play when he labels the exchange between Armado and Holofernes as "a great feast of languages" at V.i.35.

In contrast to these other characters, Anthony Dull, the Constable, is generally silent, and is not really given an opportunity to build or sully his reputation; he is called by Armado a "man of good repute, carriage, bearing, and estimation" (I.i.257). Although not mentioned by Costard as a stock character, the "dull" constable is a favorite stock character for Shakespeare. Like Dogberry in *Much Ado*, he too is noted for his malapropisms, or mistakenly used words; for example, he uses "reprehend" for "represent" at I.i.182 and "haud credo" as "awd (old) grey doe" at IV.ii.11. He is the opposite of Armado and Holofernes, who exist in a world of archaic Latin; Dull only works in a world of straight Anglo-Saxon. Like Bottom in *MND*, he lives up to his name.

Having noted the stock characters and their role in the comedy, we can now pay attention to those characters who are unique individuals. Most of the characters who can be labeled as individuals are of the upper class, with one notable exception, Jaquenetta. Although Jaquenetta appears in only two scenes, her presence is felt in several of the play's key scenes. In many ways Jaquenetta is also a stock character, a country wench, which defines much of her personality: she is uneducated, naive, sultry, and extremely fertile. But Shakespeare has some fun with her character by having not only Costard fall in love with her, but Armado as well. But Jaquenetta cannot even understand Armado's letter to her; she is illiterate and at IV.ii.91–92 she must have Holofernes read the letter for her. She is extremely passive (a trait she shares with Dull the Constable), responding only when spoken too, as she does at I.ii.126:

> *Armado:*   [*aside*] I do betray myself with blushing—Maid—
>
> *Jaquenetta:* Man.
>
> *Armado:*   I will visit thee at the lodge.
>
> *Jaquenetta:* That's thereby.
>
> *Armado:*   I know where it is situate.
>
> *Jaquenetta:* Lord, how wise you are!
>
> *Armado:*   I will tell thee wonders.
>
> *Jaquenetta:* With that face?
>
> *Armado:*   I love thee.
>
> *Jaquenetta:* So I heard you say.

This exchange borders on nonsense since, essentially, Jaquenetta and Armado speak different languages. Twice Jaquenetta speaks in provincial cliches, "With that face?" and "So I heard you say," which suggest that she is only superficially interested in what Armado says. It should be remembered that in Act I Jaquenetta was seen in a compromising situation with Costard, and her pregnancy, announced in the last act, is highly questionable in terms of who the father is. All these characteristics would suggest that Jaquenetta is firmly at the bottom of the social and cultural hierarchy of the play, except that the final songs, which are some of the most beautiful poetic passages in the play, are focused on the country stock from which Jaquenetta comes. In her passivity, it is possible that Shakespeare intended Jaquenetta to represent the simple life missing from the upper-class characters, who, in the end, unlike Jaquenetta, do not win romantic matches. If Armado has in fact been duped, Jaquenetta is the only character who goes into a relationship with eyes wide open.

The play centers around the young men and their relationships not only with the young women, but with each other. Although we have already discussed the scene in great detail, we can learn a lot about the young men from a close analysis of the scene that best defines them, the sonnet reading scene at IV.iii. Louis Montrose notes that, by line count, this scene is the center of the play (167). It is not only structurally central, but is central in terms of dramatic purpose as well. As Montrose notes, "The world of Narvarre has the appearance of a playground, a special place marked off from the pressures of social reality and the unpleasant implications of a world of fallen nature" (529). Verbal dexterity is the primary form of play for all the characters in the drama. It is easy to see the young men as cut from the same mold—all three are pretentious, witty, confused about their relationships to women, and, most important, poets. Therefore, it is through their poetry that the men reveal themselves. The play is built around "some strange pastime . . . Such as the shortness of time can shape" (IV.iii.374–375). It is the manner in which the aristocratic young men and women use their play that defines their characters. In other words, "the play is a fiction whose characters are motivated by their own responses to fictions" (530). Since each character responds differently, it can be said that they develop as characters as opposed to those stock characters already discussed.

The usual dates of composition of the play coincide with the height of the Petrarchan sonnet craze. For this reason the sonnet scene reveals that the young men are ruled by fashion. The scene also reveals that "the discrepancy between the illusory privacy and independence of action that each successive character believes he possesses and the highly formalized and predictable pattern of action they collectively present to the audience on behalf of the dramatist" (Montrose 536). In other words, because of their slavish attention to fashion, they gradually become less autonomous and begin to act more like characters in a play. In this scene, as in the play as a whole, words are action in the truest dramatic sense because it is through language that the characters are revealed and develop.

The sonnets the four young men write help to reveal their distinct character traits. Berowne, for example, focuses on "knowledge" and "oaths" in his sonnet, just as he did in the opening scene. In his sonnet, read by Nathaniel, Berowne asks, "If love make me foresworn, how shall I swear to love?" (IV.ii.101) Berowne is not a character to take anything at face value, but at the same time he is the most honest and "true" of the young men, primarily because he manages to see "through" the facade of many of his own speech acts and because he questions many of the standard conventions shared by the men. Likewise, it is Berowne who first questions the worth of the academe's aim at cloistered education: he reflects a commonsense approach to the utility of education when he asks, in his sonnet, "If knowledge be the mark, to know thee shall suffice;/Well learned is that tongue that well can thee commend." Berowne knows from the start that true knowledge lies in the love he takes an oath to deny himself. It is fitting that Berowne is the one to act as the master of ceremony for the revelations that are yet to come in the scene. Such self-awareness makes Berowne, in the words of one critic, the most "complex character created by Shakespeare before *Richard II*" (Agnew 40).

Despite his cynicism toward the art of rhetoric, Berowne's sonnet is the most fashionably "Petrarchan": he swears himself to her beauty, her voice is "dreadful thunder" and "music and sweet fire" (IV.ii.111–112). Holofernes calls Berowne's sonnet "unlearned, neither savouring of poetry, wit, nor invention" (152–153); he is wrong and right on this matter—Berowne's sonnet is conventional and fashionable, but it is also beautiful in its conventionality, a feat neither Holofernes nor Armado are ever able to accomplish.

Shakespeare has Berowne enter scene iii unaware that the audience has heard his sonnet, and he prepares to comment on the king's sonnet, which reads as follows:

> So sweet a kiss the golden sun gives not
> To those fresh morning drops upon the rose,
> As thy eye-beams, when their fresh rays have smote
> The night of dew that on my cheeks down flows:
> Nor shines the silver moon one half so bright
> Through the transparent bosom of the deep,
> As doth thy face through tears of mine give light;
> Thou shinest in every tear that I do weep:
> No drop but as a coach doth carry thee;
> So ridest thou triumphing in my woe.
> Do but behold the tears that swell in me,
> And they thy glory through my grief will show:
> But do not love thyself; then thou wilt keep
> My tears for glasses, and still make me weep. (ll. 24–37)

Poetry is so much a part of the king's existence that, once he falls in love, even his commentary on his own sonnet, which follows directly, could be seen as a seamless continuation of the sonnet: "O queen of queens! how far dost thou excel,/ No thought can think, nor tongue of mortal tell./ How shall she know my griefs?" He has become so unconsciously poetic that even his own commentary is infused with Petrarchan conceits. Navarre, who started the play attempting to separate himself from all the world's cares, is now so swept up in them that he cannot tell the difference between logic and love.

Like Berowne's, Navarre's sonnet is likewise hyperbolic: "So sweet a kiss the golden sun gives not/To those fresh morning drops upon the rose" (ll. 24–25). As Carroll notes, Navarre's sonnet is structured on "leisurely . . . parallel similes" (109) such as "so-as," "nor-so-as," "no-so." Navarre, even more than Berowne, reveals himself through this sonnet to be all surface with little depth. Berowne parodies the language of Navarre's sonnet when he comments that "in your tears/There is no certain princess that appears" (ll. 153–154); Berowne is highlighting the most Petrarchan and conceited part of Navarre's sonnet, and by doing so reveals the most substantial difference in their characters: Berowne is often insightful where Navarre is merely fashionable.

Likewise, Navarre's character does not develop as much as Berowne's. Navarre's lack of development and his general ineffectualness make him akin to the more stock characters. As a king he is limited to socially regulated behavior and must serve as "the law" to the other characters who are socially freer to transgress. Once the transgressions have occurred, which is as early as Act I, the king's dramatic purpose is gradually diminished. Given that comedy is structured on a movement away from the restraints of law to freedom, the comedy must leave the king behind.

In contrast to Navarre's sonnet, Longaville's sonnet is the product of more exercise:

> Did not the heavenly rhetoric of thine eye,
> 'Gainst whom the world cannot hold argument,
> Persuade my heart to this false perjury?
> Vows for thee broke deserve not punishment.
> A woman I forswore; but I will prove,
> Thou being a goddess, I forswore not thee:
> My vow was earthly, thou a heavenly love;
> Thy grace being gain'd cures all disgrace in me.
> Vows are but breath, and breath a vapour is:
> Then thou, fair sun, which on my earth dost shine,
> Exhalest this vapour-vow; in thee it is:
> If broken then, it is no fault of mine:
> If by me broke, what fool is not so wise
> To lose an oath to win a paradise? (ll. 57–70)

Like Navarre before him, Longaville is also conscious of the limits of
language to express the extent of his love: "I fear these stubborn lines
lack power to move. . . . These numbers will I tear, and write in prose"
(ll. 52–54) suggest the trouble he has gone through in composing them,
and the effort shows. The opening lines, "Did not the heavenly rhetoric
of thine eye/'Gainst whom the world cannot hold argument," suggest
that his poem, although Petrarchan in its conceits, is based upon a deeper
metaphor of logic and argument. As Carroll notes, the structural component of this sonnet is much deeper than Navarre's: lines six through
nine introduce a premise, while line ten produces the conclusion (113).
Whereas Navarre's logic became infused with poetic conceits, Longaville's poetic conceits are infused with logic. Either way, the stoic humanistic learning the young men earlier sought is no longer attainable
or desirable.

Dumain, who enters last, takes a different form for his expression of
love:

> On a day—alack the day!—
> Love, whose month is ever May,
> Spied a blossom passing fair
> Playing in the wanton air:
> Through the velvet leaves the wind,
> All unseen, can passage find;
> That the lover, sick to death,
> Wish himself the heaven's breath.
> Air, quoth he, thy cheeks may blow;
> Air, would I might triumph so!
> But, alack, my hand is sworn
> Ne'er to pluck thee from thy thorn;
> Vow, alack, for youth unmeet,
> Youth so apt to pluck a sweet!
> Do not call it sin in me,
> That I am forsworn for thee;
> Thou for whom Jove would swear
> Juno but an Ethiope were;
> And deny himself for Jove,
> Turning mortal for thy love. (ll. 98–117)

His poem is a standard pastoral ode, emphasizing, as do the final songs,
the beauty, innocence, and unity of the natural world. As these last two
poems suggest, in many ways Longaville and Dumain are less important,

less distinct characters than Berowne and the king. In Navarre's case, the images are fitting for his rank. However, in the case of Longaville and Dumain, the images are not of dramatic importance; in Carroll's words, "The poems of Longaville and Dumain . . . are not thematically or psychologically related to their characters at all, and might be switched with no offense to dramatic propriety" (Carroll 117).

So far we have mentioned only one female character, Jaquenetta. This is not a deliberate omission nor is it meant to suggest that the women do not play an important role in *LLL*. On the contrary, the women are the impetus for the action; from the moment of their entrance in the second act they propel the action forward. The young men fall in love with them and subsequently develop as characters, the diplomatic mission they are sent on opens up the possibility for intrigue, and it is their moral and ethical viewpoint that is the standard by which other characters come to be viewed. But, in the words of David Bevington, the young women do not develop or change in a dramatic manner in the course of the play: "The young women do not change much as dramatic characters because they are not portrayed as in need of change; the dramatic interest is instead in the men's changing attitudes toward them" (6). Ironically, it is their centrality to the play's plot that renders them so static. One important role the women serve in the play is as a moral standard by which the young men should be judged. They tend to "expose faults and correct them" (Anderson 61). Although they may not be perfect (even though there is a long critical tradition of seeing them as such; see Chapter 4), they do conduct themselves in a way that contrasts them to the frivolousness of the young men. For example, Rosaline delineates Berowne's character in a very insightful and, in her own way, polite manner:

> Oft have I heard of you, my Lord Berowne,
> Before I saw you; and the world's large tongue
> Proclaims you for a man replete with mocks,
> Full of comparisons and wounding flouts,
> Which you on all estates will execute
> That lie within the mercy of your wit. (V.ii.831–836)

Rosaline praises what the audience also sees as praiseworthy in Berowne, his wit, but she also summarizes what the audience also notes, which is that Berowne's wit needs to be tempered. Rosaline, like the other ladies, is more aware of the ironies and actions of the young men. In this way the audience is made to sympathize with the ladies. In the same manner in which only Berowne and the king can be said to stand out among the men, only Rosaline and the princess have unique personalities among the women. For example, it is Rosaline and the princess who plan and seem to take the most enjoyment out of ridiculing the young men.

In much the same way that Berowne is the conscience of much of the play, so too is the princess. Notice, for example, how she summarizes, albeit sarcastically, one of the dominant themes of the play, the importance of sincerity in oath taking:

> You nickname virtue; vice you should have spoke;
> For virtue's office never breaks men's troth.
> Now, by my maiden honour, yet as pure
> As the unsullied lily, I protest,
> A world of torments though I should endure,
> I would not yield to be your house's guest;
> So much I hate a breaking cause to be
> Of heavenly oaths, vow'd with integrity. (V.ii.349–356)

Given that this speech comes while the young women are toying with the men and teasing them about the masque, the princess, and to a slightly lesser degree Rosaline, reveal themselves to be the match for the young men, both in terms of their ability to deceive and flirt, but also to court. She knows that the vows the young men have made are not "vow'd with integrity," which is why the women get the upper hand in the closing moments of the play when they suggest a final test of the men's ability to keep a vow; it is telling that the two who make the most elaborate "rules" for their mates are Rosaline and the princess, with Maria and Katherine simply echoing their requests.

SHAKESPEARIAN META-DRAMA

Like many of his plays, most famously *Hamlet* and *Midsummer Night's Dream*, Shakespeare explores the nature of theatricality in *LLL*. *Love's Labour's Lost* contains an unprecedented three "plays-within-the play." The first, the sonnet reading scene at IV.iii, is the least self-consciously theatrical, but nonetheless it thrusts the players into the role of audience in such a way that they momentarily view each other's actions in the same way the real audience does. Bertrand Evans cites as the "perfection of the jest" the fact that we "overpeer the topmost overpeerer" (21). The scene uses five different levels of knowledge and awareness, from our own down to Dumain's at the bottom. These "exploitable gaps or discrepancies" are an "indispensable condition of comedy" (1). As I have already acknowledged in this chapter, this scene is central in developing many of the major issues of the play while also calling attention to the play as a play. It is comic, but there is also a serious dramatic purpose for it—to lead to the ultimate deflation of Berowne. William Carroll is insightful on the importance of the scene: "The sonnet-reading scene indicates how in passages like these the linguistic dimension of the play finds an exact counterpart in the dramatic structure: counterpointed levels of diction imply contending levels of awareness" (69).

The same counterpointing could be said of the other two internal dramas, the Masque of the Muscovites (V.ii) and the Pageant of the Nine Worthies (V.ii), both of which are more overtly about the nature of drama. As Carroll notes, these "sections also shape the course of the play's debate and guide the audience's response to the play as a whole" (65), not only because they reiterate important themes of the play, but because the very nature of performance or theater as play are developed in them. The Masque of Muscovites is more overtly "dramatic" since it is essentially a play with characters (who are themselves characters in a play) playing parts. As we note in Chapter 3, the masque could also have topical appeal to the Elizabethan court, and therefore could easily also serve as a mirror to the court and its courtiers. Given that it is a likely later edition to the play, its importance is not so much to character or plot development as to the overall tone and pomp of the play.

"Role playing" is an important theme in the play, and the Masque develops it in a new way—the men are wearing figurative masks all through the play, and the ladies refuse to acknowledge the masks as real. The young ladies themselves wear masks, both literally in the Masque and figuratively in that they do not show their "real" selves to the young men. Boyet reflects this theme at V.ii.296–298: "Fair ladies masked are roses in their bud;/Dismasked, their damask sweet commixture shown,/ Are angels vailing clouds, or roses blown." The entire masque and its resolution are over 300 lines long and constitute a major portion of Act V. Masques were a typical form of courtly entertainment and often reflected a simple theme of concordia/discordia, or the resolution of disorder. Most importantly to another dominant theme in *LLL*, they were a form of courtly play. However, the ladies do not allow the masque to function—they turn it into a game and undermine any serious intent on the part of the young men. The masque is even equated with courtly performance when Berowne comments that it was the ladies' intent to "dash it like a Christmas comedy" (V.ii.462).

The Pageant of the Nine Worthies is perhaps the most thematically and dramatically important of the internal plays. Like a similar scene with the rude mechanicals in *MND*, the parts are handed out, rehearsals are reportedly held, and the audiences, in this case the stage audience, are given a chance to respond. Again, as in *MND*, the performance provides an opportunity for the two camps (i.e., that is the young men and young women) to temporarily put aside their differences and join together in making sport of the play. Like the subplot in *MND*, the subplot in *LLL* centers around the lower-class characters and how those characters come together to entertain the upper class. Again like *MND*, the behavior and misadventures of the low characters parallel those of the upper class. For example, in *LLL*, Armado's totally inappropriate and unlikely love for Jaquenetta serves to reflect the more harmonious love of the young men for the young women. Likewise, in a gender reversal, the Faerie Queene's love for Bottom appears doomed from the beginning and primarily serves to highlight the more "natural" and appropriate love between the pair of wooers. The Nine Worthies performance, like the *Tragedy of Pyramus and Thisby*, is laughed at by the upper-class viewers. In both cases the play-within-the play serves to reflect major themes of the main plot, respectively, the fate of lovers and the importance of fame and worthiness.

As discussed in Chapter 4, Shakespeare takes a great number of liberties with the tradition of the Nine Worthies, liberties that are very suggestive of the main themes of the play. However, dramatically it is important to note that the casting of the roles is what first tips off the audience to the scene's comic potential. How can Moth play Hercules? When Nathaniel asks, "Where will you find men worthy enough to present them" (V.i.120–121), Holofernes and Armado offer themselves. The audience already knows the truth behind these two characters, so from the beginning the play is miscast.

The entrance of the messenger Marcade with the news of the princess's father's death at line 711 breaks down the walls of Navarre and its inherent theatricality. Again it is Berowne who states this point when he dismisses the players and states, "Worthies, away! The scene begins to cloud" (716). Death has come to a comedy, a comedy that exists on at least two levels—as a comedy written by Shakespeare that we are watching, and a (unintended) comedy performed by Holofernes and company. With the entrance of Marcade, the two worlds collide and a happy resolution is no longer possible.

It is easier, in many ways, to think of *LLL* as a play of nine scenes rather than the more traditional five acts (Heninger 53). At 922 lines, scene ii of the final act is the longest in Shakespeare. It is nearly one-third the length of the entire play, and it is four times the length of either the second or third acts. Yet, despite its lack of plot development in the scene, it holds together dramatically due not only to its spectacle, but due to the glimpse inside the characters' psyches once they cease to be characters in the play we are watching but become themselves characters in a play they are watching.

THE SONGS OF VER AND HIEMS

The play comes to stunning climax with the pair of songs inserted so as to look almost like an afterthought. The play quickly moves from dramatic artifice to lyrical poetry, but, as many critics have noted, these songs are essential to completing the language theme that runs throughout the play. The play would seem to end with Berowne's remark that "That's too long for a play," but Shakespeare delays that ending by bringing back Armado to join the princess, the king, and Dumain to read the dialogue of Hiems and Ver. (*A Midsummer Night's Dream* similarly ends with a song and dance and with Puck providing a commentary of the action of the play proper: "If we shadows have offended,/Think but this, and all is mended,/That you have but slumb'red here/While these visions did appear./And this weak and idle theme,/No more yielding but a dream.") Because they are introduced by Armado, and given what has transpired earlier, we expect the worst; the previous set pieces and plays-within-the-play have set us up to expect yet another horrible and pretentious speech. "We have every right to expect a disaster in these songs. But instead, to our delight, we witness a small miracle, one that could not have been predicted" (Carroll 208). Louis Montrose sees the songs as a way of reconfirming the essence of play: with the entrance of Marcade, Berowne and Navarre had been forced to acknowledge that their fanciful world was a "playground bounded by the world outside" (543). In this way the songs complete the outward movement of the play, from the seemingly isolated and sterile world of the academe to the universal world of nature. Shakespeare has structured the play around an ever-widening vision of how to properly communicate. The songs also allow the play to avoid a choice between an artificial happy or sad ending; as

Heninger notes, "to avoid such limitation, Shakespeare resorted to a non-dramatic conclusion, to poetry of a different order, to lyric song, where the counters are less substantial than characters in a three-dimensional setting" (45).

The ending songs are an integral part of the plot of *LLL*. In a play about its own artistry and artifice, the concluding songs are fitting in that they are complex yet simple, traditional while surprising, pleasing and harsh, and beautiful while sincere. In short, they reflect everything that the pretentious characters would like to be able to do verbally but cannot. Further, they form a thematic backdrop to the action of the play in many ways. For example, there are specific humans mentioned in the songs, Dick, Tom, Joan, Marina, rather than the types that the characters of the play tend toward (Heninger 28). The two poems offer dramatically different tones: Spring's song, while melodic and natural, is highly cynical of love, while Winter's song is more optimistic in tone and unadorned in style. In this manner the verses continue the play's debate structure while conferring linguistic stability and adeptness. Thematically, the change of seasons suggests the cyclical nature of the world, which Marcade's entrance also suggests, while the daily routine of shepherds, ploughmen, and "greasy Joan" is in opposition to the leisure of the main upper-class characters. It could further be suggested that by making the songs so beautiful while describing lower-class lives, Shakespeare was taking the opportunity to finally balance the worldview presented in the play: the songs focus on members of the lower class who show common sense, much like two characters in the play, Jaquenetta and Costard.

Just as it is throughout the play, time is a major theme of the songs. "When" is the first word of every stanza of the two songs. Every word is in the present tense (Heninger 31). Again, we should be reminded at the end of the words of the opening speech of the play:

> Let fame, that all hunt after in their lives,
> Live regist'red upon our brazen tombs,
> And then grace us in the disgrace of death;
> When, spite of cormorant devouring Time . . .

Note here the condemnation of death and the corresponding suggestion that it can be avoided. Likewise, the final poem's emphasis on those who are not famous counters the movement of the play's action as summarized in the opening speech. A little later the king charges that Berowne is intentionally malicious, and uses words that echo the final songs: "Berowne is like an envious sneaping frost/That bites the first-born infants of the spring" (I.i.100–101). This pronouncement takes on new meaning in the context of the final speeches of the play. Even Berowne is forced to admit that he is regulated by the seasons: "At Christmas I no more desire a rose/Than wish a snow in May's new-fangled shows;/But like of each thing that in season grows" (I.i.105–107).

Despite the seemingly meandering nature of the play and the unruly final act, the play does have a very tight and coherent structure that can best be appreciated by keeping the whole play in view. For a play about language and the nature of drama and poetry, and thus about itself, it is fitting that the dramatic structure of the play calls attention to the most fundamental aspects of comedy and theater. However, it is also testament to the play that while the play resists so many of the simple pleasures of comic theater, in the end it is one of Shakespeare's most satisfying comic achievements.

WORKS CITED

Agnew, Gates. "Berowne and the Progress of *Love's Labour's Lost*." *Shakespeare Studies* 4 (1968): 40–72.

Anderson, J.J. "The Morality of 'Love's Labour's Lost.' " *Shakespeare Survey* 24 (1971): 55–62.

Baldwin, T.W. *Shakespeare's Five-Act Structure: Shakespeare's Early Plays on the Background of Renaissance Theories of Five-Act Structure from 1470*. Urbana: University of Illinois Press, 1947.

Barber, C.L. *Shakespeare's Festive Comedy: A Study of Dramatic Form and its Relation to Social Custom*. Princeton: Princeton University Press, 1959.

Bevington, David. " 'Jack Hath Not Jill": Failed Courtship in Lyly and Shakespeare." *Shakespeare Survey: An Annual Survey of Shakespeare Studies and Production*. Ed. Stanley Wells. Cambridge: Cambridge University Press, 1990, 42.

Bonazza, Blaze Odell. *Shakespeare's Early Comedies: A Structural Analysis*. The Hague: Mouton, 1966.

Carroll, William. *The Great Feast of Language in "Love's Labour's Lost."* Princeton: Princeton University Press, 1976.

Coleridge, Samuel Taylor. *Writings on Shakespeare*. Ed. Terence Hawkes. New York: Capricorn Books, 1959.

David, Richard W., ed. *Love's Labour's Lost*. New Arden Shakespeare. 2nd series. Cambridge: Harvard University Press, 1951.

Evans, Bertrand. *Shakespeare's Comedies*. Oxford: Clarendon Press, 1967.

Heninger, S.K., Jr. "The Pattern of *Love's Labour's Lost.*" *Shakespeare Studies* 7 (1974): 25–53.

Montrose, Louis Adrian. *"Curious-knotted Garden": The Form, Themes, and Contexts of Shakespeare's "Love's Labour's Lost."* *Salzburg Studies in English Literature: Elizabethan and Renaissance Studies* 56. Salzburg, 1977.

Woudhuysen, H.R., ed. *Love's Labour's Lost.* Arden Shakespeare. 3rd series. Walton-on-Thames: Thomas Nelson and Sons, 1998.

4

THEMES

The title *Love's Labour's Lost* suggests two of the major themes of the play, transformation and love. The title's personification of love suggests the extent to which it serves not only as a static theme but as a dynamic player in the action of the play. Love is transformative, even if the change it effects is ultimately a negative one, a loss. Further, the word "labour" suggests the labors of Hercules, and thereby the emphasis on learned myths and images as well as the role that "work" plays in the interaction between the characters: in the play, labor is characterized as the actual work of the lower-class characters and the playful leisure that defines the upper-class characters. However, as the play develops, the two worlds come together as both groups of characters attempt to win love in the course of the play. Thus, the title reflects some of the dominant themes and images that are reiterated throughout the play.

The opening speech of the play is a remarkable example of Shakespeare's ability to intertwine several themes in a poetically and dramatically gratifying manner. Many of the play's major themes are illustrated in this speech.

> *Ferdinand:* Let fame, that all hunt after in their lives,
> Live register'd upon our brazen tombs
> And then grace us in the disgrace of death;
> When, spite of cormorant devouring Time,
> The endeavor of this present breath may buy
> That honour which shall bate his scythe's keen edge
> And make us heirs of all eternity.
> Therefore, brave conquerors,—for so you are,

That war against your own affections
And the huge army of the world's desires,—
Our late edict shall strongly stand in force:

As we will note, most of the play's main themes are suggested in these eleven lines. For example, two of the play's major themes, death and fame or reputation, are central to the play's opening situation. Ferdinand has brought together several young lords to create a "little Academe" where they might pursue humanistic studies unhampered by the outside world. The idea that studies and humanistic pursuits will bring immortality is a typical Renaissance conceit and it recalls Socrates's dialogues. This is a deliberate reference, suggesting the kind of humanism that defines the aims of the young men: they desire an idealized world free from the practical constraints of everyday life. However, throughout the play, as this academe gradually breaks down, the self-proclaimed "brave conquerors" end up violating their oaths and being conquered by the "world's desires." As in most of Shakespeare's comedies, the "war against . . . affections/And the huge army of the world's desires" is won by desire and affection. The speech continues:

Navarre shall be the wonder of the world;
Our court shall be a little Academe,
Still and contemplative in living art.
You three, Biron, Dumain, and Longaville,
Have sworn for three years' term to live with me
My fellow-scholars, and to keep those statutes
That are recorded in this schedule here:
Your oaths are pass'd; and now subscribe your names,
That his own hand may strike his honour down
That violates the smallest branch herein:

Ironically, the young men think that fame and reputation, and by extension the avoidance of death, can be won by adherence to a written oath, yet the king uses the phrase "living art," the full meaning of which is yet to be revealed to them. On the other hand, Navarre's use of phrases and terms such as "three years' term," "statutes," "oaths," "subscribe," and "violates" suggests the rigidity of law that comedies eventually break down. In fact, the breakdown of this oath in the face of love is suggested just forty-two lines later when Berowne states:

Or study where to meet some mistress fine,
When mistresses from common sense are hid;
Or, having sworn too hard a keeping oath,
Study to break it and not break my troth.

Berowne speaks of common sense, so it is fitting that he is the character to first suggest that the pretentiousness of the academe is potentially a front for romance. Also, Shakespeare sets up common sense and "living art" as the antagonist to the rigidity of arbitrary laws and artificial social codes. Berowne is the spokesman for this awareness: he knows, or at least suspects, that the plan is doomed to failure. In this way oath taking is a microcosm for language use in the play: language is trustworthy, dependent solely upon the motives of the speaker. For much of the play, language fails to mean anything certain or solid. Much of the time it simply provides an opportunity for more language. Oath taking (and breaking), therefore, serves as the thematic backbone of Shakespeare's comic intention, setting up from the beginning the expectation that love (and common sense) will win out in the end. At the play's conclusion, the young women make one final attempt at soliciting a sincere oath from the men, making them swear to perform appropriate service in order to repent their ways and show that they are worthy of love. What was at the beginning of the play a way of removing themselves from love and romance by the end of the play is used to keep the hope of love alive, even if the labors of the play are, for the time being, lost.

LANGUAGE AND THE TIMELESSNESS OF LOVE

The basic goal of the academe, to be remembered and therefore to defeat time, is a theme seen throughout Shakespeare's work, but it is seen most eloquently in the sonnets, as the first two lines of Sonnet 19 illustrate: "Devouring Time, blunt thou the lion's paws,/And make the earth devour her own sweet brood." Sonnet 16 opens with a similar war image to illustrate the defeat of time: "But wherefore do not you a mightier way/Make war upon this bloody tyrant Time?" As Anne Barton notes, in the sonnets Shakespeare "proposes two weapons against Time: children and, more persuasively, poetry. Navarre's Academe, significantly, has nothing to do either with begetting children or with the perpetuation of an actual love experience in verse" (Introduction 209). Nonetheless, by the end of the play Jaquenetta is with child and each of the lords has composed a poem to his love and done so in language fitting for love poetry.

As I noted previously, the theme of time and timelessness is important from the opening speech and continues to the dialogue that ends the play; throughout the lords continually confuse time and timelessness (Carroll 210). For example, Navarre is overconfident about time; at the end of the sonnet-reading scene, he states, "Away, away! no time shall be omitted/That will be time, and may by us be fitted" (IV.iii.378–379). Although Dumain states that love's "month is every May" (IV.iii.100), the songs show that May must be balanced by the other seasons. The seasons are "continually bound" together (222), a bounding that is illustrated by two aspects of the syntax. First is the "when . . . then" syllogistic style that opens each of the four stanzas, "a valid and natural seasonal logic which contrasts with the sophistical logic the men have used earlier. Everything is placed in its natural time and order" (222). Second is the use of conjunctives; ten of the thirty-six lines begin with "and" (223). Fittingly, the songs use language and the conventions of grammar to bridge all the oppositions and dichotomies of the play.

The women, however, are the true "custodians of time" (Carroll 212), as Berowne himself notes:

> What? I love, I sue, I seek a wife?
> A woman that is like a German clock,
> Still a-repairing, ever out of frame
> And never going aright, being a watch,
> But being watched that it may still go right! (III.i.186–190)

As with many of the passages in the play, this one is rich in metaphoric meaning. First, clocks were suggestive of male and female sex organs (as were watches and dials). Second, according to H.R. Woudhuysen in a note to this passage, German clocks were more valuable and beautiful than reliable, and thus Berowne is suggesting the same of women. Longaville, after hearing of his penance, says that "the time is long" (V.ii.825); he has finally arrived at a more realistic view of time and its relation to love than he or the other young men had at the beginning of the play. This theme is highlighted by the fact that the play literally runs out of time.

As Shakespeare's sonnets suggest, one of the ways to defeat time is to write poetry, and this is a lesson each of the young men learns in the course of the play. Even though the lord's poetry is ultimately sterile love poetry, given that the only hope of begetting lies with Jaquenetta and the father of her child, be it Costard or Armado, it is language that the lords utilize to present themselves to the world. Ultimately their eloquence is not an empowering trait in the play; the young women being wooed by the lords are not impressed by their eloquence, as Maria states after receiving a letter from Longaville: "The letter is too long by half a mile" (V.ii.54).

In the Renaissance "love" could mean either physical love (i.e., love for a material thing or person) that when allowed to rule unchecked turned into lust, or, in a Petrarchan sense, a higher, Platonic spiritual love. The latter, which served as a fashionable conceit in love poetry thanks to the popularity of Italian Petrarchism, saw love as a microcosm of divine love and an ennobling force. The clearest example of Platonic love is seen in Edmund Spenser's "In Honour of Love":

> For having yet in this deducted spright,
> Some sparks remaining of that heavenly fire,
> He is enlumind with that goodly light,
> Unto like goodly semblant to aspire;
> Therefore in choice of love, he doth desire
> That seems on earth most heavenly, to embrace,
> That same Beauty, born of heavenly race. (ll. 106–112)

Shakespeare is having some fun with this notion of Platonic love, first by having the young men escape the world to study in a Platonic academy, and second by having them fall in love so quickly and so deeply. The latter trait is a common one in Renaissance comedies, but in *LLL* it takes on a new depth due to its juxtaposition to the goals of the academy. However much the young men are overpowered by the women's beauty, the play parodies Petrarchan love. When the young men withdraw to write their sonnets, Shakespeare's parody becomes overt. "Feminine beauty and the Platonic pursuit are placed at odds with one another, and Berowne's initial misgivings about the wisdom of the Academy are, in the context of the play, proven correct" (Goldstein 342). Rather than emphasizing how love leads to knowledge of all things, in *LLL* love serves as a distraction. The whole play is "an attack on the very notion of the Platonic Academy" (340), and, by extension, the verisimilitude of poetic language.

Another way to think about the importance of language is to consider how language can portray heavenly truth, or even true earthly love. In short, this is the difference between proper and improper language. The most comic example of improper language occurs in IV.i when Boyet reads Armado's love letter:

> By heaven, that thou art fair, is most infallible; true, that thou art beauteous; truth itself, that thou art lovely. More fairer than fair, beautiful than beauteous, truer than truth itself, have commiseration on thy heroical vassal! The magnanimous and most illustrate king Cophetua set eye upon the pernicious and indubitate beggar Zenelophon; and he it was that might rightly say, Veni, vidi, vici; which to annothanize in the vulgar,—O base and obscure vulgar!—videlicet, He came, saw, and overcame: he came, one; saw two; overcame, three. (ll. 61–72)

This speech is a perfect parody of Petrarchan love conventions seen through the eyes of an overly pedantic writer. "By heaven that thou art fair" is itself a typical Petrarchan conceit, but "infallible" is not a properly tuned word for love poetry, suggesting as it does unrefined learning and Latin scholasticism. In the letter, Armado notes that there is a difference between the way the educated upper class speak and the way the "base and obscure vulgar" lower-class characters understand. Despite the comparison of himself to Cophetua and Jaquenetta to Zenelophon, his declaration is not metaphoric; rather it is highly literal ("thou are lovely"). It achieves whatever "literary" merit it has by a heightened vocabulary, which renders it almost nonsensical to the average ear. Again, language fails to communicate.

POETRY

Even Berowne, who is the most suspicious of the formal conventions and speech acts in the play, can never acknowledge that nature is prior to experience or language:

> From women's eyes this doctrine I derive:
> They are the ground, the books, the academes
> From whence doth spring the true Promethean fire. (IV.iii.298–300)

Even in love, Berowne still relies on a conventional metaphor, that a woman's eyes are the source of all knowledge, defined tellingly by him as books. He knows that the academe is a bad idea, but he still sees the world through a contrived and scholarly lense. Like Armado, he contemplates whether or not language is equitable with beauty, whether, to paraphrase Keats, truth is beauty and beauty is truth. All the men are, to some extent, limited by their belief in Petrarchan conceits.

In the sonnet-reading scene all the previous themes of oaths, language, and artifice come together. When Berowne first sees Longaville enter with his sonnet, he says, "He comes in like a perjure, wearing papers" (IV.iii.45). Longaville responds: "Am I the first that have been perjured so?" The language of law and order permeates the lord's private discourse, but Longaville's real concern is that his poem might not be good enough to affect his love:

> I fear these stubborn lines lack power to move:
> O sweet Maria, empress of my love!
> These numbers will I tear, and write in prose.

Longaville knows that language must communicate, that it must be productive and fruitful. In this scene we are able to see the young men struggle with language and its impact on their intended audience. Later in the play, at Act V, scene ii, we see the young women's reaction to the poetry, which is predictably critical:

> Nay, I have verses too, I thank Berowne;
> The numbers true, and, were the numbering too,
> I were the fairest goddess on the ground. (34–36)

Berowne got the meter correct, as one might predict from a scholar of fashionable poetry, but Rosaline doubts the verisimilitude of his "numbering," or reckoning. Maria says of Longaville's verses, which he sent along with a necklace of pearls, that she wishes, "The chain were longer and the letter short" (56). Berowne, however, reassures Longaville that verse is the proper language of love:

> O, rhymes are guards on wanton Cupid's hose:
> Disfigure not his slop.

Much like Shakespeare's sonnets, the play investigates the nature of poetic imagery. Likewise, the women are not standard, stereotypical Petrarchan ideals, rather, Rosaline is born "to make black fair./Her favour turns the fashion of the days" (IV.iii.257–258). Likewise, in sonnet 130,

"My mistress' eyes are nothing like the sun;/Coral is far more red than her lips' red"; Shakespeare parodies the fashionable love poetry of his time. This is quite fitting for a play that has "fashion" as a central theme. For example, Longaville and Dumain's sonnets are more traditional in their Petrarchanism. Longaville's sonnet opens with a very traditional conceit: "Did not the heavenly rhetoric of thine eye,/'Gainst whom the world cannot hold argument,/Persuade my heart to this false perjury?" (IV.iii.59–61). On the other hand, Berowne calls attention to their unreflective Petrarchanism; Berowne could be commenting on Spenser when he writes:

> This is the liver-vein, which makes flesh a deity,
> A green goose a goddess; pure, pure idolatry.
> God amend us, God amend! We are much out o' th' way. (IV.iii.74–76)

It could be argued that Berowne ends up a Petrarchan, and this could be the joke Shakespeare intended. Berowne, who, after being revealed as a hypocrite, acknowledges that "For where is any author in the world/ Teaches such beauty as a woman's eye?" (IV.iii.312–313). Unreflective and stereotypical imagery becomes yet another example of the lack of "honest" language on the part of the young men. In a much discussed passage, Berowne and Ferdinand debate about the appropriateness of black as a poetic image:

> *Berowne:*   Is ebony like her? O wood divine!
> A wife of such wood were felicity.
> O! Who can give an oath? where is a book?
> That I may swear beauty doth beauty lack,
> If that she learn not of her eye to look:
> No face is fair that is not full so black.
>
> *Ferdinand:* O paradox! Black is the badge of hell,
> The hue of dungeons and the school of night;
> And beauty's crest becomes the heavens well.
>
> *Berowne:*   Devils soonest tempt, resembling spirits of light.
> O! If in black my lady's brows be deck'd . . .
> (IV.iii.244–254)

In this exchange, both Berowne and Ferdinand estimate a woman's worth by her relation to poetic standards of beauty. Berowne wishes to take an oath, as he did in the first scene, swearing that black is the very color of beauty. Oath taking again becomes a way of positively proving sincerity and of fixing speech acts in relation to the truth of the "real" or material world. Yet Berowne cannot be trusted to keep his oath given how quickly he and his fellow lovers broke their original oaths.

Contrast these formulaic descriptions to the following exchange between the forester and the Princess on the true praise of beauty:

> *Princess:* Nay, never paint me now:
> Where fair is not, praise cannot mend the brow.
> Here, good my glass, take this for telling true:
> Fair payment for foul words is more than due.
>
> *Forester:* Nothing but fair is that which you inherit.
>
> *Princess:* See see, my beauty will be saved by merit!
> O heresy in fair, fit for these days!
> A giving hand, though foul, shall have fair praise.
> (IV.i.17–23)

Again we see an example of the women refusing to use language in a less than sincere manner. The object of the princess's scorn is opportunistic, stereotypical praise. For her, sincerity is defined as natural, and nature is prior to language; hence, "praise cannot mend the brow."

The real difference between the women and men in the play is that the men insist that language is an artificial system whereas the women see it as "living art." The concluding lines of the play are seen by Malcolm Evans as exemplifying this difference and the inherent difficulty of pursuing human reason via isolated study and printed books. This is reflected when, after the songs have ended, Armado steps forward to announce: "The words of Mercury are harsh after the songs of/ Apollo. You that way: we this way." Whether later additions of an editor or director, for Evans these lines suggest that Mercury is opposed to the "rhyming" of Apollo—that is, the pursuit of the beauty of the spoken word as opposed to the silent written word. Throughout the play the stability of the written word is juxtaposed to the relative instability of the spoken word, which is seen in the huge number of puns and malapropisms in every scene, practically every speech, of the play. However, spoken language is more fruitful and capable of conveying useful meaning. The two miscarried letters are good examples of the insufficiency and unreliability of the written word. Such juxtaposition typically defines characters according to their education and economic class, but just as often Shakespeare uses them to challenge the conventional categories of characters and uses the resulting linguistic tension to heighten the comic inversion of the upper and lower classes. This reversal is inherently comic and is one of the reasons for the play's success on stage.

ELOQUENCE AND GRACE

As Moth notes, "They have been at a great feast of languages, and stol'n the scraps" (V.i.39–40). For Costard, language is a material commodity, in this case food, or as in III.i, literally a coin ("remuneration"). The plural "languages" is important—Moth notices that the upper class prides itself on amalgamating different languages and the word "feast" suggest the leisure with which they do so. C.L. Barber, in *Shakespeare's Festive Comedy*, concludes that "the more one reads the play, the more one is caught up by the extraordinary excitement it expresses about what language can do—the excitement of the historical moment when English, in the hands of its greatest master, suddenly could do anything" (153). As this scene suggests, even the lower-class characters see language as playful and as a source for social advancement. No scene is without some exchange between characters that is primarily about exercising language creatively. The upper-class characters have the luxury of using their witty exchanges purely for fun and playful competition. For the lower-class characters, language is useful for social betterment: they emulate the upper-class characters so as to sound like them.

The men must learn that language, like love, must be sincere and suitable to be legitimate. Legitimacy, therefore, whether in oath taking or paternity, is another important linguistic theme. Holofernes is a character who continually calls attention to his own misguided eloquence and pointless learning; nothing new is created when Holofernes speaks since he usually speaks in synonyms: "Sir Nathaniel, as concerning some entertainment of time, some show in the posterior of this day, to be rend'red by our assistance, the king's command, and this most gallant, illustrate, and learned gentleman, before the princess—I say, none so fit as to present the Nine Worthies" (V.i.119–124).

Not only are the men the most suspect in their linguistic methods, they are very critical of the language of other characters. For example, it is the men who react the most harshly to the Pageant of the Nine Worthies, cruelly making sport of it. Correspondingly, it is the young women who see the lord's reaction as a sign of their hypocrisy. Throughout the play, as we shall see, the women stand for honesty and sincere language use:

Rosaline: A jest's prosperity lies in the ear
Of him that hears it, never in the tongue
Of him that makes it; then, if sickly ears,
Deaf'd with the clamrs of their own dear groans,
Will hear your idle scorns, continue then,
And I will have you and that fault withal;
But if they will not, throw away that spirit,
And I shall find you empty of that fault. (V.ii.861–868)

Rosaline clearly calls a fault a fault; language is only effective when it is shared. Rosaline knows that effective language results in communication, in hearing as well as speaking. As with the other young ladies, she has willingly entered into the wooing game with the men, but she is clear that victory in wooing is reliant on appropriate discourse. Jaquenetta aside, sexual and romantic union is reserved only for those whose language is appropriate for representing love.

The conclusion of the play suggests that Shakespeare uses the theme of language and wit to investigate a larger theme, one he would soon return to in *A Midsummer Night's Dream*: the limits and conflicts between fancy and imagination. Joseph Westlund explores this theme in his essay "Fancy and Achievement in *Love's Labour's Lost*." "*Love's Labour's Lost* presents a conflict between fancy and achievement, a conflict which is ultimately one between artifice and nature" (37). The king's first speech proposes that the academe will be "Still and contemplative in living art"; the young men, via their academe, fail to see how language and wit work in relation to nature. Likewise, the lords fail to see what love truly is (38)—their concept of love is a literary one, an artificial witty love taken straight from the sonnets of Petrarch. Only the young ladies can be said to align their emotional responses with their intellects, and this fact alone gives them dramatic moral superiority over the men.

NATURE AND ARTIFICE

Even though the Pageant of the Nine Worthies is deserving of some ridicule, it still serves as an attempt to creatively manipulate language for ceremonial purposes. But it is ultimately uncreative and as such is suggestive of death, a theme that inevitably arises in Shakespeare when creative or procreative tendencies are denied. Echoing the opening speech, the Pageant of the Nine Worthies is "naturally evocative of death and time" (Barton 210), as is the entrance of Marcade and, in a meta-

phoric way, the songs of Spring and Winter. Armado comments that
Hector, who has just been introduced in the Pageant, is "dead and rotten.
Sweet chucks beat not the bones of the buried. When he breathed, he
was a sweet man" (V.ii.656–659). From the very beginning the play is
"evocative of death and time"; the second and third lines of the play,
"brazen tombs/ And then grace us in the disgrace of death," announce
the theme and do so in relation to verbal acts, in this case oath taking
and the written epitaphs of tombs. As the title tells us in advance, love
does not win in the end, of course, and these lines set up the darker tone
of the play. The theme of death returns most overtly at the end of the
play with the entrance of Marcade and the announcement of the death
of the princess's father:

> *Marcade:* I am sorry, madam, for the news I bring
> Is heavy in my tongue. The King your father—
> *Princess:* Dead, for my life!
> *Marcade:* Even so: my tale is told. (V.ii.710–713)

The leisure and happiness of the garden are interrupted by the reality of
the world outside Navarre. With this news, the illusion of comedy and
happy endings is removed, and the theme of language is again made
relevant by a reminder that the most important things in life, such as
death, do not need to be represented by words. Berowne acknowledges
that with the news of the death, stylized language is not appropriate:
"Honest words best pierce the ears of grief" (V.ii.747). The play moves
to its more somber and unadorned conclusion, including the final debate
between Winter and Spring, which links death to nature.

> *Spring:* When daisies pied and violets blue
> And lady-smocks all silver-white
> And cuckoo-buds of yellow hue
> Do paint the meadows with delight,
> The cuckoo then, on every tree,
> Mocks married men; for thus sings he, Cuckoo;
> Cuckoo, cuckoo: O word of fear,
> Unpleasing to a married ear!
>
> When shepherds pipe on oaten straws
> And merry larks are ploughmen's clocks,
> When turtles tread, and rooks, and daws,
> And maidens bleach their summer smocks

> The cuckoo then, on every tree,
> Mocks married men; for thus sings he, Cuckoo;
> Cuckoo, cuckoo: O word of fear,
> Unpleasing to a married ear!

The song of Spring renews the implied theme of legitimacy and happiness in marriage. For a play that withholds the marriage usually associated with comedy, and given the questionable nature of Jaquenetta's impending marriage, the only one promised in the play, the cuckoo is a suitable image, since in the Renaissance the cuckoo was often associated with cuckoldry.

Nature, or the sum of the world outside of Navarre, is unpleasant to a married ear, suggesting that marriage itself is unnatural. Ironically, this reversal of the usual Petrarchan conceit of heavenly harmony through marriage or requited love suggests that there is a positive side to the loss of love that characterizes the dramatic ending of the play. Further, both songs focus on lower-class characters who are laboring; in Spring the shepherds "pipe" and the maidens "bleach." Perhaps most fittingly, a play that is so much about the power of language ends with the imitation of the sounds of nature. Since the entrance of Marcade, language has ceased to be a fitting conduit of emotions, and these songs are perfect examples of "silent" or natural eloquence.

The song of winter develops several of these themes, but does so in a "debate" structure; Winter stands in stark thematic opposition to Spring:

> *Winter:* When icicles hang by the wall
> And Dick the shepherd blows his nail
> And Tom bears logs into the hall
> And milk comes frozen home in pail,
> When blood is nipp'd and ways be foul,
> Then nightly sings the staring owl, Tu-whit;
> Tu-who, a merry note,
> While greasy Joan doth keel the pot.
>
> When all aloud the wind doth blow
> And coughing drowns the parson's saw
> And birds sit brooding in the snow
> And Marian's nose looks red and raw,
> When roasted crabs hiss in the bowl,
> Then nightly sings the staring owl, Tu-whit;

> Tu-who, a merry note,
> While greasy Joan doth keel the pot.

Again, real people are working real, and most important, seasonal jobs. This time the birds sing joyous songs while "brooding in the snow." Thus, the songs encompass all the emotions of the play that proceed them, ultimately ending on a positive note. Taken together, the two songs suggest that marriage can be either a happy institution or a mockery; the marriage of Jaquenetta and Armado, in comparison to the withheld marriages of the young men to the women, reflects the same dichotomous relationship.

William Carroll notes that the final dialogue "serves as a suggestive emblem of the basic structural principle of *Love's Labour's Lost*" (170). The play is constructed on several dualistic principles. Given the basic theme of art versus experience, the following dualisms, represented in the final songs, are noted by Carroll as running throughout the play:

Spring vs. Winter

Learning vs. Experience

Rhetoric vs. Simplicity

Affectation vs. Self-Knowledge

Wearing a Mask vs. Revealing Oneself

Playing a Role vs. Being Oneself

Style vs. Matter

Words vs. Things

Form vs. Content

Mind vs. Body

Paradox vs. Common Sense

Carroll sees it as ironic that modern critics affirm a victory of the right side of the list over the left; for Carroll the songs suggest that it is the "interplay" between the two forces that is of interest (173) and that the play resists "easy dualisms" (174). The songs also serve as a reaffirmation of the power of poetry and language. Given all the attempts at poetry that have failed in the play, the fact that the songs are as perfect and beautiful as they are comes as a very pleasant surprise and serves as a fitting conclusion to the play.

These two songs are examples of a medieval tradition of seasonal debates, but, in the context of the play, they remind us of one of the major themes of the play: artificiality versus nature. Throughout the play we see this dichotomy played out in various themes, such as language, which is either highly artificial or quite natural and sincere, and thus appropriate, and in love, which is either forced, mannered, and thus insincere, or, as in the case of the love of the women, more natural and sincere, even if it is withheld at the end of the play. The Spring dialogue describes nature in terms of art; for example, the meadows are "painted" and the flowers are described metaphorically (McLay 124). The song of Winter, on the other hand, seems more "natural" and "merry." This could be taken to mirror the movement of the play, from artifice to nature, or from illusion to reality (125). It is also another example of the reversals that define the play: the usual conventional metaphor of winter as death or melancholy and spring as life are here reversed in a manner that the young men would never accept as poetically fashionable.

EDUCATION

From the very beginning of the play we are in a world defined by education. There is the formal education of the young lords who seek to sequester themselves in humanistic study, and there is Don Armado who sees himself as highly educated. There are also Holofernes and Nathaniel, who attempt to teach anyone who will listen, and finally there are the lower-class characters who are infected by the pretentiousness of the upper class. For all these characters, their education, whether formal or informal, is usually centered around linguistic competency. However, it is only the male characters who are consistently tied to education, either as willing or reluctant students or as teachers. On the other hand, it could be said that by the end of the play the young women have become teachers in that they set out to "educate" their suitors in proper behavior. Early in the play it is Berowne, typically, who illustrates the dichotomy between education and experience:

> Study is like the heaven's glorious sun
> That will not be deep-search'd with saucy looks:
> Small have continual plodders ever won
> Save base authority from others' books
> These earthly godfathers of heaven's lights
> That give a name to every fixed star
> Have no more profit of their shining nights

Than those that walk and wot not what they are.
Too much to know is to know nought but fame;
And every godfather can give a name. (ll. 84–93)

Education, like oath taking and foreswearing of love, is called into question. For Berowne, education is compared to "real life" and comes up wanting. To the extent that Ferdinand's academe represents one stereotypical image of the Renaissance, the power and unlimited nature of knowledge, Berowne's assessment of the limits of knowledge reflects another extreme, the significance of everyday life. Berowne's assertion that "too much to know is to know nought but fame;/And every godfather can give a name" directly contradicts Ferdinand's aims. Of the men, Berowne's enlightened common sense accords the most moral and ethical viewpoint. Berowne is, as Bobbyann Roesen [Barton] has noted, a chorus character throughout the play (Roesen 127), serving as the commentator on the action, more often than not reflecting a more commonsensical approach to the various situations and comic qualities of the other characters.

More than any other facet of the play, it is education that ties the lower-class characters to the upper class. In the second scene of the play there is an exchange that is typical of this association; Moth, a young page, is talking to Armado. Their subject is love, with Armado quizzing Moth on other famous men who were in love, asking Moth to describe their complexion.

> *Armado:* Tell me precisely of what complexion?
>
> *Moth:*   Of the sea-water green, sir.
>
> *Armado:* Is that one of the four complexions?
>
> *Moth:*   As I have read, sir; and the best of them too. (I.ii.79–82)

When Armado asks about complexion, he means what "humour" (i.e., disposition) were they. Moth's response is much simpler—he thinks of complexion as skin color. Armado, rather than dismissing Moth's comment due to ignorance, accepts it and allows it to lead to the exchange that follows. As in this scene, much of the comic banter centers around bookishness, and in this case a lack of formal education does seem to limit the knowledge of the lower-class characters, but what makes the scene comic is that Armado, who fancies himself among the learned, must stoop (literally, given Moth's stature) to gain knowledge from

Moth. One of the most consistent comic attributes of the play is the reversal that so often occurs when a young student gets the best of his master, or when a supposedly less-educated character "teaches" the supposed master, as in the previous exchange. Another example of ironic role reversal occurs at III.i.79–101:

Armado: No, page; it is an epilogue or discourse, to make plain
Some obscure precedence that hath tofore been sain.
I will example it:
The fox, the ape, and the humble-bee,
Were still at odds, being but three.
There's the moral. Now the l'envoy.

Moth: I will add the l'envoy. Say the moral again.

Armado: The fox, the ape, and the humble-bee,
Were still at odds, being but three.

Moth: Until the goose came out of door,
And stayed the odds by adding four.
Now will I begin your moral, and do you follow with my l'envoy.
The fox, the ape, and the humble-bee,
Were still at odds, being but three.

Armado: Until the goose came out of door,
Staying the odds by adding four.

Moth: A good l'envoy, ending in the goose: would you desire more?

Costard: The boy hath sold him a bargain, a goose, that's flat.
Sir, your pennyworth is good, an your goose be fat.
To sell a bargain well is as cunning as fast and loose:
Let me see; a fat l'envoy; ay, that's a fat goose.

Again, the two players are Moth and Armado, but this exchange is a bit more combative than the previous one. Moth is playing with the idea of an "envoy" being the final word or moral of a given story or fable. He does not allow the parable to end the way Armado would like it to; instead, Moth turns it into a bawdy joke on "goose," which means, among other things, whore. Moth appropriates the role of teacher and turns Armado into a goose, or in this case fool. Costard sides with Moth by pointing out that Moth has sold Armado an envoy. Again, for many of the lower-class characters, language is a material entity, capable of buying and selling.

Most of the learning that occurs in the play is based on language and eloquence; therefore many of the comic exchanges occur when characters of both classes are attempting to understand each other. Several characters, including most of the lower-class characters, utter malapropisms. However, once a "student" has learned a new word, they make the word their own and bring new comic life to it. After receiving his "remuneration" (i.e., payment) for delivering a letter from Armado to Jaquenetta, Costard says:

> Now will I look to his remuneration. Remuneration! O, that's the Latin word for three farthings: three farthings—remuneration.— 'What's the price of this inkle?'—'One penny.'—'No, I'll give you a remuneration:' why, it carries it. Remuneration! why, it is a fairer name than French crown. I will never buy and sell out of this word. (ll.136–143)

Initially Costard did not understand Armado's Latinate word for "payment." Although Costard quickly learns from Armado that this word means payment, his learning has symbolically bought his freedom, not only from Armado's bondage, but "economic" freedom to discourse with others using his new word, which is what he does a short time later when conversing with the upper-class Berowne:

> *Costard:* Pray you, sir, how much carnation ribbon may a man buy for a remuneration?
>
> *Berowne:* What is a remuneration?
>
> *Costard:* Marry, sir, halfpenny farthing.
>
> *Berowne:* Why, then, three-farthing worth of silk.

Costard is now teaching the upper-class Berowne how to use this word. It is fitting that the word used here is "remuneration" since its literal meaning represents what new words can do for the lower-class characters—buy them the respect which comes from proper, educated language.

WIT

This type of exchange is common in the play, with characters often challenging each other to keep up or to exercise their wits. One nineteenth-century critic, Thomas Price, has counted 250 puns or word plays in *LLL*, with Berowne alone responsible for forty-eight of them and Costard thirty-four (71–72). As with most themes in the play, it culminates when the young women challenge the lords to refrain from wit for a period of one year. Rosaline, who puns a mere twenty times, "sentences" Berowne to one year among the sick and dying so that he will learn a lesson one would have thought he knew, given his tribute to learning earlier in the play—namely, that there is a limit and place for wit:

> *Rosaline:* Oft have I heard of you, my Lord Berowne,
> Before I saw you; and the world's large tongue
> Proclaims you for a man replete with mocks,
> Full of comparisons and wounding flouts,
> Which you on all estates will execute
> That lie within the mercy of your wit.
> To weed this wormwood from your fruitful brain,
> And therewithal to win me, if you please,
> Without the which I am not to be won,
> You shall this twelvemonth term from day to day
> Visit the speechless sick and still converse
> With groaning wretches; and your task shall be,
> With all the fierce endeavor of your wit
> To enforce the pained impotent to smile. (V.ii.833–846)

Rosaline's sentence of punishment is designed to test the limits of Berowne's wit, and given that Berowne is the wittiest of the characters, wit in general. Her brilliant joke on weeding his "fruitful brain" suggests that wit is not what is faulty in the young men; in fact, at the proper time and in measured doses, it is one of the most charming aspects of their personality. Rosaline understands that it is only once the young men have tested their wit in the larger confines of the world, where audiences are not so polite or willing to laugh, that they will truly be witty.

MARRIAGE AND THE LABOR OF LOVE

The theme of language and learning is closely aligned with the theme of marriage and love. The play withholds a happy ending, yet it is typically comic in its focus on courtship and elaborate romantic festivities. In fact, Shakespeare develops three wooing couples in a complex thematic structure that highlights the characteristic trappings of Elizabethan comedy. In Act III, scene i, it is Berowne who again views love from a comic/subversive angle:

> O! and I forsooth in love!
> I, that have been love's whip;
> A very beadle to a humorous sigh;
> A critic, nay, a night-watch constable;
> A domineering pedant o'er the boy;
> Than whom no mortal so magnificent!
> This whimpled, whining, purblind, wayward boy;
> This senior-junior, giant-dwarf, Dan Cupid;
> Regent of love-rhymes, lord of folded arms,
> The anointed sovereign of sighs and groans,
> Liege of all loiterers and malcontents,
> Dread prince of plackets, king of codpieces,
> Sole imperator and great general
> Of trotting 'paritors:—O my little heart:—
> And I to be a corporal of his field,
> And wear his colours like a tumbler's hoop!
> What, I! I love! I sue! I seek a wife! (ll.168–184)

Berowne relies on comic personifications of love, such as Cupid as a blind, wayward, and mischievous boy, and he points to the Petrarchan behavior of sighing and sonnet writing as tokens of love. Also tellingly, Berowne utilizes military metaphors to describe Cupid, "liege," "dread prince," "great general," and "corporal of his field" wearing "colours." Caroline Spurgeon notes the predominance of military metaphors and images in the play (275). Just as the young women "lay seige" to the men by camping outside their academe, the Petrarchan conceit of the beseiged lover is developed alongside the image of wit and conversation as combative. The young men have armed themselves against the world's desires; Cupid becomes a "regent" and a "great general" who reduces Berowne to a "corporal of his field." Likewise, Armado, whose name suggests war via the Spanish Armada, is a braggart who often uses military terminology at the least appropriate times, as he does in the following exchange where he declares to Moth his love for Jaquenetta:

> I will hereupon confess I am in love: and as it is base for a soldier to love, so am I in love with a base wench. If drawing my sword against the humour of affection would deliver me from the reprobate thought of it, I would take Desire prisoner, and ransom him to any

French courtier for a new-devised courtesy. I think scorn to sigh: methinks I should outswear Cupid. Comfort, me, boy: what great men have been in love? (I.ii.57–65)

Armado continues the metaphor of the soldier of love. Armado sees love as a type of war or joust. Moreover, by asking Moth what great men had been in love, Armado turns his proclamation of love into an exercise in humanism: he desires to put his emotions into an historical context, while his language describing his love, "drawing my sword against the humour of affection," "reprobate" and "new-devised courtesy," suggest his reliance on overly artificial language and Latinate words. The fact that his pretentiousness is used to describe his love for a "base wench" makes this scene all the more amusing. Shakespeare highlights this pretentiousness at the end of the scene when Armado speaks of his love:

I do affect the very ground, which is base, where her shoe, which is baser, guided by her foot, which is basest, doth tread. I shall be forsworn, which is a great argument of falsehood, if I love. And how can that be true love which is falsely attempted? Love is a familiar; Love is a devil: there is no evil angel but Love. Yet was Samson so tempted, and he had an excellent strength; yet was Solomon so seduced, and he had a very good wit. Cupid's butt-shaft is too hard for Hercules' club; and therefore too much odds for a Spaniard's rapier. The first and second cause will not serve my turn; the passado he respects not, the duello he regards not: his disgrace is to be called boy; but his glory is to subdue men. Adieu, valour! rust rapier! be still, drum! for your manager is in love; yea, he loveth. Assist me, some extemporal god of rhyme, for I am sure I shall turn sonnet. Devise, wit; write, pen; for I am for whole volumes in folio. (I.ii.157–175)

Like Berowne before him, Armado turns a discourse on love into an oration on Cupid, and acknowledges that, like any self-respecting educated man, he will become a writer of sonnets. Unlike Berowne's speech, which has some wit and charm to it and a hint of sincerity, Armado's is laughable because it is so artificial and stilted. By choosing metaphors from dueling ("first and second cause," "passado" and "duello"), Armado makes a poetic mistake probably noticeable by even the least educated audience member, that of a mixed or inappropriate metaphor. He awkwardly mixes his dueling and military metaphors with language from formal logic, such as "great argument" and "first and second cause," and in so doing only distances himself further from the object of his love. However, like the lords, he too is fashionable in matters of love, acknowledging that he will "turn sonnet."

Although Berowne attempts to distance himself from these behaviors, he will, like the other young men, write sonnets and sigh, and, by choosing to act out the role of love's soldier, becomes another literary stereotype. Meanwhile, Katherine gives her own opinion of love, one that fittingly is not as overtly witty as Berowne's, but more sincere and serious.

> [Love] made her melancholy, sad and heavy,
> And so she died. Had she been light like you,
> Of such a merry, nimble, stirring spirit,
> She might'a' been a grandam ere she died.
> And so may you; for a light heart lives long. (V.ii.14–18)

For Katherine love is tragic, and this reminds us of the theme of death prevalent throughout the play. Although it could be argued that Katherine's melancholic condition is itself a literary posture, the past she refers to suggests that she has the experience to make her melancholic demeanor authentic. As these examples suggest, throughout the play love is a type of gestalt—each character sees in the abstraction some projection of their personality. Berowne cannot see beyond his education and drive to be witty; Katherine sees in love a potential tragedy, and as such she is careful about proceeding into blind love. The various love intrigues in the play could be summarized by Costard's observation that "such is the simplicity of man to hearken after the flesh" (I.i.215). But as Berowne's reference to blind Cupid suggests, love is blind, and no relationship shows that more than that between the simply country wench Jaquenetta and Armado.

LABOR

Armado's reference to "Cupid's butt-shaft is too hard for Hercules' club" is one of several references to the labors of Hercules, a theme that is suggested in the title and culminates in the Nine Worthies performance. In the Renaissance, the nine worthies represented fame, virtue, honesty, and achievement. In the Pageant, all these traits are undermined simply by the performance: those who are playing the parts are not worthy to do so. In a play about oath taking in which all the characters break their oaths, the truth of the real world stands in stark contrast with the allegorical lessons the worthies are meant to manifest. Shakespeare makes this clear by emphasizing the "reality" of the players in the king's introduction:

> Here is like to be a good presence of Worthies. He
> presents Hector of Troy; the swain, Pompey the
> Great; the parish curate, Alexander; Armado's page,
> Hercules; the pedant, Judas Maccabaeus: And if
> these four Worthies in their first show thrive,
> These four will change habits, and present the other five. (V.ii.530–535)

The king repeats the players commedia dell'arte personas (see Chapter 4 for a more complete discussion of the commedia dell'arte tradition). Whereas the worthies were to represent consistency and stability, these "worthies" will have to "change habits" to present the final five worthies.

The casting of Moth as Hercules is perhaps the most egregious example of the ironic performance. Through its absence in the play proper and its emphasis in the final song, we are made aware that the labor of the title is more than simply the efforts of the young men to find love. Rather, it becomes an important poetic motif. For example, *LLL* mentions Hercules' labors more than any other Shakespeare play. Joseph Westlund notes that "the minor but persistent allusions to famous men and their accomplishments are part of an interesting mock-heroic strand which runs through" the play (40). Again, the opening speech reveals this theme when the king's grand and eloquent speech is so quickly and easily undercut by the ladies. At IV.iii.166–169 we see the culmination of this theme when Berowne comments upon the irony of the performance:

> To see a king transformed to a gnat!
> To see great Hercules whipping a gig,
> And profound Solomon to tune a jig,
> And Nestor play at push-pin with the boys.

In other words, the fame called for in the first speech has been reduced to playfulness and the characters themselves are ironically presented in antithesis to famous worthy persons, a point made by Costard on his own performance of Pompey: "For mine own part, I know not the degree of the Worthy, but I am to stand for him" (504–505). As Joseph Westlund notes, "The show is the climax of an apparently fruitless courtship:

the lords are presented with famous models of achievement at the moment they begin to realize their own labors have been in vain" (41). We are reminded that this is a play in which "great things labouring perish in their birth" (V.ii.521). The list of those great things that perish consists of the most prominent themes in the play: love, language, fame, and honor.

WORKS CITED

Barber, C.L. *Shakespeare's Festive Comedy: A Study of Dramatic Form and Its Relation to Social Custom*. Princeton: Princeton University Press, 1959.

Barton, Ann. Introduction. *Riverside Shakespeare*. 2nd ed. Ed. G. Blakemore Evans. Boston: Houghton Mifflin, 1997. 208–212.

Carroll, William. *The Great Feast of Language in "Love's Labour's Lost."* Princeton: Princeton University Press, 1976.

Evans, Malcolm. *Signifying Nothing: Truth's True Contents in Shakespeare's Texts*. 2nd ed. Athens: University of Georgia Press, 1989.

Goldstein, Neal L. *"Love's Labour's Lost* and the Renaissance Vision of Love." *Shakespeare Quarterly* 25 (1974): 335–350.

McLay, Catherine. "The Dialogues of Spring and Winter: A Key to the Unity of *Love's Labour's Lost." Shakespeare Quarterly* 18 (1967): 119–127.

Price, Thomas. "Shakespeare's Word-Play and Puns: *Love's Labour's Lost. "Love's Labour's Lost"*: *Critical Essays*. Ed. Felicia Hardison Londré. New York: Garland Publishing, 1997. 71–76.

Roesen, Bobbyann (Ann Barton). "Love's Labour's Lost." *Shakespeare Quarterly* (1953): 411–426.

Spurgeon, Caroline. *Shakespeare's Imagery and What It Tells Us*. New York: Macmillan, 1935.

Westlund, Joseph. "Fancy and Achievement in *Love's Labour's Lost." Shakespeare Quarterly* 18 (1967): 37–46.

Woudhuysen, H.R., ed. *Love's Labour's Lost*. Arden Shakespeare. 3rd series. Walton-on-Thames: Thomas Nelson and Sons, 1998.

5

CRITICAL APPROACHES

It is telling that one of the first commentaries on *LLL*, found as a part of Robert Tofte's *Alba: The Month's Minde of a Melancholy Lover* (1598), and which describes an early performance of it, was also a negative criticism of the play. As Tofte's opinion suggested, the play can be difficult to simply enjoy. Although we must take Tofte's comments with a grain of salt, he does make some noteworthy comments about the play. He wrote of the play:

> LOVES LABOR LOST, I once did see a Play,
> Ycleped so, so called to my paine,
> Which I to heare to my small Ioy did stay,
> Giuing attendance on my froward Dame,
> My misgiuing minde presaging to me Ill,
> Yet was I drawne to see it gainst my Will.
> This Play no Play, but Plague was vnto me,
> For there I lost the Loue I liked most:
> And what to others seemde a Jest to be,
> I, that (in earnest) found vnto my cost,
> To every one (saue me) twas Comicall,
> Whilst Tragick like to me it did befall.
> Each Actor plaid in cunning wise his part,
> But chiefly Those entrapt in Cupids snare:
> Yet All was fained, twas not from the hart,
> They seemed to grieve, but yet they felt no care:
> Twas I that Griefe (indeed) did beare in brest,
> The others did but make a show in Jest.
> Yet neither faining theirs, nor my meere Truth,

Could make her once so much as for to smile:
Whilst she (despite of pitie milde and ruth)
Did sit as skorning of my Woes the while.
Thus did she sit to see LOVE lose his LOVE,
Like hardned Rock that force nor power can moue.

Besides a commentary of a single performance, Tofte could be criticizing the play itself. For example, while the audience found it a comedy, Tofte found it to be "feigned" and to be more of a tragedy than a comedy. Tofte's opinion of *LLL* as feigned, as not from the heart, is typical of criticism of the play, much of which tends to see it as primarily concerned with artifice and rhetoric. Although Tofte's poem was developed around the conceit of the scorned lover, and therefore his role as critic of the play must be tempered, he did seem to report a successful performance. His criticism of the players as "cunning wise" but "not from the heart" could be read as a condemnation of the play; certainly, as we will see, the play has suffered from criticism that it is, for a modern audience, feigned. Most important was the response Tofte got from his "frowrad Dame," who, like the young women in the play, refused to smile at his wit and scorned his love. Like that of the young gentlemen in the play they are watching, Tofte's own "labour" of love was lost. Tofte's own ironic distance from the events he narrated mirrors the irony of *LLL* itself.

Tofte's comments innocently set the stage for much of the criticism that would follow. For example, few modern readers can fully understand, and therefore fully appreciate, the play without some textual support. Unlike Tofte, however, Harold Bloom writes of *LLL* that "I take more unmixed pleasure from *Love's Labour's Lost* than from any other Shakespearean play" (121). As Bloom goes on to note, the play seems to him to be the play Shakespeare most enjoyed writing and which contains the most exuberant language and, as a result, it is the play that has often struck many critics as unique among Shakespeare's work for what it reveals about the author. As any good performance of the play will illustrate, it is a highly enjoyable and very exuberant experience, but from a textual level the play demands close attention and rewards readers with an unparalleled richness of language. Bloom's appreciation of the play highlights the two main areas of critical discussion of the play: first, its linguistic density and its variety of poetic forms, and, second, the presence, albeit shadowy and undefined, of Shakespeare the man and writer. These two topics have been the focus of the vast majority of scholarship on the play, and as such will be the focus of much of the discussion that follows. The "traditional" schools of criticism, such as post-structuralism, Marxism, and psychoanalytical, have been over-shadowed by the critical focus on the play's language and topical allusions; however, these topics have informed and influenced a variety of critical approaches, namely, as we will see, feminism.

EARLY COMMENTARIES

Two of the earliest commentaries on the play were also among the most negative. Samuel Johnson, in his *Notes to the Edition of Shake-speare's Plays* (1765), argued that the play was vulgar and contends that "it must be confessed that there are many passages mean, childish . . . and some which ought not to have been exhibited, as we are told they were, to a maiden queen" (Johnson 182). This opinion is revealing not only of the taste and manners of the eighteenth century, but also for the way it directly opposes one of the most prevalent opinions about the play held since that time—namely, that the play was written for a courtly and aristocratic audience. Rarely have critics since Johnson emphasized the play's bawdiness. However, Johnson also acknowledged that "there are scattered, through the whole, many sparks of genius; nor is there any play that has more evident marks of the hand of Shakespeare" (182).

Johnson also famously stated in his *Preface to the Edition of Shake-speare's Plays* that a major fault in Shakespeare was his occasional pre-occupation with language for the sake of language. He could easily have been thinking about *LLL* when he wrote:

> A quibble is to Shakespeare what luminous vapours are to the trav-eller! He follows it at all adventures; it is sure to lead him out of his way, sure to engulf him in the mire. It has some malignant power over his mind, and its fascinations are irresistible. Whatever be the dignity or profundity of his disquisition, whether he be enlarging knowledge or exalting affection, whether he be amusing attention with incidents, or enchaining it in suspense, let but a quibble spring up before him and he leave his work unfinished. A quibble is the golden apple for which he will always turn aside from his career, or stoop from his elevation. A quibble, poor and barren as it is, gave him such delight, that he was content to purchase it by the sacrifice of reason, propriety, and truth. A quibble was to him the fatal Cle-opatra for which he lost the world, and was content to lose it. (132)

If there was a single statement that summarizes the temptation to damn Shakespeare with praise, it is this one, and that tendency has influenced the critical reception of *LLL* since Johnson. Johnson's own remarks on the play reflect this tendency: of lines I.i.31, Johnson wrote: "The stile of the rhyming scenes in this play is often entangled and obscure. I know not certainly to what 'all these' is to be referred; I suppose he means that 'love, pomp, *and* wealth *in* philosophy' " (180). However, having acknowledged, as many critics have, that the language of the play is occasionally obscure or convoluted, Johnson found room for great praise: "I know not well what degree of respect Shakespeare intends to obtain for this vicar, but he has here [V.i.2] put into his mouth a finished representation of colloquial excellence." Johnson was acknowledging the power of the colloquial exchanges in the play, and went on to praise Shakespeare's description of the "schoolmaster's table-talk." From the earliest criticism of the play, astute critics, of whom Johnson is the most astute, have noticed the meta-linguistic theme in the play, which calls attention to its own artifice. However, even the best critics can confuse Shakespeare's often convoluted syntax as an inexperienced weakness rather than a dramatic and ironic statement on the nature of formal language.

The first critical edition of Shakespeare's plays, Nicholas Rowe's edition of *The Works of Mr. William Shakespeare*, published in 1709 and republished in 1710, included a volume by Charles Gildon, "Critical Remarks on His Plays." Gildon was particularly hard on *LLL*, calling it "the very worst" of Shakespeare's plays (quoted in Londré 45). But it is possible Gildon's dislike of the play was based on a misunderstanding of its basic aims; he acknowledged that "I can't well see why the Author gave this Play this Name." Gildon, like so many critics who followed, attributed weaknesses in the play to the youthfulness of the playwright, and concluded that since it is the worst, it must be the first (45). Without understanding the inherent irony of the play, Gildon could not possibly have appreciated the play's deeper meanings.

Such extreme criticism continued when in 1817 William Hazlitt remarked that "if we were to part with any of the author's comedies, it should be this" (quoted in Londré 61). Despite this declaration, Hazlitt admitted that certain characters such as Berowne, Costard, and Holofernes should not "be lost to the world," and given the necessity of the minor characters in setting up the situations that surround these characters, he concluded that "we believe we may let the whole play stand as it is." Hazlitt's main complaint about the play was, like Johnson's, centered on the language of it. He called it "pedantic" and wrote that it sounded more like "the logic of Peter Lombard, than of the inspiration of the Muse" (Londré 61). Although he acknowledged that this was deliberate and that the language of the play was an imitation, Shakespeare was, to Hazlitt's taste, too successful since "he has imitated it but too faithfully" (61). Again, we see a tendency to damn Shakespeare with praise: the play is too successful at what it sets out to do.

Samuel Coleridge's criticism best represents what the Romantics saw as Shakespeare's greatest legacy. For Coleridge, as well as many early nineteenth-century critics, Shakespeare's strongest dramatic talent was in the creation of character, and *LLL* is no exception. Coleridge also asserted that based on the characters developed in the play, the play must be an early one: "The characters [are] either impersonated out of his own multiformity, by imaginative self-position, or of such as a country town and a school-boy's observation might supply—the curate, schoolmaster, the Armado" (82). Also, "*LLL* contains the "germs of characters afterwards more fully developed." For example, Coleridge saw Berowne and Rosaline as precursors to Benedict and Beatrice (83). In keeping with the Romantic tendency to privilege character over other aspects of drama, Coleridge cited several speeches from the play as exemplary of Shakespeare's early ability to develop consistent and deeply drawn characters. For example, Coleridge saw Berowne's "Promethean fire" speech at IV.iii.320–361 as "remaining faithful to the character supposed to utter the lines, and the expressions themselves constituting a further development of character" (85). Likewise, Coleridge singled out Rosaline as the most developed female character, citing her speech at V.ii.833–846: "Oft have I hear of you." At this point of the play, in this speech, Coleridge believed that Rosaline is Beatrice's equal.

Perhaps the most insightful nineteenth-century criticism of the play comes from Walter Pater, who in 1878 published his *Appreciations*. He compared *LLL* to Shakespeare's sonnets, with which it shares "their conceits of thought and expression" (65). Pater also acknowledged that the play is very serious, despite the frivolity of many of its scenes. One of the serious issues underlying the comedy is that of language; the Elizabethan preoccupation with "dainty language and curious expression" reflects a "real sense of fitness and nicety" (67), and it is this topic that Shakespeare turns to in the play. This is a very modern view reflecting much of the best and most insightful of twentieth-century scholarship on the play. In speaking of Berowne, for example, Pater noted that he is the character who best represents the limits and appropriateness of formal language: "What is a vulgarity in Holofernes, and a caricature in Armado, refines itself in him into the expression of a nature truly and inwardly bent upon a form of delicate perfection, and is accompanied by a real insight into the laws which determine what is exquisite in language, and their root in the nature of things" (68). This is an exquisite summation of what is the dominant theme of the play, the nature of language and its effect on character.

But Pater's critical influence is felt in other aspects of the critical tradition of the play as well. The play's overall formality, which extends from the theme of language to the setting, class structure, and spectacle of the play, was noted by Pater as a defining characteristic of the play. Pater undoubtedly influenced productions of the play when he wrote the following: "The scene—a park of the King of Navarre—is unaltered throughout; and the unity of the play is not so much the unity of a drama as that of a series of pictorial groups, in which the same figures reappear, in different combinations, but on the same background" (66). Pater goes on to compare the play to a tapestry to which Shakespeare has given voice. This is a wonderful way of describing what Shakespeare has done in *LLL*, and rather than damning the play for its seeming lack of character development, Pater acknowledges that Shakespeare clearly set out to reproduce a highly formal world and that the play's inherent drama is the result of the grouping of characters in different situations. As we will note in the next chapter, after Pater many modern productions of the play used visual metaphors drawn from art to recreate the mood and tone of the play.

LANGUAGE AND IMAGERY

Bloom's assertion that *LLL* is the play that Shakespeare most enjoyed writing is most clearly illustrated by the play's linguistic exuberance. Shakespeare's earliest reputation was as a stylist, as three contemporary critics of Shakespeare all note. Thomas Green's pamphlet of 1592 refers to Shakespeare as "garnisht in our coulours" and as a playwright who thinks he "is as well able to bombast out a blank verse as the best of" other playwrights. In 1592, the playwright Henry Chettle defended Shakespeare and referred to Shakespeare's "facetious grace in writing, that approves his Art." Finally, Francis Meres wrote of Shakespeare: "The English tongue is mightily enriched, and gorgeously invested in rare ornaments and resplendent abiliments" and "the sweete wittie soule of Ovid lives in mellifluous & hony-tongued Shakespeare" (quoted in

Cunningham 93–94). All this early commentary suggested that *LLL* was most representative of what Shakespeare was famed for early in his career, and those modern critics who focus on this aspect of the play are helping modern readers to reconstruct how linguistically sophisticated Shakespeare really was in the context of his time.

Love's Labour's Lost is undoubtedly one of the densest of Shakespeare's plays. Two important modern studies of Shakespeare's comedies focus on the play's rich language. William Carroll's *The Great Feast of Language in "Love's Labour's Lost"* is the most thorough study of Shakespeare's linguistic achievements in the play. Along with Carroll's book, Keir Elam's *Shakespeare's Universe of Discourse: Language Games in the Comedies* provides us with a deep understanding of the depth and brilliance of Shakespeare's conception of language. Most of the criticism written on the play, whatever the theoretical orientation, begins with a consideration of the density of language. For example, one of the best Marxist readings of Shakespeare, Malcolm Evans's *Signifying Nothing*, notes that the linguistic excess of the play allows for many different interpretations, each of which reflects their own ideology, yet the play has a meaning that is historically and culturally specific (103). For many Marxist critics one of the questions that arises is what Shakespeare's puns suggest about language acquisition and Shakespeare's multifaceted audience.

William Carroll took the "great feasts of language" as his title for what remains the most in-depth and revealing treatment of the play. Carroll notes that "*Love's Labour's Lost* offers in its characters a wide range of attitudes toward the power of language, from skeptical positivism to an almost primitive belief in the inner life of words" (11). Carroll's book is especially helpful since he considers the impact the language was meant to have on an audience: "The immense power inherent in language is not being mocked, but the traditional means of access, through the rhetorical training of the schools, is" (40–41). In other words, much of what Shakespeare is doing in the play is meant to be comic and his contemporaries would see the parodic nature of it.

> In my view, *Love's Labour's Lost* has been oversimplified even by its recent critics, who tend to be dogmatic where Shakespeare is tentative and ambivalent. The standard reading of the play today is that it finally illustrates the rejection of Art for Life, or Nature. I will try to correct this one sided view by leaning the other way: by beginning with the assumption that the play is 'sophisticated,' that

it is largely exploratory, and that it offers multiple viewpoints in order to set them in conflict and create debates. Its strategy is to encourage 'dialogue,' in all the connotations of that term, and its goal, beyond sheer entertainment, is to reject, not Art, but bad art— something rather different. (9)

For example, "we listen in full admiration" to Berowne's Promethean Fire speech at IV.iii (57), which is an exploration of art, and foregrounds artifice as the primary concern of the characters in the play. With Armado and other examples of "verbal licentiousness" the audience reacts with both condemnation and admiration at the fun of the exchanges and characters (57).

In *Shakespeare's Universe of Discourse: Language-Games in the Comedies*, Keir Elam sets out to study the "self consciousness of Shakespeare's language" (1). After noting that the Renaissance was "an age in which language occupied a central place in all areas" of culture, Elam notes that *LLL* is the play that most "exemplifies Shakespeare's baroque poetics" (32). By using Wittgenstein's theory of language-games Elam is able to explore Shakespeare's verbal activities within the context of the theatrical and dramatic purposes for which they were created. For example, there are theatrical and semantic games acted out on stage that call to mind words as words, or, in the words of Ernst Cassirer, the "game of the pure self-activity of the word" (quoted in Elam 1). Keir Elam reminds us that the tradition that categorizes *LLL* as an early play solely due to its linguistic preoccupation does so based on a suspicion of rhetorical patterning, especially the kind of extended patterning that occurs throughout the play (243). However, these self-conscious patterns call to mind the "plastic medium" of language itself. Given that many modern readers/viewers are no longer able to process or pay attention to this medium over long stretches of discursive development, we tend not to praise rhetorical strategies that rely on syntactic ordering as much as metaphor or metonymy (242). With this in mind, Elam treats *LLL*, as well as other comedies, most notably *Twelfth Night, Much Ado about Nothing, Merchant of Venice, Midsummer Night's Dream*, and *As You Like It*, as self-conscious commentaries on discourse and the game of language. Elam's cataloging and description of the various language-games reveals the extent to which Shakespeare was a product of the various language theories of his contemporary Renaissance, theories that arose as a result not only of the new learning but also as a product of the Reformation, and why *LLL* cannot be read and fully appreciated without the context provided by these various theories.

Malcolm Evans's main interest in how the final words of the play, "The Words of Mercuries/Are harsh after the songs of Apollo:/You that way; we this way," are thematically important. After noting the editorial controversy about whether these lines are the intended final words of Shakespeare or whether they are an editor's addition (the final line is only found in the folio, where the lines are given to Armado, whereas in the 1598 quarto the first two lines are set in type much larger than that of the rest of the play, suggesting that it was intended to be read as part of the play proper), Evans notes that the opening speech sets the world of books, to which the lords plan to escape, against the world of common sense and world knowledge. Mercury is traditionally the patron of "solitary learning" (54) while Apollo is the god of "rhyme, the seasons and speech" (56); the two are set against each other beginning with Berowne's questioning of the king's edict. Throughout the play writing only gives the appearance of the kind of immortality and stability the king desires; in fact, it is the spoken word that comes to have the most credibility in the course of the play. "If the opening scene of *Love's Labour's Lost* is an initiation into the world of reading and writing, the penances that conclude the play are an induction into the order of speech" (62). Evans sees the play as a "symmetrical production of a diversity of sixteenth-century ideological materials associated with speech and writing" (63). Evans is particularly insightful as to how Shakespeare plays out the tension between the artifice of writing and the spontaneity of speech and the linguistic attributes of both.

Throughout the play Shakespeare explores how language means what it means. In the course of the play Shakespeare nearly makes language "an autonomous symbolic system" (Calderwood 317). He does this by treating it as simply a phonetic aggregation of sounds, such as the emphasis on how simple sounds can be combined to form words, as seen in the wonderful passage at V.i. 41–62, where Costard creates a new Latin word from its aggregate components, "honorificabilitudinitatibus," and where, a little later, Holofernes and Moth make a joke out of the English vowels. This same creative manipulation of letters and sounds is seen in the pun on "sorrel" at IV.ii.36–61. In this way Shakespeare emphasizes language as language—as an entity with a separate existence in the word outside of its ability to communicate.

Love's Labour's Lost contains more "verbal humour" than any other Shakespeare comedy, notes Herbert Ellis in *Shakespeare's Lusty Punning in "Love's Labour's Lost."* By examining Shakespeare's puns (he counts about 210 in the play), Ellis's aim is to "offer a few conclusions about the nature of Shakespeare's comic art in" *LLL* (11). In the introduction Ellis conjectures that puns were part of the "national interest" in witty language, and that popular literature, in the form of sermons, jest-books, ballads, and broadsides, reflected this interest. Further, Ellis reminds us that such fancy language was fashionable during the Renaissance (13). But Shakespeare was also interested in how language is rhetorically creative, that is, how the figures and tropes of the language can be manipulated. Sister Miriam Joseph has explored the debt Shakespeare owes to the traditional rhetorical and logical theory of his time. As she notes early in her book *Shakespeare's Use of the Arts of Language*, "Elizabethans were eagerly and patriotically bent on creating literature in the vernacular inspired not only by the ancient classics but also by the new vernacular literature of Italy and France" (5). Sister Joseph notes that Shakespeare had a deep knowledge of English rhetorical texts by such writers as Richard Puttenham and Henry Peacham's *Garden of Eloquence* (44). Although her book contains numerous examples of various tropes and figures of both rhetoric and logic, it should come as no surprise that the most concentrated discussion of *LLL* occurs in the chapter dedicated to "The Vices of Language," pages 64–78.

T.W. Baldwin, in his *William Shakespeare's Small Latine and Lesse Greeke*, sets out to correct the misinterpretation of Jonson's famous aphorism, from the preface to the first folio, that Shakespeare "hadst small *Latine*, and less *Greeke*"—that is, that he suffered somehow from a lack of classical learning. Baldwin uses all of Shakespeare's plays, including, not surprisingly, *Love's Labour's Lost*, to support his contention that Shakespeare's education served the writer well, and that rather than lacking in education, Shakespeare's knowledge of Latin and Greek was deep and widespread. He writes that "if we are to understand how Shakespeare developed, we must know something of the formal education to which he was exposed" (1). Baldwin notes that Jonson called Shakespeare the "Soule of the Age" in the first line of the preface, and that Jonson emphasized the comedies as the best example of Shakespeare's excellence. Throughout his book Baldwin cites examples of where Shakespeare either borrowed or was directly influenced by Greek and Roman writers, both classical and Renaissance. His brief illustrations from *LLL* are spread throughout the book and serve to remind us how widely read Shakespeare was. Even if we admit that in many cases Shakespeare could have found his definitions, examples of word play, or rhetorical models in a number of other sources that Baldwin cites, Baldwin's classic study illustrates that Shakespeare was well versed in the same kind of rhetorical handbooks and models of eloquence as his characters in *LLL*.

Sister Joseph and Baldwin are traditional in their approach to Shakespeare's language: they both are dedicated to exploring Shakespeare's early education and its impact on his conceptualization of literary language. Further, they both attempt to explain Shakespeare as a product of this culture. Many critics have taken different paths toward the exploration of this important topic, ones more theoretically informed. But most critics of Shakespeare, even where their work differentiates itself from that of Joseph and Baldwin, owe a debt to their work. It is inevitable that, when exploring the language of the play, critics emphasize the cultural and societal influences that came to bear on Shakespeare in the writing of it.

Jane Donawerth has also explored Shakespeare's language in her *Shakespeare and the Sixteenth-Century Study of Language*. She notes that Elizabethans were greatly interested in how the power of language could reflect, and in some cases affect, the world. Renaissance writers such as Thomas Wilson, Richard Puttenham, and Richard Mulcaster all wrote about the need to find fit words for their ideas. Likewise, throughout *LLL* characters struggle with finding "fit words" for their ideas. Donawerth notes that the early plays dating from 1594–96, including *Titus Andronicus, LLL, King John, Richard II*, and *Romeo and Juliet*, have the highest frequency of key terms referring to language (142). She notes that as Shakespeare was experimenting with form and style he was also interested in finding a suitable verbal style. In this way *LLL* is autobiographical: like Berowne and his companions, Shakespeare was struggling with how to represent the reality he wished to recreate. One of the aspects of language that most interests Shakespeare is the generative nature of it, how words can be taken apart and recreated to form witty puns and new words; see, for example, IV.ii.58–61: "Of one sore I a hundred make by adding but one more L." By adding one letter to "sorel" (a deer of four years), he makes it a "sorel" (a deer of three years), and then, by identifying L as the Latin numeral for "fifty," he makes fifty sores (sore-L), or with another L, one hundred (sore-LL) (144). [In a more traditional vein, Sister Joseph labels this as an example of proparalepsis, the addition of a syllable at the beginning of a word (51).] Either way, what is important to note is the generative nature of Shakespeare's language: new meanings are created and generated out of simple and colloquial words and letters. Given that the young men have come to study books, the lessons and "words" of those books are an extension of the basic linguistic feats found throughout the play. Characters literally devour words, as seen in the words of Costard, who says to Moth, "I marvel thy master hath not eaten thee for a word, for thou art not so long by the head as *honorificabilitudinitatibus.*" Such a word, the longest, according to Samuel Johnson, in English literature, is itself a result of the generative nature of Latin. This word, like so many uttered by the pedagogues in the play, is completely artificial; the likelihood of *honorificabilitudinitatibus* being unselfconsciously used is nil, as any actor who has been asked to pronounce the word on stage would attest. In short, *LLL* represents language as reflecting the world around it—the artificial world of the academy, separated from the natural world of love and social relations, results in an artificial language.

Samuel Johnson was the first critic to take Shakespeare to task for his preoccupation with "quibbling," or the overreliance on clever word play. Donawerth notes the following comment by Boyet as a commentary on quibbling:

> The tongues of mocking wenches are as keen
> As is the razor's edge invisible,
> Cutting a smaller hair than may be seen,
> Above the sense of sense; so sensible
> Seemeth their conference, their conceits have wings
> Fleeter than arrows, bullets, wind, thought, swifter things. (V.ii.256–
>   262)

The artificiality of language also influences another theme of the play, the relationship between social classes. Moth, who is almost eaten by his master who is able to chew big words, is a prime example of how the ability to use language distinguishes the upper class from the lower class. But as is typical of comedies, such a distinction is not allowed to operate unreflectively. Throughout the play both the lower- and upperclass characters play games with language: "The lower characters delight in language as sound and pattern; the higher characters, especially the women, see that the order of language becomes a way of generating surprising meanings: mankind is guest, not host, at the great feasts of language" (Donawerth 151).

Barbara L. Parker takes a different stance in discussing the importance of the characters' language. She notes that the language used by the young lords is overly rhetorical and sophistic, and as such is "calculated to ensnare" love rather than arrive at it naturally and logically (85). In contrast, the ladies insist that word and matter or deed be in alignment, that they be sincere and natural. As an example, the princess condemns the forester for "painting" her beauty (89) in Act IV, scene i. Parker goes one step further and suggests that all the linguistic differences between the characters serve as a commentary on Catholic concepts of both grace and merit, as represented by the opportunistic and overly rhetorical stance of the young men, versus a Protestant concept of merit as proof of righteousness. "See, see! my beauty will be saved by merit? O heresy in fair, fit for these days!/A giving hand, though foul, shall have fair praise." (IV.i.21–23). From a Protestant point of view, Catholic concepts of good works and merit as a necessity for achieving grace suggested that grace could be bought and that good words were commodities; hence, the young men are using language to "buy" grace from the ladies, as opposed to the more sincere speech acts of the ladies that are in alignment with righteousness and sincerity. In a similar vein, James Calderwood, in his *"Love's Labour's Lost*: A Wantoning with Words" states that in the play "words have the function, not so much of expressing the truth of either things or feelings, but of eliciting, through puns, metaphors, syntax, rime, alliteration, coinage . . . verbal relations that are in themselves aesthetically pleasing" (318). The worthiness and merit of a character are based on their "generative potential," that is, their ability to be "procreative" in their verbal interaction with other characters (319). As both Calderwood and Parker suggest, language is a commodity with a very specific, culturally defined use; even the aesthetic has a function that goes beyond merely pleasing.

Another example of the social function of language is seen in the oath taking of the young men. The men bind themselves to each other through oaths and statutes. However, as the play proceeds, the social order is threatened by verbal "promiscuity"; language that is divorced from "the realities of human nature" (Calderwood 321) cannot be procreative. It is the women who prevent the total disintegration of language, and by extension social order, since the ladies have respect for language and the "genuine marriage between word and meaning" (326). Much as women often function to maintain social order in the comedies through fidelity and fertility, in *LLL* they stabilize language and give it a firm social foundation. Berowne's sentence to "Visit the speechless sick and still converse . . . With all the fierce endeavour of your wit/To enforuce the pained impotent to smile" (V.ii.861–864) is meant to ensure that he learns that language must be in accord with the audience and social situation.

Love's Labour's Lost is also a play rich in imagery. As Caroline Spurgeon notes, *LLL*, along with *As You Like It*, has more images than any of the other comedies. "But this large number does not in *Love's Labour's Lost* denote, as it would in most other plays, a high percentage of sheer poetry, for the images chiefly go to form the tissue of verbal wit, puns and double meanings, of which the fabric is woven" (275). This is an important point for it suggests that Shakespeare makes the images a part of the texture of the play; in other words, verbal dexterity is not an exception, but a fact of life in Navarre. Of the 164 images she counts in the play, only eleven are really poetic (275). This imagery appears in almost all facets of the play—rich, poetic imagery pervades the poetry of the young men, and comic imagery, often in the form of puns, informs most of the comic banter. Spurgeon, who defines an image as "any and every imaginative picture" (5), finds "running symbolic imagery" (a continued series of images that highlight a major theme or themes of the play), throughout the tragedies, yet in only three of the comedies—*LLL, Much Ado,* and *All's Well* (271). The main images in *LLL* are of war and weapons, which serves to emphasizes the war of wits theme (271).

THE COURT AND TOPICALITY

Since the nineteenth century there has been a critical assumption that *Love's Labour's Lost* is a highly topical play and that it was probably written for a courtly audience. Although these assumptions are looked at more closely in Chapters 1 and 6, much of that criticism does not stand up today in light of more sophisticated textual analysis. However, there is no doubt that the play does set out to mimic, on some level, the life of the court, at least the life of the court of Navarre. To that end many modern critics have viewed the play through historical lenses, looking for what the play might reveal about Shakespeare's conception of courtly life. For example, as Caroline Spurgeon reminds us, the war of wits is an important aspect of courtly life. In *"Love's Labour's Lost*: The Court at Play,"* John Turner argues that inherent in courtly life was competition, both between individuals for power and fame and between court and country, as well as political intrigue and ecclesiastical debates. By calling itself an academe, Navarre's court highlights the separation of court from country and the implied pretentiousness that such a separation brings. In Act II of *LLL*, Boyet describes the court as "he [Navarre] and his competitors in oath" (II.i.82); Turner notes that "competitor" had a double meaning in the Renaissance, meaning either partner or rival, and thus the court could be seen as either a group gathered as rivals or as partners, and the play acts out this ambiguity (19). Turner notes three kinds of competition in the play: (1) the competition within the court, (2) the competition between Navarre and the court of France, and (3) the competition between the court and the country it represents (21).

Berowne represents one paradox inherent in courtly love: that it is both a necessary and rule-oriented activity while also serving as a source of freedom. It is Berowne who sees the pursuit of love as providing a freedom from the drudgeries of scholarship, and it is Berowne who also speaks of the "purblind, wayward boy" Cupid, who is the "Regent of love rhymes, lord of folded arms,/The anointed sovereign of sighs and groans" (III.i.174–177). Love, like so much else in the court, is governed by unwritten rules of behavior and affectation (26–27). It is Armado, however, who best represents the "entrapment of court life" (27). Armado's excesses, both in speech and melancholy, parody the social role that courtiers such as the lords play in Elizabethan society.

Turner sees the entrance of Sir Nathaniel, Dull and Holofernes at the beginning of Act V as representative of the three agents that maintain social order: religion, law, and learning (30). The sonnet reading scene at IV.iii is also a central turning point in the play for it is the moment when "fellowship becomes open rivalry" (31). These various social rituals are themselves political and when uncovered by satire, the tensions inherent between self-proclaimed fictions about the court and the realities of the court are articulated. The tension between court and country can best be seen in Costard, who is drawn to the language of the court (see, e.g., his use of "remuneration" and "guerdon"), but he is also resistant to it, which is best seen in the "competition" between Costard and Armado (40). "We see a society bound together in all the exclusiveness of cultural snobbery; a punctiliously deferential courtesy together with a competitive display of wit; a presumption of prestige swollen into gorgeous vanity; and a pedantic parade of variations played upon the restricted themes of polite conversation" (42).

Throughout the play, the word "grace" is used to in a variety of ways to suggest a desired characteristic of a gentleman or woman. The word appears twenty-nine times in the play, but despite this presence it is never a stable referent. Navarre's first speech sets up the ambiguity: "Let fame, that all hunt after in their lives,/Live regist'red uppon our brazen tombs,/ And then grace us in the disgrace of death." Navarre's opposition of fame's grace to death's disgrace "secularizes" the theological meaning of "grace" so that it becomes a "form of humiliation or dishonor, a consignment of one's name to oblivion" (Montrose 532). Closely aligned to this secularized grace is the stylistic connotation of grace, what was referred to as "sprezzatura," a spontaneous wit or linguistic skill that has the appearance of effortlessness. Wit or linguistic grace should appear effortless and natural, but in fact this kind of grace is dependent upon proper education or instruction (532). The final connotation of the word, also used throughout the play, is theological—the gift of God which saves man from sin, and it is this meaning that suggests that salvation and charity are related to grace. The grace the women withhold from the young men ("And not a man of them shall have his grace,/Despite of suite, to see a lady's face" at V.ii.128–129) suggests this kind of grace. Berowne acknowledges that there is such a thing as "natural grace" when he states that "every man with his affects is born/Not by might mast'red, but by special grace" (I.i.151–152). But when he breaks his oath, he stands in "eternal shame" (I.i.157). All these connotations come together in the play via the characters' emphasis on "natural" and appropriate language and the "secular religion" of courtship (534). In the largest sense "grace" means approval in all these contexts, and as such it is closely aligned with the theme of language and the desire for approval each of the character's possesses (534).

John Dixon Hunt, in "Grace, Art and the Neglect of Time in 'Love's Labour's Lost' " also notes the importance of the idea of "grace" in the play. As with most words in the play, it takes on many different connotations in the course of the play. Hunt defines it, according to the *OED*, as "attractiveness or charm belonging to elegance or proportions" and as "divine influence operating in men to regenerate and sanctify." For Hunt, the "lesson" of the play, which the young lords of the Academe must come to learn, is how to achieve both of these graces "within the world of nature and time" (77). Hunt does not see the play as built upon a dichotomy between art and nature; rather, it is grace that allows both to ideally live in harmony. When Berowne, in I.i.80–83, uses a theological conceit to describe beauty, he is also reaffirming a common Renaissance conceit regarding heavenly grace:

Study me how to please the eye indeed,
By fixing it upon a fairer eye;
Who dazzling so, that eye shall be his heed,
And give him light that it was blinded by.

Unwittingly, Navarre wishes to withhold grace by denying the young men access to women. Likewise, the young women deny the men the grace of beauty by wearing masks in V.iii.128–129: "not a man of them shall have the grace, / Despite of suit, to see a lady's face."

The theme of grace is so prevalent in the play that it touches upon many other themes. For example, grace can also be seen in the sense of linguistic decorum—doing or saying the right thing at the right time and place, another lesson the lords must learn. The "harmony" of decorum and its relationship to harmonious nature are illustrated in the exchange between Berowne and the King at I.i.100–106, in which Berowne concludes that "proud summer should [not] boast/Before the birds have any cause to sing?" and that he no more desires "a rose/Than wish a snow in May's new-fangled shows." With this insight, Berowne and the lords begin to gradually move toward "some consonance between their art or language of living and the world in which they have to live," a movement that culminates in sonnet writing and their attempt to put on the masque (91). By interrupting the comedy we are watching with the announcement of death, and by acknowledging that life "is too long for a play," the audience is reminded that natural grace lies outside the game of the theater.

For Thomas Green the word "grace" takes on a very specific social connotation: the "enlightened intercourse between the sexes, with gaiety and true wit, with poise, taste, decorum, and charity" (328). The play is essentially about the pursuit of these goals, which remain out of reach until the final songs, which form an "ideal ending" to a play about the abuses of language. These final songs suggest that Shakespeare firmly believed in the power of rhetoric and poetry, but that he does not include an example of it within the play proper. Rather, playtime is too "short." Since grace is absent from the play proper, so is any solid and undebatable social underpinning (315) that comes from the proper use of language and decorum. Despite being a play about "civil" society (i.e., ladies and gentlemen in formal discourse), the gentlemen have only a vague understanding of what civility is, at least in its relationship to decorum, and therefore each of them violates the rules of civility (318). Berowne, more than the others, at least knows that he muddles through and makes mistakes, but he cannot stop himself. For Green, the turning point in the play occurs when Berowne "forswears,"

Taffeta phrases, silken terms precise,
Three-pil'd hyperboles, spruce affectation,

Figures pedantical—those summer flies
Have blown me full of maggot obstentation. (V.ii.406–410)

Berowne finally arrives at the kind of self-knowledge and criticism he has searched for throughout the entire play. His conclusion that he is "blown full of maggot obstentation" is a realization that true grace comes not from formal rules of rhetoric but from natural speech.

Love's Labour's Lost plays out the relationship, sometimes tense in Elizabethan society, between court and country. This was a cultural tension as well as an economic and social one: the court was defined by certain fashionable modes of behavior and learning, and it is this tension that *LLL* most cleverly reveals. Richard Cody, in *The Landscape of the Mind: Pastoralism and Platonic Theory in Tasso's Aminta and Shakespeare's Early Comedies*, calls "pastorlism" the "poetic expression *par excellence* of that cult of aesthetic Platonism which arose in Florence" in the Renaissance (6). During the Italian Renaissance the "thisworldliness" of courtly culture was reconciled with the "otherworldliness" of Platonic ideals (12). Hercules, a mythic figure who represented the struggle between these two ideals, is a prominent figure throughout *LLL* and his struggle is essentially the major theme of the play. For example, Berowne's speech at I.i.1–14 represents a choice between the "erotic and academic way to virtue" (106). The Pageant of the Nine Worthies likewise develops around the theme of worldly appetites as a potentially destructive force.

In the pastoral tradition, nature was an extension of courtly culture. The play is united by the concept of "landscape," a point that Cody acknowledges was made by Pater in his *Appreciations*: "the unity of the play is not so much the unity of a drama as that of a series of pictorial groups, in which the same figure reappears, in different combinations but on the same background" (quoted in Cody 109). This unifying principle reminds us that *LLL* is essentially a pastoral. For Cody, pastoral is a way for the courtier to have it both ways: to take delight in a sensible universe and to have a vision of divine perfection (7). In short, it means having a good "inner life." This good, balanced life is reflected in the language of the play: "The virtue of *Love's Labour's Lost* is stylistic" and it reflects the importance of "the right degree of self-consciousness in all the actions of life" (125).

META-DRAMA AND THE PAGEANT OF THE NINE WORTHIES

Structurally *Love's Labour's Lost* presents critics with several problems. First, it is a very asymmetrical play. The last scene of the play, the longest in Shakespeare, foregrounds artifice—that is, calls attention to itself as drama—which leads to a second problem, the (seeming) overreliance on spectacle at the expense of plot. Throughout the play, artifice is seen in the language used by the characters as well as in the dramatic performances (the masque of the Muscovites and the Nine Worthies). In the words of Louis Montrose, "playwright, actors, and audience are engaged in the purposeful playing of a play whose fictional action is generated almost entirely by characters at play" (529). G. Beiner notes that there are two kinds of artifice in *LLL*: the use of (and references to) conventions and the "meta-dramatic dimension" that is created when Shakespeare calls the spectator's attention to the artifice (49). Shakespeare often includes reflective elements in his comedies; see, for example, *The Taming of the Shrew, A Midsummer Night's Dream*, and *Twelfth Night*. In the latter two, Shakespeare waits until the drama is over to present meta-dramatic references, bringing characters from the play out of the play to address the audience. *Love's Labour's Lost* presents the most drastic use of meta-drama (52). By refusing to provide the "usual" comic conclusion, Shakespeare is calling attention to the play as a comedy. Specifically, it is the entrance of Marcade that calls to an end the "game" of the comedy and festivities. The conclusion renders it impossible for *LLL* to "end like an old play" (V.ii.874). The disruptions and interruptions deliberately frustrate the comic form and by doing so the play provides a more active role for the reader than might otherwise be afforded (64). "The play tackles the very basis of any verbal art, and specifically of comedy: language and form" (69). It should be noted that much modern criticism on Shakespeare's self-conscious use of comic form owes its existence to the archetypal criticism of writers such as Northrop Frye, most significantly his "The Argument of Comedy" (1948), which provided a great deal to the understanding of Shakespeare's comedies. Likewise, C.L. Barber's 1959 *Shakespeare's Festive Comedy* exposed the anthropological basis for the comedies: *Love's Labour's Lost*, like *A Midsummer Night's Dream*, ends with the archetypal "holiday sequence of release and clarification" (11). Although many critics now view the play as resisting the "holiday" spirit at the end, Barber brought to Shakespearian criticism a new understanding of how deeply ingrained the comic spirit is in our collective unconscious and what an important role it plays in our social and cultural existence.

Although Barber managed to suggest a certain verisimilitude to Shakespeare's art, *LLL* is especially noteworthy for its emphasis on deliberate artifice. The deliberate foregrounding of artifice contrasts with the sense of realism Peter Berek notes as a characteristic of Shakespeare's advances over his "teacher," John Lyly. Berek defines "realism" as the presentation of "basic human emotion as necessary qualities of specific characters in specific situations" (207). Shakespeare develops this realism in stark contrast to the formalities of courtly drama that he inherited from Lyly and which were influential on his plays. Although many of the themes of *LLL* are to be found in Lyly's plays, Shakespeare adds a twist in that he shows how formal artifice fails. Throughout the play, "the verbal is as much a foil for the real as the way in which real feeling is displayed" (215). In fact, it is the failure of artifice in the play that gives us a glimpse of real human emotions.

One of the most "artificial" passages in the play is the Pageant of the Nine Worthies. The tradition of the Nine Worthies dates to France in the early fourteenth century and was widely used in Renaissance literature. Usually the worthies were grouped as pagans (Hector, Alexander, Julius Caesar), Jews (Joshua, David, Judas Maccabaeus) and Christians (Arthur, Charlemagne, Godfrey of Boulogne), and the pageants typically presented them in that order. The idea of the timelessness of fame is a fitting theme for *LLL*, yet Shakespeare takes several liberties in his presentation. Are these alterations the result of ignorance or, more likely, deliberate thematic alterations? Thematically important is the medieval tradition that the Worthies were the highest example of heroic behavior, and in the play the pageant brings out "the inhumanity" and the "blindness and folly of the noblemen's behavior" (Anderson 60). The Nine Worthies reminded audiences (and in *LLL*, the characters) that arrogance is counterproductive since wit is not enough to overcome death.

Perhaps Shakespeare's most obvious alteration is his inclusion of Pompey and Hercules, and that he only includes three of the standard Worthies, Alexander, Judas Maccabaeus, and Hector. The comic limitations of the players accounts for why Holofernes can only come up with nine, but why add Pompey and Hercules? Judith Perryman notes that Shakespeare first deviates from the tradition by bringing Pompey "on stage" first, followed by Alexander, Hercules, Judas, and finally Hector, thereby losing any sense of thematic order imparted by the traditional order. This could point either to ignorance on Shakespeare's part or, more likely, to his appreciation of the thematic similarities these characters have to the original Nine Worthies (157). She also notes that in one of Shakespeare's possible sources, John Eliot's *Ortho-epia Gallica*, Hercules kills serpents, as Moth maintains that Hercules does. Perryman also observes that each character has a thematic role in the play, but generally their presence is a parody of the king's academe.

The first Worthy, Pompey, is represented by a threefold pun: the first is "Pompion," or pumpkin, for Pompey, as noted in Costard's "mistake" at V.ii.502. Perryman notes that "pompions" were newfangled vegetables often associated with foreigners. A second pun is suggestive of the theme of "pomp" or ceremony and show that runs through the play. To introduce the pedants as "Pompion the Great . . . " "Pompey surnam'd the Big! . . . " and "Greater than great, great, great Pompey!/ Pompey the Huge!" (V.ii.550–686) serves as a reminder of the self-importance these characters represent. The third possible pun, "pomewater," or apple, connects Costard, or "a kind of apple of large size" [*OED*], with his role as a fool who serves as a foil for many of the other characters. All the puns suggest "things inflated" that are somehow "deflated"(158). By leading with Pompey, Shakespeare successfully deflates the entire tradition as well as the players.

The second worthy to be introduced, Alexander "the conqueror," reminds the audience of the king's description of his academe members as "brave conquerors" conducting war against their "own affections" (I.i.9–10). Again, by this point in the play, the young men are no longer conquerors but lovestruck. Hercules is an important referent throughout the play: it could be that Hercules's labors are referred to in the title of the play, and Hercules is mentioned more times than any other mythological figure except Cupid (Perryman 160). In keeping with the theme of "deflation," given that he is played by Moth, Hercules is deflated or reduced to an "imp . . . a babe, a child, a shrimp" (V.ii.588–590).

Holofernes as Judas Maccabaeus lends itself to an obvious reference, that of Judas Iscariot, called a "kissing traitor" by Berowne at line 595. The traditional association of Hector with boasting is also fitting for the worthies tradition since he is played by Armado, the stock braggart character in the play. Although the classical Hector was known for wisdom and moderation as well as strength, Armado is not so noteworthy. Finally, Perryman quotes Anne Barton, who noted that "the Pageant of the Nine Worthies, naturally evocative of death and time, seems to concentrate and draw to itself all those images of mortality which have begun to make themselves felt in the last movement of the play" (*Riverside*

176). In Shakespeare's hands, each of the Five Worthies has met defeat and has had his weakness revealed. Armado notes that "the sweet warman is dead and rotten" (V.ii.660), while Berowne states that "Judas was hang'd on an elder" (V.ii.601), and finally Nathaniel acknowledges that Alexander, despite his fame, died: "When in the world I liv'd" (V.ii.562) (Perryman 161).

After pointing out that every model, or representation, is dictated by the nature of the artistic medium and is therefore a simplification of the thing represented, Philip Edwards, in *Shakespeare and the Confines of Art*, applies this Platonic understanding of art to the theater: the "imitation of life has the beginning and the middle and the end that life itself lacks" (5). *Love's Labour's Lost* has no ending, however, at least not an ending that is prescribed by the rules of comedy. Edwards cites Northrop Frye's contention that comedy has three stages: separation, bewilderment, and harmony (33). *Love's Labour's Lost* does not end properly, with harmony, which traditionally takes the form of music and marriage in Elizabethan comedies. "*Love's Labour's Lost* is the comedy which denies itself and refuses to behave" (37). It ends with the mocking of comic conventions by the songs of the cuckoo and the owl and a "wintry" twelve months in a hermitage or hospital. Edwards suggests that Shakespeare is refusing to end on a note of harmony since he is asking his comedy to conform to "ordinary experience" (46). He has not yet learned how to include real pain and real union, something he will learn to do in *Romeo and Juliet*, for example (48). However, it should not be assumed that this is a weakness of this comedy, as Edwards suggests it is; after all, it is Edwards who quite correctly notes that Shakespeare was an experimenter whose skepticism of the value of his own art as an adequate model of life itself kept him altering and mocking the art of theater (10). Shakespeare was undoubtedly calling attention to the conventions of the theater in order to parody them. Likewise, the play does end in harmony, as many critics have shown us, with the beautiful songs of the cuckoo and owl, songs that, while calling attention to the standard metaphoric roles of the seasons, reverse them in accordance with the play.

Edwards is not the only critic to make connections between the relative inexperience of Shakespeare at the time he wrote the plays and the lack of development in the characters themselves. Understanding how characters are rendered is the most important component in understanding Shakespeare's comedies, according to Larry S. Champion in *The Evolution of Shakespeare's Comedy: A Study in Dramatic Perspective*.

Love's Labour's Lost is an early play: the princess and her ladies are "puppet like" compared to Ferdinand and his lords (9) since Shakespeare was still developing as a playwright. In regards to characterization, *LLL* is comparable to *Two Gentlemen of Verona* since both depend on caricature, minor characters as "comic pointers," and zany figures whose actions parallel the main plot (41). The humor of the play resides in the impossible and extreme posture of Navarre and its turn to farce. What we end up seeing is the downfall of the characters, not their actual transformation, which is so often the focus of later, more mature comedies (42). Any actual growth on the part of the characters must occur "beyond the limits of the stage-world" (45), as is evidenced in the final act. However much of a critical mainstay it might be, the notion that the play suffers from a lack of deep and "realistic" character development due to its reliance on situation is contradicted by several critics who have praised how Shakespeare manages to develop multifaceted, if not "realistic," characters from the transformative situations of the play. For example, John Cutts writes that *"Love's Labour's Lost* derives much of its permanent dramatic interest from the results of its characters' 'unseeing' "(22). Whereas Champion sees the dependence on character development as a negative attribute of the play, Cutts sees it as a strength. The failures of the young men to lead lives of contemplation offers them "the opportunity to look into the mirror of themselves, to see themselves for what they are and learn to live with the reality" (33).

This "mirror" can also be seen as a meta-dramatic element in the play. "In a critical approach to *Love's Labour's Lost*, we must distinguish carefully between the intention of the playwright and the intentions of his characters," writes Louis Montrose, "and try to assess the dynamics of audience response to the disjunctions that Shakespeare's ironic strategies are intended to generate" (530). In the case of *LLL*, the lords create their own play world in which they will "act out" their living play, except that the world and other characters refuse to cooperate. In turn, the play studies how humans at large play, that is, how they use rituals, games, myths, social institutions, and language; the play is itself a manifestation of Elizabethan culture since "its author, actors, and audience are social players engaged in the same kind of strategies as those of the characters" (530). Throughout the play, Shakespeare manipulates the audience's response by revealing the different levels of awareness between the characters and between the characters and the audience (536). Such constant unveiling forbids the characters the "grace" they desire from other characters and from the audience. Additionally, the audience is put at an ironic distance from the action of the play by the breaking of theatrical contract at the end when Berowne announces, "That's too long for a play" (542). In the end, the play is full of denials: the "rituals" of bonding are denied, along with the lords' denial of their own oaths, the ladies' denial of grace, and the playwright's denial of an expected comic conclusion (548).

FEMINISM AND GENDER CRITICISM

Feminist critics have typically viewed *Love's Labour's Lost* as, in the words of Marilyn French in *Shakespeare's Division of Experience*, "Shakespeare's freest comedy" (94) since it ends not with the traditional marriage and dominance of men over women, but with the women victorious and delaying the finality of marriage. As both feminist and queer theorists point out, *LLL* is typically comic in that institutional love is questioned and the separate worlds of men and women gradually break down as the play unfolds, yet Shakespeare self-consciously delays the final movement of comedies. *Love's Labour's Lost* teaches us what a comedy is by example as well as exception.

Any play that ends with delayed nuptials and women making demands of their wooers is ripe for the kind of insight afforded by modern feminist theory. Jeanne Addison Roberts states that "the temptation is strong to argue for *Love's Labor's Lost* as Shakespeare's most feminist play" (75). At the same time, *LLL* is a perfect example of the contradictions that feminist scholarship must face: whenever women appear in control or fully self-aware, we are reminded that the plays were written by a man, and a man of his time who undoubtedly had some reservations about the autonomy and independence of women. Is *Love's Labour's Lost* an exception, a play that is wholly "feminist" in the most contemporary sense, (i.e., that presents women as wholly equal to men), in many cases superior, or is it more typical in the sense of presenting strong women for the sake of laughter, as some critics have suggested about Kate in *The Taming of the Shrew*? Roberts suggests that *LLL* is not actually about women since the ladies appear in only three scenes (although one of them is the longest scene in Shakespeare) and they do not appear at all in Acts I and III. Jaquenneta, who appears in only three scenes, represents the most basic stereotypical characteristics of women: she is appealing and fertile (78). However, as Katherine Eisaman Maus notes, "the linguistic pleasures and perplexities of *Love's Labor's Lost* are inseparable from its sexual politics, as the play calls the relations between the sexes and the appropriateness of names into question by the same means and for similar reasons" (221). Even if the play is more about the men than the women, it is about the men's reaction to the women.

On one level *LLL* is surely about the differences between the sexes. Irene G. Dash, in *Wooing, Wedding, and Power: Women in Shakespeare's Plays*, sees the play, and more specifically the issue of oath taking, as revealing "how men and women characters perceive the meaning of truth and honesty" (9). Women are the subject of the men's vows, from the initial vow to reject them to the final vow to marry them. Of the men it is Berowne, always the rational and quick-witted one, who believes the initial oaths to be too harsh and doomed to failure:

> As not to see a woman in that term,
>
> .   .   .
>
> And not be seen to wink of all the day,
> When I was wont to think no harm all night,
>
> .   .   .
>
> O, these are barren tasks, too hard to keep. (I.i.37–47)

Navarre, however, the figure of authority, insists on total compliance with the oath, and Berowne submits. Whereas oaths "link the men," the play questions the wisdom of this oath taking, and it is the women who are the "chief challengers" (11). It is also the women who inherently understand the importance of keeping oaths: after the king asserts that the "virtue of your eye must break my oath" (V.ii.348), the princess objects, "You nickname virtue; vice you should have spoke,/For virtue's office never breaks men's troth" (349–350). Dash discusses several other examples of oath making and breaking, yet it is always the women, usually the princess, who point to the hypocrisy and futility of oath taking. Dash notes the remarkable independence and intelligence of the princess and further sees exchanges such as in IV.i.34–38 as examples of Shakespeare's "remarkable insight into the mind of a woman and his ability to create individualized women" (23). The princess represents the superiority of the women in the play because of her awareness ofthe weakness of oaths as proof of love, a lesson the men never learn. Dash's conclusion is an important one for Shakespearian feminist criticism: "Writing at a time when new perceptions of women were challenging the old, the dramatist molded a character who was individual, one who drew her strength from understanding herself—a woman functioning in a man's world and questioning that world's values." (29).

As David Bevington observes, the "male point of view" inherent in comedy, at least in those comedies in which a female becomes a prize, is something the male dramatist is only partially aware of. Shakespeare is not unique in withholding the prize at the end of the play; John Lily's *Sappho and Phao* also delays or collapses marriage negotiations. Lily and Shakespeare "are alike in dramatizing not so much the success of courtship as its hazards and uncertainties" (2). In Lily's play it is a gap in political and social roles that causes the collapse: Sappho must reject the advances of the lowly Phao. Yet Bevington notes that as spectators we "see that Lily objectifies the plight of the male to a significant degree by bestowing on women a cutting wit and an ironic sense of what is so discrepant about male behavior" (3). Like Dash, Bevington sees the young women in *LLL* as more self-knowing, citing the first scene of Act II, in which the young women make honest appraisals of the men, as an example of such self-awareness. While the women never lose themselves, rationally or emotionally, to love, we watch amusingly as the men proceed to make fools of themselves.

The men are essentially "unselfknowing" (7), unable to accurately appraise their own affections; it is this inability that makes them foolish, notes Bevington, not the announced aims of the Academe. The comic embarrassment of the men depends on "a deeper embarrassment, the feeling of male inadequacy before such an exalted and goddess like creature as a woman" (7). Berowne's comparison of a woman to a German clock at III.i.186 reveals the misogyny of the young men who see love as enslavement and as leading to a threat of cuckoldry. The women understand this, at times jeering the young men: "Thou canst not hit it, hit it, hit it,/Thou canst not hit it, by good man" (IV.i.132). As Bevington notes, the "men are driven into love, then, by a desire that at once makes them anxious" (98). In the end the women are unknowable to the men, or to the "male point of view" (10), and Shakespeare, more than Lily, is aware of this irony. The two plays discussed are "alike in providing women with a matriarchal power structure in which the authority of affirmation or denial remains in women's hands" (13), even though this authority is resistant to the comic structure of the play.

Although the language of the play has been closely examined by many critics, few have noted how the linguistic gymnastics of the play impact the various gender issues inscribed in the play. Legitimacy and fame, two issues of importance at the opening of the play in Navarre's newly founded academe, involve an assumption that names are "fixed," that they are permanent and can even overcome death: "Let fame, that all hunt after in their lives,/Live register'd upon our brazen tombs,/And then grace us in the disgrace of death." For many of the male characters, there is a "close connection . . . between a name and a title to property" (Maus 210), as seen in II.i.201–207. However, patronage and title by name are not as easily discernible as the men would like. James Calderwood, for example, notes how the young men must come to see language as either legitimate or illegitimate—a genuine marriage of word and meaning is necessary for a faithful and procreative union. Katherine Eisaman Maus explores the importance of names and titles in her essay, "Transfer of Title in *Love's Labor's Lost*: Language, Individualism, Gender." Maus argues that in making the penalty against an encroaching woman the cutting out of her tongue, the men imagine women as speechless and passive (214). (In 1710, Charles Gildon called this "a perfect penalty.") Women can only corrupt the clear relationship between name and title. The princess does indeed threaten this male homogeny, but as several critics have noted, she does so with a great deal of independence: although she speaks for her father, and thus represents his title and claim to property, he is distant, remote, and by the end of the play, dead. The princess becomes "the object and subject in a system of exchange" (215).

However, Maus reminds us that the women, unlike the men, do not have surnames, and in Renaissance England, a woman's property, like her name, disappears into her husband's (216), which is why when Longaville learns that Maria is "the heir of Falconbridge," he can assume that he, eventually, will be the true heir. For women, the "truth" of language is a moral issue—the men can have fun with exuberant word play and luxurious wit, but the women must see the "truth of names in patriarchy" as the "consequence not of some intrinsic connection between names and things but of female sexual fidelity" (218). Hence, the women often strike critics as more serious, earnest, and self-restrained.

Cuckoldry is one of the ways patrimony is questioned in Renaissance comedies. The Song of Spring and Winter both close the play with suggestions of cuckoldry. In "Jaquenetta's Baby's Father: Recovering Paternity in *Love's Labor's Lost*," Dorothea Kehler explores the question of paternity in great detail. Like Maus, Kehler notes that "the play insists that hierarchical and patrilineal systems remain vulnerable to female subversion due to the nature of the reproductive process" (51). She notes that the theme first arises when Longaville first sees Maria, and he asks, "Pray you, sir, whose daughter?," to which Boyet responds, "Her mother's, I have heard" (II.i.201–202). The same type of quip occurs in *King John, The Taming of the Shrew, The Tempest*, and *Much Ado about*

Nothing. Paternity is important to the men in *LLL* because what is their father-in-law's will someday be theirs. As Kehler observes, there is a deep significance to the issue of paternity in *LLL*: it is very possible that Costard is the father of Jaquenetta's baby, not Armado, and that either Armado is being deceived or he is consciously trying to woo his competitor's beloved (47). "In that subtext not only are male/female and menial/non-menial binarisms reversed but also the stigmas attaching to cuckoldry and female promiscuity disappear" (47). In the first act and scene of the play Costard is caught with "the wench." By Act V, scene ii, we hear that Jaquenetta is pregnant, and that "the child brags in her belly already. 'Tis yours" (676–677). Costard is not only punning on Armado's reputation and comic role as a braggart, but undermining it by questioning his manhood. Kehler cites several examples to support the possibility of Costard's fathering the baby rather than Armado, but perhaps the most convincing is Costard's admittance that he did "follow" her into the park, which could be read as a reference to sexual intercourse given that "follow" was pronounced like "fallow," which in turn meant "to plow" (49). Likewise, at IV.iii.208, Berowne refers to Costard and Jaquenetta as "turtles" or "turtledoves." Jaquenetta ends up being just as independent as the higher-class women in the play, and she does so in a similar manner, by acknowledging that it is through the woman that names and lineage are linked.

Undoubtedly, power is at the root of male/female relationships, in literature as in life. As long as the women in the play retain power, there is no way for the play to end happily and in accordance with the rules of comedy. This play is remarkable for it suggests that as long as we have strong, autonomous women, "Jack hath not Gill" (V.ii.875). As Peter Erickson notes, in the play "women are given the power to be disruptive" (66). The play also calls attention to the nature of literary language, especially Petrarchan love conceits, as artificial and as a "closed linguistic system" (69). Throughout the play the men automatically associate being in love with writing poetry. For example, Berowne ends his sonnet by resigning himself to the necessity of poetry: "Well, I will love, write, sigh, pray, sue, groan" (III.i.204). Petrarchan conceits empower women in the sense that they are able to either redeem or repel their admirers; either way, however, they remain objects and their autonomy is limited by what or whom they choose to be dominated. The same conceits give to the male poet the role of interpreter of love and of the beloved (72), as Berowne notes:

Never durst poet touch a pen to write
Until his ink were temp'red with Love's sighs:
O then his line would ravish savage ears
And plant in tyrants mild humility. (IV.iii.343–346).

Caroline Asp takes this power to interpret as an attempt to "master" women and therefore to "exclude disruptive elements by concentrating on surfaces of perceptions . . . as the sum of knowledge and truth" (4). Asp also notes that this attempt at mastery is reflected in the decree to cut out the tongue of any woman who violates their decree. If you deprive a woman of speech then you deny her the ability to speak from the "masculine" position and she more easily becomes "susceptible to objectification" (5). Poetry is power, at least it is the power to control and persuade. But Shakespeare does not allow the lord's poetry to persuade: in the end, the women resist it and almost all manifestations of courtly relationships. As Ericson notes, the only true evidence of a "connection" between men and women is between Armado and Jaquenetta, but that connection is an embarrassment for all concerned (78). In short, "Shakespeare shows that this hierarchical conception of masculine and feminine roles is unworkable" (74). But throughout the play power relationships are portrayed in literary concepts; for example, the good deeds the lords are sentenced to perform are suggestive of Christian knights performing chivalrous deeds for the sake of their beloveds.

Not all critics have sided with the women in the play. Responding to Ralph Berry's observation that the princess is "beyond question the internal arbiter of the values of *Love's Labour's Lost* . . . The Princess's court . . . upholds the value of truth, or reality," John Wilders conjectures that the princess misjudges most of the situations in which she finds herself (quoted in Wilders 28). For example, he sees Rosaline's response to Berowne's courtship at V.ii.60–68 ("That same Berowne I'll torture ere I go") as arrogant and spiteful. He also condemns the women for not seeing beneath the surface of the Masque of Muscovites, which Wilders sees, against the grain of most of the scholarship on the play, as "an elegant but genuine process of courtship" (29). Rather than regarding the women's condemnation as appropriate, he sees them as misreading the genuineness of the lords. This favoritism is complicated, however, with the Pageant of the Nine Worthies, where the men are the cruel ones, and therefore the audience's sympathies are conflicted: earlier, according to Wilders, our sympathy was with the men when the women reacted harshly to them. Now, we must respond against the men for misinterpreting the aims of the actors. For these reasons, Shakespeare shows an advancement beyond the contemporary debates regarding illusion versus reality or art versus nature. Shakespeare shows us the true "conflicting impulses" within humans: we are social yet solitary, and we wish to be part of the world and to transcend it (33). Perhaps the most important role the women play, according to J.J. Anderson, is to expose faults: the women "are presented not as perfect, but as embodying norms of human conduct against which the aberrations of the noblemen are to be measured" (61).

Love's Labour's Lost is a play of reversals. It reverses, or withholds, the typical comic ending by delaying the union of the lovers. And as we have seen in the scholarship already discussed, it sets out to reverse the "typical" hierarchy of male over female that is inherent in comedies. There is also an implicit reversal based on class: the language as well as demeanor of the high-born characters are brought down by the "lower" born characters. Patricia Parker analyzes these "reversals" in her article "Preposterous Reversals." The word "preposterous," found in Armado's condemnation of Costard's dalliance with Jaquenetta as an "obscene and most prepost'rous" event (l. 242), suggests the theme of reversal that runs through the play: the word is made up of "posterus," meaning "after" or "behind," and "prae," "in front of" or "before." Why was it "preposterous" that Costard would follow Jaquenetta into the park? Given that Jaquenetta is referred to as "a child of our grandmother Eve" (l. 264), we can read the word to suggest that Costard not only reversed the edict of Navarre, but reversed the proper ordering of genders in Genesis where Eve is meant to be subordinate and to follow Adam (436). Parker sees allusions to Genesis throughout the play and suggests that they serve as the basis for the theme of reversal; for example, Costard's name means "apple" and therefore suggests original sin, as does his "hearkening after the flesh" (218). Parker's argument is too subtle and thorough to summarize here, but she notes that most of the situations in the play illustrate reversals. For example, Armado's letter to Jaquenetta betrays his class, just as the lords "follow" the base Costard in falling in love. Similarly, when Berowne derides "base authority from others' books" at I.i.86–87, he is foreshadowing the reversals that will occur when Costard and Moth appropriate Latin terms for their own gain. The play begins with the women acting as the "besiegers" camped outside the male enclosure and ends with the Pageant of the Nine Worthies and the "preposterous" reversals acted out in it. Throughout the play there occurs the "repeated reduction of the decorous, elevated, or high to the 'base, bodily, and low.' "

One of the most basic literary motifs in Renaissance literature, the seduction of a passive women by active men, is effectively reversed in the play. As Jeanne Addison Roberts notes, in the opening of the play, the king "takes on the aura of the female virgin immured in a secluded garden" (76). The women seem, in the opening, the more aggressive sex; Boyet notes that the women are more like invaders who have come to besiege the court. Further, the women are suitors for "money and land" (77), not husbands, which simultaneously masculates them and removes them from their ascribed gender roles. Many of these themes of gender reversal, patrimony, and marriage are highlighted in a 1668 closet drama by Margaret Cavendish, Duchess of Newcastle, whose *The Convent of Pleasure* seems likely to have been based on *LLL*. Cavendish, an early commentator on Shakespeare and praiser of his dramatic women (Roberts 83), reverses the genders in her play and creates a young Lady Happy, who is rich due to her father's death, and vows to retire with her female friends to live "incloister'd from the world" (quoted in Roberts 83). Unlike the young lords, she intends to "enjoy pleasure, and bury [herself] from it" (83). Like *LLL, The Convent of Pleasure* has a play within a play. Likewise, young men appear on the scene as wooers who are, in turn, ridiculed by the women (84). Cavendish's play ends, however, with a conventual marriage, but the internal play suggests that marriage is not a pleasurable experience or necessarily a good choice for a young woman. Thus, the same ambiguity is seen in her play as in *LLL*. Unlike Shakespeare's version, however, Cavendish's young Princess Happy does marry, "loses her name and seems to dwindle complacently into a conventional New Comedy wife" (86).

As much of the criticism of the play suggests, *LLL* is Shakespeare's most ambiguous comedy. Its emphasis on death from the opening speech to the final dialogue gives it some affinity with Shakespeare's tragedies. For example, the play is not alone in its suggestion that marriage can be an unpleasant arrangement. Carol Thomas Neely notes that, in the comedies, often "the cuckoo then, on every tree,/Mocks married men" (v.ii.896–897), but in the end, the mockery strengthens relationships. In a tragedy such as *Othello*, the power of women is incapable of bringing a bad situation to a happy ending (215). Othello does have a Rosaline to temper his "idealism," as is noted in the following from *Othello*:

If it were now to die,
'Twere now to be most happy, for I fear
My soul hath her content so absolute,
That not another comfort, like to this
Succeeds in unknown fate. (II.i.189–1193)

Othello cannot accept cuckoldry, or even joke about it, nor can he let any other character joke about it. The presence of Iago does not allow the mocking yet "realistic" voice of women to intrude, and thus, the play is a tragedy rather than a comedy (217).

As the criticism of *LLL* suggests, the play holds a privleged place in Shakespeare's canon, not only for its own beauty and dramatic effectiveness, but for what it suggests about Shakespeare's conception of his own art and dramatic power. For example, as a comedy, the play is noteworthy not only for what it exemplifies about the genre, but what it calls into question. Robert Tofte, the play's first critic, likewise saw the play as "tragic," and although his reason for doing so is not to be taken seriously, between the criticism of Tofte and much contemporary criticism, the play's ambiguous nature is one of the characteristics that makes it most interesting and most entertaining to today's audiences.

WORKS CITED

Anderson, J.J. "The Morality of 'Love's Labour's Lost.' " *Shakespeare Survey* 24 (1971): 55–62.

Asp, Caroline. "*Love's Labour's Lost*: Language and the Deferral of Desire." *Literature and Psychology* xxxv (1989): 1–21.

Baldwin, T.W. *William Shakespeare's Small Latine and Lesse Greeke*. Urbana: University of Illinois Press, 1944.

Beiner, G. "Endgame in *Love's Labour's Lost.*" *Anglia* 103 (1985): 48–70.

Berek, Peter. "Artifice and Realism in Lyly, Nashe and *Love's Labour's Lost.*" *Studies in English Literature 1500–1900* 23 (1983): 207–221.

Berry, Ralph. *On Directing Shakespeare: Interviews with Contemporary Directors*. London: Hamish Hamilton, 1989.

Bevington, David. " 'Jack Hath Not Jill': Failed Courtship in Lyly and Shakespeare." *Shakespeare Survey: An Annual Survey of Shakespeare Studies and Production*. Ed. Stanley Wells. Cambridge: Cambridge University Press, 1990. 42.

Bloom, Harold. *Shakespeare: The Invention of the Human*. New York: Riverhead Books, 1998.

Calderwood, James. *"Love's Labour's Lost*: A Wantoning with Words." *Studies in English Literature 1500–1900* 5.2 (1965): 317–332.

Carroll, William. *The Great Feast of Language in "Love's Labour's Lost."* Princeton: Princeton University Press, 1976.

Champion, Larry S. *The Evolution of Shakespeare's Comedy: A Study in Dramatic Perspective.* Cambridge: Harvard University Press, 1970.

Cody, Richard. *The Landscape of the Mind: Pastoralism and Platonic Theory in Tasso's Aminta and Shakespeare's Early Comedies.* Oxford: Clarendon Press, 1969.

Coleridge, Samuel Taylor. *Writings on Shakespeare.* Ed. Terence Hawkes. New York: Capricorn Books, 1959.

Cunningham, J.V. " 'With That Facility': False Starts and Revisions in *Love's Labour's Lost."* *Essays on Shakespeare.* Ed. G.W. Chapman. Princeton: Princeton University Press, 1965. 91–115.

Cutts, John. *The Shattered Glass: A Dramatic Pattern in Shakespeare's Early Plays.* Detroit: Wayne State University Press, 1968.

Dash, Irene G. *Wooing, Wedding, and Power: Women in Shakespeare's Plays.* New York: Columbia University Press, 1981.

Donawerth, Jane. *Shakespare and the Sixteenth-Century Study of Language.* Urbana: University of Illinois, 1984.

Edwards, Philip. *Shakespeare and the Confines of Art.* London: Methuen, 1968.

Elam, Keir. *Shakespeare's Universe of Discourse: Language-Games in the Comedies.* Cambridge: Cambridge University Press, 1984.

Ellis, Herbert. *Shakespeare's Lusty Punning in "Love's Labour's Lost": With Contemporary Analogues.* The Hague: Mouton, 1973.

Ericson, Peter. "The Failure of Relationship Between Men and Women in *Love's Labour's Lost."* *Women's Studies* 9 (1981): 65–81.

Evans, Malcolm. *Signifying Nothing: Truth's True Contents in Shakespeare's Texts.* 2nd ed. Athens: University of Georgia Press, 1989.

Green, Thomas M. *"Love's Labour's Lost*: The Grace of Society." *Shakespeare Quarterly* 22 (1971): 315–328.

Hunt, John Dixon. "Grace, Art and the Neglect of Time in 'Love's Labour's Lost.' " *Shakespearian Comedy.* Ed. D. Palmer and Malcolm Bradbury. Stratford-Upon-Avon Studies 14. London: Edward Arnold, 1972.

Johnson, Samuel. *Samuel Johnson on Shakespeare.* Ed. H.R. Woudhuysen. London: Penguin, 1989.

Joseph, Sister Miriam, C.S.C *Shakespeare's Use of the Arts of Language.* New York: Columbia University Press, 1947.

Kehler, Dorothea. "Jaquenetta's Baby's Father: Recovering Paternity in *Love's Labor's Lost."* *Renaissance Papers* (1990): 45–55.

Londré, Felicia Hardison, ed. *"Love's Labour's Lost": Critical Essays.* New York: Garland Publishing, 1997.

Maus, Katherine Eisaman. "Transfer of Title in *Love's Labor's Lost*: Language,

Individualism, Gender." *Shakespeare Left and Right*. Ed. Ivo Kamps. New York: Routledge, 1991.

Montrose, Louis A. " 'Sport by sport o'erthrown': *Love's Labour's Lost* and the Politics of Play." *Texas Studies in Literature and Language* 18 (1977): 528–552.

Neely, Carol Thomas. "Women and Men in *Othello*: "What should such a fool/ Do with so good a woman?" *The Woman's Part: Feminist Criticism of Shakespeare*. Ed. Carolyn Ruth Swift Lenz, Gayle Greene, and Carol Thomas Neely. Urbana: University of Illinois Press, 1980.

Parker, Barbara L. *A Precious Seeing: Love and Reason in Shakespeare's Plays*. New York: New York University Press, 1987.

Parker, Patricia. "Preposterous Reversals: *Love's Labour's Lost*." *Modern Language Quarterly* 54.4 (1993): 435–482.

Perryman, Judith. "A Tradition Transformed in *Love's Labour's Lost*." *Etudes Anglaises* T.XXXVII. no. 2 (1984): 158–162.

Roberts, Jeanne Addison. "Convents, Conventions and Contraventions: *Love's Labor's Lost* and *The Convent of Pleasure*." *Shakespeare's Sweet Thunder: Essays on the Early Comedies*. Ed. Michael J. Collins. Newark: University of Delaware Press, 1997.

Spurgeon, Caroline. *Shakespeare's Imagery and What It Tells Us*. New York: Macmillan Co., 1935.

Turner, John. "*Love's Labour's Lost*: The Court at Play." *Shakespeare: Out of Court: Dramatizations of Court Society*. Ed. Graham Holderness, Nick Potter, and John Turner. New York: St. Martin's Press, 1990.

Wilders, John. "The Unresolved Conflicts of *Love's Labour's Lost*." *Essays in Criticism* (1977): 20–33.

6

THE PLAY IN
PERFORMANCE

Although the play is once again becoming a popular one, *Love's La-bour's Lost* has the dubious distinction of being the only play of Shake-speare's not performed between 1700 and 1800. Why the silence in the eighteenth century? The answer could lie in the nature of the play as a literary text; when read as opposed to seen, the play can strike a reader as dense and frivolous. As a whole, the play presents a finely crafted comic world, and what on the page appears as linguistic gymnastics comes across on the stage as almost musical. This opinion of the play is supported by George R. Foss, the director of a 1918 performance at the Old Vic, who noted that "what had been somewhat vague, pedantic and uninteresting to read, became quaint, bright, and amusing when acted" (Foss 152; quoted in Gilbert 38). Theatrically, the play has a great deal to offer: some of Shakespeare's most humorous characters and his most well-crafted scenes are contained in it. The play is also one of Shakespeare's most spectacular, containing two masques and several elaborate set pieces; for example, the sonnet-reading scene in Act IV, scene iii, is one of Shakespeare's great comic achievements. Although no reader or viewer of the play who was familiar with the nature of comedy would be surprised to discover that the oaths taken by the young men in the first scene of the play were destined to fail, the pacing and arrangement of the young men's changing demeanors make this one of Shakespeare's great comic achievements.

The major problem the play has traditionally faced in performance is the proliferation of "inside" jokes, or topical allusions. As Granville-Barker noted in 1947: "Here is fashionable play; now, by three hundred years, out of fashion. Nor did it ever, one supposes, make a very wide appeal. It abounds in jokes for the elect. Were you not numbered among them you laughed, for safety, in the likeliest places. A year or two later the elect themselves might be hard put to remember what the joke was" (413). Granville-Barker, an actor, director, and later a critic whose *Prefaces to Shakespeare* have influenced generations of directors, sees the play's textual nature as getting in the way of the dramatic. "[Shakespeare] is still too occupied with the actual writing of the play, with himself, in fact, and his own achievements, to spare to his characters that super abundant strength which can let them seem to develop a life of their own" (433). Granville-Barker also views the play as an early one, and typically regards that as the primary fault of the play: "We find in it Shakespeare the dramatist learning his art" (414). What praise he does have for the play is reserved: the play is "well enough done to show that he quite enjoyed doing it, but the sort of thing that almost anyone could learn to do." Here Granville-Barker is specifically concerned with the opening scene of the play, but he could be describing almost any scene in the play given that one of its defining characteristics is "word gymnastics" (414).

Because of Shakespeare's focus on word gymnastics, it is easy to see the main characters as lacking life, especially if one refuses, as Granville-Barker does, to see the language as a necessary component of the characters' dramatic existence. However, Granville-Barker does note some signs of Shakespeare the great dramatist; for example, the character of Berowne achieves "dramatic stature" and the princess is made "flesh and blood" (417). Dramatically, these characters are more than simple stereotypes. Granville-Barker notes that Costard's speech about "great Pompey" (Costard: 'Tis not so much worth . . .") is a great one that reveals Costard the man, not just the fool. As in all the greatest plays, the characters are what make the play timeless, but one must be careful how the characters are interpreted. Whether Holofernes, for example, is simply a type of character (i.e., a pretentious teacher) or whether he is a deeply felt human being is largely dependent on how the character is presented to the audience. If a director is too concerned with presenting Holofernes as a stereotype, and therefore seeing the play as a satire, she runs the risk of rendering the play an historical curiosity. Again, Granville-Barker: "But the producer must consider carefully just what the carrying-power of this embryonic drama is, and how he can effectively interpret to a modern audience the larger rest of the play." The play as Shakespeare wrote it was a satire and "as satire it means nothing to us" (421). I would argue, along with most modern critics, that the "carrying-power" of the play lies in its richly poetic and sardonic language, not in any satirical allusions within it; in fact, as we have already noted, it is doubtful that the play was ever really a topical satire. Nonetheless, the dated nature and density of the word play do present serious potential problems for any production. Modern directors negotiate the historical nature of the play in a variety of ways. Most often, directors choose to highlight the play's formal and "artificial" nature. Granville-Barker, for example, calls for a "fine and rhythmical" delivery (422). The whole play demands a highly formal and stylized approach. In keeping with the historical nature of the play, the costumes should be contemporary with Shakespeare [at most the costumes can date back "fifty years or so back—or forward" (425)]. Despite the words of warning from Granville-Barker, in a theater, in front of an audience, as the play was meant to be seen, the play is hilarious and entertaining. As critic Kenneth Muir wrote of the play, "I have seldom heard so continuous a sound of thoughtful laughter—of laughter mingled with surprise that we had not realized what a good comedy it was" (quoted in *Triple Bond* 25). The same revelation came to John Dover Wilson who notes that in his 1923 edition, he, like earlier editors, missed the main point and art of the play because they had not seen it performed (63). Finally, in 1936, Wilson saw a performance at the Old Vic directed by Tyrone Guthrie, which revealed "a first-rate comedy" (64). Wilson argues that since the public had been "infected" by the critics, this production could not find an audience and closed soon after it opened. The play is best read, perhaps, from the point of view of a playgoer rather than a textual critic. Wilson notes that what makes the play successful is, first, its vivacity and spirit of merriment (65). He cites Dull in V.i.148–149, "I'll make one in a dance, or so; or I'll play/On the tabor to the worthies, and let them dance the hay." Second is the play's plot, which "contains much more than has hitherto been allowed." Audiences take great joy in watching the inevitable occur, such as seeing oath takers breaking their oaths (67) and the later "campaign for love" (68). Third is the play's focus on patterning, such as the abundance of rhyme, which gives the play much of its vivacity and beauty (69). There is also a clear pattern in the two parts of the play, the events leading up to the masque and the pageantry after it, the two parts of which are almost the same length (70). Finally, there is the grouping of characters according to Lylian patterns of conflicting personalities.

So, when critics follow William Hazlitt in his pronouncement that if we were to part with any of the comedies it should be *LLL*, they are probably speaking from only a reading of the play. Twentieth-century scholarship has the benefit of wonderful performances of the play that earlier criticism, especially in the nineteenth century, did not, and these performances have provided a refreshing perspective on the play that can account for many of its peculiarities—namely, the reliance on word play and a thin plot. As we will see, the play benefits from live performance for two reasons: one, the reliance upon word play makes it necessary to be heard as opposed to simply read and, two, the pageantry of the play overshadows any difficulties the language might present. Given that the play's greatness can best be seen in its performances, a brief look at the history of its staging will suggest how audiences and directors have conceived of the play.

In terms of staging, the play is typically Elizabethan, and one could easily imagine the play staged both in a great hall or on a public stage. Very little is necessary for performing the play: in Act IV, scene iii, Berowne needs a tree, one of the few properties called for by the play, in which to sit. Even this seemingly exotic prop would likely have been common property for most theater companies; for example, the 1598 list of properties held by the Lord Admiral's Men mentions a "j. braye tree" (*Henslowe's Diary* 319; quoted in Gilbert 8). The entire play takes place inside Navarre's park, and even though some modern productions have created elaborate sets, a park setting is not a challenging set to design or build. The Pageant of the Nine Worthies requires some simple costumes, the cheaper the better since the play smacks of the same amateurism of the performance by the Rude Mechanicals in *MND*. Finally, the Masque of the Muscovites necessitates masks and there is an exchange of gifts, but again, nothing is required beyond simple stage props. The most demanding aspect of the play in performance is undoubtedly the elaborate word play and complicated dialogue, which accounts for why the play is often cut down a great deal in most modern productions. However, as anyone who has ever seen or acted in the play will attest, an audience does not need to know what "costard in a shin" means to find it funny: delivery is everything.

As for actors, again *LLL* presents no special problems. Depending on how true you are to the original script, Moth is a role for a child actor. In fact, Alfred Harbage argues that the play was written for an acting company of boys (Harbage 27), and there are six roles for boys in the play; of those roles, Moth's is the most complicated, and great care should be taken with casting that part since it involves a great deal of punning and circumlocution.

Of all the characters, Berowne's is the most important, if for no other reason than that he speaks between a fifth and a quarter of all the play's lines; his speech at IV.iii.285–360 is the longest speech in Shakespeare. Therefore, a successful performance is dependent on a fully realized Berowne. The role of Berowne has been played by such notable actors as Kenneth Branagh and Timothy Dalton. There have also been several examples of surprising casting choices in the twentieth century; for example, in 1985, the Royal Shakespeare Company cast a black actress, Josette Simon, as Rosaline, and in Kenneth Branagh's film version, Carmen Ejogo played Maria. There is some textual support for the former choice: for example at IV.iii.257 Rosaline is described by Berowne as being "born to make black fair." Finally, several productions have cast women as Moth. Although there is no textual support for such casting, it does not do damage to the play. Kenneth Branagh cast a woman to play Holofernes, or, as it was, Holofernia.

EARLY PRODUCTIONS

It is easy to assume that Shakespeare's play performed well in front of his contemporaries. However, what cannot be known with certainty is what made a "good" performance for a Renaissance audience. What makes a play performance successful or enjoyable to an audience is just as dependent on the collective aesthetic of a culture as the text itself. At least one of Shakespeare's contemporaries, Robert Tofte, did not find the performance of *LLL* that he witnessed enjoyable:

> This *Play* no *Play*, but Plague was unto me,
> For there I lost the Loue I like most;
> And what to others seemede a Jest to be,
> I, that (in earnest) found unto my cost,
> > To every one (save me) twas *Comicall*,
> > Whilst *Tragick* like to me it did befall.

Tofte goes on to assert that the performance was feigned and "not from the heart." We must take Tofte's criticism with a grain of salt; his poem is about lost love. As H.R. Woudhuysen notes, there is no evidence that Tofte was ever at the English court and therefore it is likely that the performance he witnessed was in one of the public theaters (77). We should not assume that his commentary means that *LLL* did not play well in Shakespeare's time. However, it can be safely assumed that the play was well enough known for Tofte to make a witty comparison to it in his own poem, and his reference to "every one (save me)" suggests the performance was a successful one. What did this performance look like? And how did it compare to modern productions of the play?

We should remember that, in the 1580s, Elizabethans were somewhat inexperienced theatergoers; regular playgoing (i.e., in the modern sense of paid performances of works written for popular audiences) only started in the 1570s and it was only during Shakespeare's life that it gained a sense of consistency and maturity. As any student of Shakespeare knows, the audiences for his plays were often riotous. Yet this play seems, to modern audiences, sophisticated and learned. Many modern performances start from the premise that modern audiences are not as well prepared as Elizabethan ones to understand the play, and in certain ways this is true. A semi-well-educated Elizabethan would know far more Latin than most well-educated theatergoers today, and slang being for the Elizabethans what it still is today, they would understand many of the allusions much more easily than even the most informed scholar does today.

We have very little information on the supposed first performance of the play. The title page of the first quarto states that it was "presented before her Highness this last Christmas." This performance, whenever it occurred, might be fodder for Berowne's statement at V.ii.462, the reference to a "Christmas comedy." "This last Christmas" does not necessarily have to refer to 1597–98 since, as we noted in Chapter 1, title pages were notoriously inaccurate about such matters. Nonetheless, the fact that it was performed for a courtly audience does not necessarily mean it was written for one; the assertion that it was "newly corrected and augmented" likewise makes it impossible to know for whom or when the play was originally written.

The second quarto, published in 1631, refers to public performances at Blackfriars and the Globe (Gilbert 6), thus we know the play had a life in the public theater. But perhaps the most significant early performance of the play occurred in 1605. In a letter from Sir Walter Cope to Sir Robert Cecil, Cope suggests *LLL* for a performance in front of the new Queen Anne:

> Sir—I have sent and been all this morning hunting for players, jugglers & such kind of creatures, but find them hard to find; wherefore leaving notes for them to seek me, Burbage is come, and says there is no new play that the queen hath not seen, but they have revived

an old one, called *Love's Labour's Lost*, which for wit and mirth he says will please her exceedingly. And this is appointed to be played tomorrow night at the my Lord of Southampton's, unless you sent a [note] to remove the corpus cum causa to your house in Strand.

The date of the letter is 1604 and the probable dates of performance are between January 8 and 15 of 1605. The fact that the queen had not yet seen it could be read to suggest that the play had fallen out of favor or that it was not a popular one. But the statement can also be read as evidence against those who argue that the play was originally written for a courtly audience; if Queen Anne, who evidently prided herself on seeing many plays, had not yet seen it, it certainly was not a court favorite just a few years after its composition. Likewise, the play is clearly meant as entertainment—Cope puts it in the company of jugglers and "such kind of creatures." Cope's description does not make it out to be a highly topical work filled with serious commentary on court politics or personages.

After this performance, there are no references to the staging of the play until 1771 when the actor David Garrick commissioned a musical version of it. This version cut over 800 lines and eliminated the scene of the Nine Worthies. However, it was never staged (Gilbert 21). Despite this fact, the inclination to see the play in terms of music is frequently found in many modern productions, including, as we will see, a twentieth-century opera and the contemporary film version of the play by Kenneth Branagh. Although we will treat these productions in detail later, it is important to note that the play has drawn musical comparisons throughout its stage history. It is undoubtedly the formal nature of the play and its emphasis on decorum and language that generated Garrick's version as well as the two modern productions.

Although the play itself remained absent throughout the eighteenth century, there was an adaptation attempted in 1762 when *The Students* (anonymous) was published. Like Garrick's later version, there is no evidence it was ever performed. It was a much shorter play, at 1,625 lines, versus *LLL*'s 2,785 (Gilbert 22). In addition to the typical cuts of the Pageant of the Worthies and the Masque of the Muscovites, it cut IV.iii, the most dramatically successful scene in the play (22). The closing lines of the play became "Our wooing now doth end like an old play;/Jack hath his Jill; these ladies' courtesie/Hath nobly made our sport a Comedy" (24). Also, at one point Berowne steps forward to announce that he heard the ladies speak of their love for the young men, thus imposing a happy ending and making the play unambiguously a comedy. This adaptation suggests that one of the factors that made the original unpopular in the eighteenth century was the lack of a happy ending (Gilbert, "Disappearance and Return" 26).

Miriam Gilbert discusses the absence of the play in the eighteenth century and its gradual reappearance in the nineteenth in "The Disappearance and Return of *Love's Labor's Lost*." She notes that in addition to the happy ending, *The Students* added intrigue by adding scenes in which Berowne is disguised as Costard and during which he flirts with Jaquenetta. In addition, Dumaine asks the real Costard about a letter he thought he gave him to deliver to Katherine, but which was taken by the real Berowne, recalling a similar situation in *A Comedy of Errors* (156). Inexplicably, *The Students* does away with the sonnet-reading scene, and instead has Berowne/Costard finding the king's sonnet. According to Gilbert, *The Students* has more plot and comic incidents and "offers no challenge to the notion that men do, and should, dominate all romantic relationships" (158).

The play returned to the London stage on September 30, 1839, when Madame Vestris, a singer, actress, and theater manager, opened the Covent Garden season with it (27). The production did not lead to a revival of interest in the play and closed after only eight more performances. The Folger Shakespeare library has a prompt book that shows a large production number with the final song ("Spring") with twenty-seven actors and children on stage. Likewise, "Winter" contains another procession with over fifteen persons. Again, music drives the production. It seems clear that the director wanted to emphasize spectacle at the end of the play, rather than Shakespeare's somewhat ambiguous ending. However, as one writer (Arthur Colby Sprague, in *Theater Notebook*) notes, the messenger Marcade wore black, but there is no evidence in any other contemporary reviews that the role was emphasized at all. The ending of the play and the entrance of Marcade remain problems for directors to this day, but this is the first performance in which there is any clear evidence of how it was handled. As we will see, the manner in which the ending is produced, and Marcade's entrance in particular, influences the overall tone of a given production.

A much more successful, and subdued, performance was mounted by Samuel Phelps in 1857 at Sadler's Wells theater in London. He used painted backdrops, and the courtiers appeared in medieval attire (Gilbert, "Disappearance and Return" 32). The performance was reviewed by John Oxenford for *The Times*, who praised it as a "charming picture of a medieval Court" and commended the set. This production is important as it emphasized the artifice of the play via the set design (Gilbert, "Disappearance and Return" 32). Oxenford praised the actors' performances: however, in the end he called the play an "elaboration of trifles" (Gilbert 34). There is a lesson in both descriptions of this production and in Oxenford's criticism of it—namely, that the play benefits from careful consideration of staging and set design so as to bring out the play's emphasis on artifice and decorum. Second, the play is clearly an ensemble piece; even critical reviews often acknowledged that the play allows for constant interaction between characters. John Oxenford, for example, noted this aspect of the play when he wrote that it is one "over which a great deal of good acting may be diffused, for even the smallest parts are marked characters and some of the themes very strongly and very strangely defined" (quoted in Gilbert, "Disappearance and Return" 160.) Another review of the production likewise emphasized the performances:

> He [Armado] affects finery of speech, and is so utterly destitute of ideas, that to count three he must depend upon the help of a child who is his servant. . . . He carries a brave outside of clothes, but cannot fight in his shirt, because, as he is driven to admit, "the naked truth of it is, I have no shirt." This is the view of his character to which Mr. Phelps gives prominence by many a clever touch, such as the empty drawl on the word love, whenever Armado uses it, or the lumbering helplessness of wit displayed by the great Spaniard when magnificently and heavily conversing with the tiny Moth, in which part Miss Rose Williams has been taught to bring out very perfectly some little points. (quoted in Gilbert, "Disappearance and Return" 160)

Besides the emphasis on the interpretation of Armado, Phelps chose to cast a woman in the role of Moth. Many contemporary reviewers noted that the play calls for a strong ensemble, rather than one or two star roles, given the importance of the interrelationship between characters, even minor characters such as Moth.

The next major production of the play and the last in the nineteenth century was directed by Augustin Daly in New York City in 1891. In a review dated March 29, 1891, the *New York Times* observed that Augustin Daly produced a "well-arranged" version of *LLL*. The reviewer noted that the play is a "merry conceit" and further acknowledged that the production was well acted but also noted that even the role of Berowne was not deep. However, in a typical comment of the play and various productions of it, the setting and stage production were highlighted: "Indeed, no hansomer setting of a play by Shakespeare was ever seen in this country—or in any other, probably. Every picture is a noble example of the scene painter's art" (350). This production may have set the standards for those that came after it, for if this reviewer's description is accurate, then future directors were inspired to represent the play's formal tone by elaborate sets, most often influenced by highly mannered and expressionistic painting. Daly himself might have been influenced by Walter Pater's critical commentary on the play in his *Appreciations*, in which he wrote that the play was structured like a living work of art, or, more precisely, a tapestry. This interpretation of the play as a static still life of upper-class manners and highly artificial dress and speech influenced not only how the play was conceived of dramatically, but how it was staged, how the characters were costumed, and how the lines were spoken.

The *New York Times* review ends by noting that the "groundlings" of Shakespeare's day were entertained by the "horse-play" of the Nine Worthies episode, but that today the groundlings are not touched by "Shakespearean comedy even when it is combined with horse-play" (351). Thankfully, such misguided and ill-informed elitism is no longer fashionable, and as we will see, many modern productions have found a way to make this comedy, perhaps Shakespeare's most linguistically sophisticated one, entertaining to people of all walks of life.

The next significant production occurred at London's Westminster Theater in 1932 and was directed by Tyrone Guthrie. He used a permanent set and cut the text so that the running time was ninety minutes. This was an important production, for it was this performance that influenced John Dover Wilson to reappraise the play. One of the reasons for its success was undoubtedly the casting of Alec Guinness as Boyet (40). But, as Wilson notes, the play closed early in its run. However, four years later Gutherie again directed the play, this time at the Old Vic. As in the previous production, Gutherie had evidently noted Granville-Barkers's advice about the play demanding style: his production was highly formal and stylized, according to G.R. Hibbard in his Oxford edition of the play (6).

MODERN PRODUCTIONS

Peter Brooks

In 1946, Peter Brooks produced the play (and repeated it in the 1947 season). In his production he emphasized the play's darker aspects, such as death and the play's potential for tragedy (41). This interpretation stands in stark contrast to Gutherie's staging, if we are to believe John Dover Wilson, which was generally a happy and merry one. Brooks's is an important and insightful interpretation of the play, and one that would influence many later productions. What is of special interest in Brooks's production is not only the dark and somber tone he added, but the way in which he, like his precursors, also brought out the painterly qualities of the play. In his memoir, *The Empty Space*, Brooks notes that *LLL* was his first "big production" (119–120). In another memoir, *The Shifting Point* (1988), Brooks states, "When I directed Shakespeare's *Measure for Measure* in 1956, I thought the director's job was to create an image which would allow the audience to enter into the play, and so I reconstructed the worlds of Bosch and Brueghel, just as I had followed Watteau in directing *LLL* in 1950" (11).

The French painter Antoine Watteau (1684–1721) has been an influence on modern productions of *LLL* throughout the twentieth century. Watteau's paintings usually represent idealized human society, and as such serve as a parallel to *LLL*. Second, many of his paintings feature human subjects in park or country settings. His women are often characterized as remote or inaccessible, only partly engaged by the entertainment around them. All these characteristics could explain the attraction of directors to Watteau's painting. However, perhaps the most important influence would be Watteau's style: his work is very dark and somber in tone, despite the subject matter, and has often been critiqued as more crafted that inspired. Watteau was not a painter of daily life or of the "real" world; instead, he painted well-dressed ladies and gentleman at ease in leisure activities, usually involving music. All these elements explain why Watteau's paintings are visual metaphors for the world Shakespeare has created in *LLL*. Mannered paintings such as the "Age of Gold," in which it is springtime and yet the world seems melancholy, recreate a formal tableau much like Shakespeare's play. Finally, many critics since Samuel Johnson's original observation have suggested that *LLL* is the play in which we most clearly see the hand of Shakespeare the man. Likewise, art historians see the dark figure in the background

of most Watteau paintings as the painter himself; Marcade in *LLL* is that
same dark figure (Gilbert 138). We can see this in Brooks's production
with the entrance of Marcade; to Brooks it seems obvious that with
Marcade's entrance the play's tone changes: "because he came into an
artificial world to announce a piece of news that was real." Marcade,
like the dark figure in Watteau's paintings, serves to remind us that this
is not the real world but a created, artificial, albeit beautiful, one. This
reverses the opening action of the play in which the lords attempt to
close themselves off from the "real world." This interpretation is clear
in Brooks' own words:

> And it was through this that I brought Mercade over a rise at the
> back of the stage—it was evening, the lights were going down, and
> suddenly there appeared a man in black. The man in black came
> onto a very pretty summery stage, with everybody in pale pastel
> Watteau and Lancreet costumes, and golden lights dying. It was very
> disturbing, and at once the whole audience felt that the world had
> been transformed. (*Shifting Point* 12)

In an interview, Peter Brooks explained that the play suggested a tableau
very early in his experience with it. Brooks first directed *LLL* at the age
of nineteen or twenty. "When I did *LLL* I had a set of images in mind,
which I wanted to bring to life just like making a film. So *LLL* was a
very visual, very romantic set of stage pictures which I then did in a
Watteau-costume, eighteenth-century Romantic manner" (Berry 135).
But in addition to the formal and static Watteau world, Brook's injected
a bit of "reality" and lower-class mischief into the play, more in keeping with Shakespeare's complex dramatic world. Brooks's production
opened with prostitutes milling about the set, only to be chased off stage
after the announcement of the proclamation (Gilbert 45). Brooks also
wanted to emphasize the artifice of the play by using elaborate stage
frames and setting the garden/outdoor scenes in front of a grand staircase
suggesting a large patio.

One cannot overestimate the importance of Brook's production to the
reappraisal and renewed popularity of *LLL*. It was Brooks who first revealed for modern audiences the complexity and beauty of Shakespeare's
little world. Watteau would again be referenced by the director of the
BBC television production, and painters would inspire the Stratford production in 1984 (directed by Barry Kyle, who used Manet and Monet)

and a 1990 production (by Terry Hand), which likewise evoked Impressionist paintings.

No modern directors attempted to present the play as "topical satire" until Michael Kahn's Stratford, Connecticut production of 1968 (Gilbert 78). The play opened in late June 1968, about four months after the Beatles had left the world of media and stardom to study in India with a guru. In the first scene the young men are pursued by photographers and young fans. Kahn filled his stage using a 1960s pop-culture setting and costuming. Otherwise, the stage was left relatively bare, leaving the focus on the characters. He included references to the Beatles, Truman Capote, "hippie" culture, and other contemporary icons. Navarre was renamed India and he was "accompanied by incense-bearers and a sitar player" (78). Boyet recalled Truman Capote. Kahn's belief was that the play "was such a specific satire on Southampton's court and friends that the Elizabethan audience would have realized the topicality" (quoted in Gilbert 79). One specific scene, IV.iii., the sonnet reading and overhearing scene, recalled the Beatles' *A Hard Day's Night* (1964). Kahn admitted to not being able to find a "type" or modern equivalent for Armado in the contemporary setting (84), which should remind us how much of a product of the sixteenth century Armado really is. Many years later, Kahn said that "when I did *LLL* in 1968 I was concerned with manners—we seemed to be in a time of superstars of one form or another whose fame was really based upon personality and modes of behavior. That's not true right now, and *LLL* does not interest me now" (Gilbert 90).

John Barton and The Royal Shakespeare Company

All the productions so far considered suggest a world of high formality and material excess, a world that was fitting for the play's emphasis on the formalities and richness of language. Another side of the play, however, was exemplified by John Barton's 1978 Royal Shakespeare Company production, a world that was, according to Gilbert, "gentle and friendly rather than elegant or beautiful" (115). As one reviewer noted, "Barton is more interested in the idea of intellectual arrogance and posturing romanticism being brought down to earth" (*The Manchester Guardian Weekly*, August 27, 1981, 21; quoted in Londré 385). This aspect of the play was exemplified by the quiet entrance of the young men at the beginning of the play; in Barton's production the men enter without fanfare, whereas in many of the earlier productions the opening is used as an opportunity for spectacle and pageantry. The result was that in Barton's production the language "sounded less like the witty badinage of sophisticated people and more like the attempts of immature people to impress each other" (116). To this end, Barton made numerous cuts to the text, including Berowne's "Light, seeking light" I.i.77, but, as Barbara Hodgdon notes in her diary of the production, this line, and several others, were later reinstated when their dramatic necessity was uncovered.

This cutting points to a major issue for directors: how true must one remain to the original text? Granville-Barker's opinion on the acceptability of cutting scenes for performance is typical of many directors of *LLL*: "We need hardly hold sacred all that the printer has left us" (Granville-Barker 439). He would cut the "redundant" passages in Act IV, scene iii, and Act V.ii "may go." He would cut out all of the "l'envoy" speech to "We will talk no more of this matter" since, in his opinion, a modern audience cannot enjoy it (440–441). Many modern directors, including Barton, Elijah Moshinsky, the director of the BBC production described later, and Kenneth Branagh in his film adaptation follow Barker's advice and make large cuts to the play, so much so that it is likely that most people who have only seen the play performed have never experienced all the riches it has to offer. In the end, Barton worked with a text cut by approximately 400 lines, a figure noted by Hodgdon as a bit heavy for a Royal Shakespeare production (388). Barton's aim was to tighten the narrative and dramatic focus while sharpening the relationships between characters. As Hodgdon notes, "*playing* [i.e., performing] a 'full text' remains the ideal, even in the light of contemporary textual scholarship," which makes questions of what is the text difficult to answer (389).

John Barton's interpretation suggested that the linguistic acrobatics of lower-class characters such as Moth and Costard were similar in spirit to those of the more sophisticated characters such as Berowne and Armado; although the upper-class characters may be more "correct" when they speak archaically, they are experimenting with the possibilities of language in a manner similar to the lower-class characters and all the communication in the play is an attempt at sounding sophisticated. Barton's production was potentially inspired by his wife Anne Barton's influential writings on the play, as illustrated in her introduction to the *Riverside Shakespeare*, as well as her own essay from 1953 [as Bobbyann Roesen] *Shakespeare Quarterly* (Gilbert 116). In fact, her *Riverside* introduction appeared in condensed form as the program note for the 1978 production. After Anne Barton, John Barton's production emphasized "the sense of two worlds, the emphasis on the importance of keeping oaths, the necessity of growing up" (Gilbert 116). Anne Barton made standard the importance of the ending in understanding the intent of the play. Miriam Gilbert notes that more and more productions of comedies stress the "darker" side of them, but with *LLL* "the 'darker' side is built explicitly into the structure of the play" (166). The relationship between critical assessment and theatrical production is an important one and is seen most clearly in the case of *LLL*: the revival of *LLL* as a favorite critical text is at least partially due to its renewed popularity as a piece of theater; likewise, as the Anne Barton example suggests, directors often look to critics for inspiration in producing plays. "[W]ithout an appreciative critical tradition, directors may chose not to stage the play at all, preferring to work instead with plays they know and with plays they feel sure their audiences will both know and like. Critical disdain leads to theatrical neglect" (Gilbert, "Disappearance and Return" 162).

Perhaps Barton's production is most noteworthy for its attempt to distance itself from the "Watteau-like preciosity of tradition" (392) and instead to give the play a sense of comfort and hominess. Even the language comes to serve the characters' personalities, rather than the reverse. "Barton stresses relishing the artificiality and advises the actors to think of rhyming as a part of the characters' consciousness" (401). For example, rhyming is used by the young men as part of their wooing, yet it also suggests wit and immaturity. Armado and Holofernes are not nearly as witty as they think they are, and their speech habits reflect their pretentiousness and Old World ways. Barton succeeded in deflating his characters through hilarious visual jokes; for example, when Nathaniel enters playing Alexander the Great, only his feet are visible from under the huge hobby horse, with his weak voice repeating, "When in the world I lived, I was the world's commander" (V.ii.558) (Gilbert, "Disappearance and Return" 173).

Joseph Papp and Shakespeare in the Park

The favored staging of the play stresses artifice and elegance, usually suggesting wealth and upper-class gentility. However, two modern productions stage the play in more contemporary settings, perhaps in response to the play's playfulness and sensual nature.

One of the great American theatrical projects of the twentieth century would be the series founded by Joseph Papp in 1957, Shakespeare in Central Park. This series presents a challenge for directors, especially when faced with a play such as *LLL* that is based on word play and linguistic displays. The Delacorte Theater in Central Park is a large outdoor theater with a diverse audience, thereby making subtlety less effective than grand gestures. In 1989, Gerald Freedman directed a production of *LLL* in Central Park. He faced the particular challenges of the play by using physical action, rather than language, to set the scene ("Directing *Love's Labor's Lost*" 28–29). He also relied on modern dress, as Clive Barnes noted in his review of the play for the *New York Post*, on February 28, 1989: "[H]ere modern dress has a classic purpose—not to remind us, as if any reminder were needed, of the 'universality' of Shakespeare, that crutch of modish directors, but to transform the play's original fashionable text into a fashion closer to our own comprehension and understanding" (quoted in Londré 421). Barnes goes on to note that "getting" all the references is not necessary for a good production:

> To be sure, we either get, or miss, the outlandish puns with some relevant portion of our senses. But the sensibility of the piece, the concept of harsh, callow youth having its foolish fling before the onset of life's maturity, is made as immediate as a newsflash from our soul.

Not only does Barnes remind us of the importance of production values, but he rightly summarizes one of the themes that makes the play successful to a varied audience and from which Shakespeare's "universality" comes. This theme of youthful fun is evident in the opening scene: the production opens with King Ferdinand watching Berowne, Longaville, and Dumaine playing tennis, having fun (28). (This could be compared to Brooks, who as we noted, opened his production with prostitutes milling around the set.) After signing the oath, a nude statue was carried off and replaced with a telescope as a visual way of suggesting that frivolity and sexual desires were now replaced by serious educational concerns (30). In doing so, Freedman created a clear visual metaphor for the substitution of one pastime for another.

Like Brooks, Freedman notes that the key to the play is found in the pivotal final scene and the entrance of Marcade and the corresponding sudden change in tone. What might seem clumsy to a reader "works beautifully on stage, the place for which the scene was, after all, meant" (Freedman, *Love's* 22). For Freedman, *LLL* is a play filled with human feeling. Any production that overemphasizes frivolity does not set up the viewer for the final scene (23–24). "As far as I am concerned, the best way to approach style is not to approach it at all" (24). This is a refreshing approach to a play that, as we have noted, has tended to inspire the opposite priority. However, it is a comedy with very traditional themes—namely, the inevitability of love—and as long as those themes are emphasized, the play's power can be made evident to any audience. Freedman notes that many critics have complained that the gender relationships in the play are unbalanced and that the women are not fully developed, but he disagrees: the princess is a complete human being who can be silly and serious at the same time (40). "Throughout the play the girls seem far superior to the men" (43).

For Freedman, King Ferdinand and the princess were the two most important characters (25). Berowne, Longaville, and Dumain have been "constant companions since childhood," like the women in the play, and therefore, the director needed to create an "ensemble effort" (26). The most difficult passages and most obscure dialogue could be clarified by focusing on the speakers rather than the words alone. For example, at Act I, scene ii, Freedman asks, "What are they doing?" The scene seems to be all talk. However, the answer lies in character—Armado is man of pretension and appearance, for example at I.ii.43, Armado, in response to Moth's acknowledgment that he is a "gentleman and a gamester," replies, "I confess both. They are both the varnish of a complete man" or, in other words, the outer appearance of a complete man. But Armado also does not have more than a single shirt, as he later acknowledges. From this characterization Freedman came up with a costume for Armado that consisted of castoffs, including rusted pieces of armor and an old feather for his hat (36). This created a visual metaphor that caused the audience to have some pity for his character (37).

However, no director can ignore the verbal aspects of the play. In the punning section of Act III, scene i, the "egma" and "plantain" speech, Freedman realized that audiences would have difficulty following the meaning. Simply knowing that these are mispronounced words does not help on a modern stage where what the words should sound like are not common knowledge. Rather, what works is playing the section as a semi-burlesque "who's on first" routine (47). In this production, every line after "O, Marry me to one Francis! I smell some l'envoy, some goose, in this," received a laugh; although the audience did not understand the literal meaning, they understood the sense of it (48). At various places in the scene Freedman considered cuts, but the "actor was able to clarify the rather difficult words with mimicry and mime so that the speech turned out to be a very delightful moment, instead of awkward or obscure" (181). For the "remuneration" exchange, the director had Costard adopt an attitude of cynicism "about the low value of the tip."

Gerald Freedman notes that there are several factors that make *LLL* a good choice for production, and he has directed it five times. He notes that it needs a cast of young actors, that it demands ensemble playing, and that the plot is centered on love and the "immediacy" of young lovers (Freedman 423). In the end, it doesn't matter what the class or education level was of the Central Park audience. "In every case, the audience response was identical" (429). As Gerald Freedman notes, the characters of Holofernes and Nathaniel are easy characters to successfully portray: "They work beautifully for the modern audience; they are classic types, Holofernes being the dogmatic, narrow-minded, superior tyrant of the pedantic intellect, and Nathaniel representing the hostile sycophant that one often finds close at the heels of a Holofernes" (51). An actor's confusion with language, especially Latin, is a good thing, not a problem, since the characters are likewise often confused by it (51–52). As a result, a director does not have to worry about the verbal density of much of the play. This is a good point to remember when producing this play, but this observation must be balanced by an awareness that the "average" Elizabethan was a lot less confused than even a well-educated audience member today and that it does add to the enjoyment of certain passages to know what the character meant to say or thought he or she was saying. Nonetheless, "those who maintain that the humor in *LLL* is impossible for a contemporary audience to enjoy, or try to make sense of footnotes, would save themselves both time and anguish by simply performing it in front of an audience" (52).

The 1987 production of *LLL*, directed by Karel Kríz, at the National Theatre in Prague, provided one of the most interesting visual designs and interpretations of the play. Using the theory of "action design," or the use of "real objects to make metaphorical connections" (Christilles 136), Kritz designed a "totally synthetic production style" and employed "space as text" in which the stage design became a visual text, paralleling the words of the text (135). For the production, the dominant element on stage was a ornate fire curtain. The stage also featured "real" trees, designed to be leafless, but gilded, positioned in the center of the acting area. All of the scenery rested upon a white floor cloth. But the scenery also called for a particular style of acting; Malina, Kríz, and dramaturge Jaroslav Kral "synthesized a style out of their collaboration, opening up multiple levels of communication and perception" (135). The two edited the play to two hours, giving the play a more relaxed, "almost indolent style of acting" (136). In an interesting addition, they included seven of Shakespeare's sonnets at selected moments in the script to highlight key events or themes.

The production opened with an empty stage and with Navarre walking toward the audience, speaking the opening lines regarding the edict and his plans for the academe. But as he walked toward the front of the stage, the fire curtain slowly descended, eventually cutting the stage from view and requiring Navarre to finish his speech lying down. The fire curtain was further emphasized as each man pledged his oaths; as they did so they threw their jackets into a trap door in the stage and changed to "academic" shirts. With this change, "the fire curtain, and the rest of the stage was revealed" (Christilles 136). For the remainder of the play, until the last scene, the main stage decoration consisted of panels painted with foliage, and a painted, decayed fire curtain hung at the rear of the stage. "The self-referential, recursive quality of this drop clearly communicated the idea of an ongoing and endless battle of the sexes. Metaphorically, had that curtain risen, an even more decayed version of the ornate fire curtain would have been visible behind it, and so on and so on" (136).

Once the men joined the company of women, their costumes changed to more contemporary dress, such as blue jeans. With the news of the king's death, the lighting, which had been bright, became "stark and expressionistic" and the fire curtain again descended, again blocking the rest of the stage. For the rest of the play the actors played on in front of the fire curtain, until the conclusion, when the fire curtain was again raised, only to reveal an empty stage. As the characters made their exit, a black curtain rose at the back of the stage revealing a small garden with bushes and trees (Christilles 138). "By turns realistic and romantic, theatrical and illusionistic, employing period elements and staging techniques that were rearranged for contemporary sensibilities, Malina created a powerful, synthetic production" (138). As with many of the productions considered in this chapter, it was their intention to have the stage emphasize the "self-referential and recursive" nature of the play. "The production was as self-absorbed as the action of Shakespeare's characters and the words they spoke."

The 1995 production by the Washington, D.C. Shakespeare Theater, directed by Laird Williamson, emphasized time with a large clock serving as the dominant image. Likewise, books were strewn about in large and small stacks and what appeared to be torn manuscripts covered the wall; a passage of Chaucer was discernible on the back wall. On one end of the stage stood a bright yellow piano. These props and stage decorations served to anchor all of the action within the context of the worldly and temporal nature of learning and academic pursuits. The actors were costumed in Edwardian dress, with the king and lords dressed as English university students, and with the lower underclassmen sporting "Navarre Academy" jackets. Don Armado, played by the great comic actor and mainstay of the Shakespeare Theater Floyd King, wore shoes with hilariously long toes. Overall, the production was frivolous, almost slapstick: at one point Ferdinand balanced the three lords on a bicycle as he road around the stage. The characters threw paper airplanes at each other, and when they come out to meet the young ladies, they had been playing soccer and were covered in mud. But the festive tone was used, as it is so many productions, to highlight the change in mood of the last few lines of the last act. In the same way Kenneth Branagh would later use a prewar setting (in his case World War II), Williamson set his play in pre-World War I Europe. In the Pageant of the Nine Worthies we are reminded that many of them were, historically, soldiers since they were dressed in brown uniforms. Finally, the news of the death of the princess's father is delivered by French soldiers, and the play ends with the sound of distant artillery fire.

The BBC Shakespeare

The BBC Shakespeare began in 1975 as the first attempt to film the entire Shakespearian cannon (Willis 4). In all it took six years to produce and a total budget of $13.5 million by 1982. *Love's Labour's Lost* is a reminder of the aims of the BBC Shakespeare, to bring Shakespeare to the masses in an entertaining manner, and why *LLL* was one of the last plays to be filmed. The director, Elijah Moshinsky, who is noted for his opera productions, was influenced by Peter Brooks's production almost forty years earlier (56). Moshinsky saw the play as presenting "formalized rules between men and women, sense against sensibility" (quoted in Gilbert 56). Again, Watteau's paintings were very influential on how Moshinsky conceptualized the play; he saw the play as "a painting momentarily come to life" (Willis 160). The production's design stressed the formality of the character's world; this is particularly evident in the opening scene in the king's library, which features a gold clock and large tables on which the men sign their oaths. This production also seems to have influenced Branagh, who, like Moshinsky, set the sonnet reading scene in a library rather than the garden called for by the stage directions. Moshinsky directed five plays for the series: *All's Well that Ends Well, MND, Cymbeline, Coriolanus,* and *LLL.* In all his productions he cut lines, eliminated quibbling, and sometimes rearranged scenes. For example, there are eighteen scenes in the BBC production as opposed to the nine in the play (Willis 84). Moshinsky cast an adult, John Kane, in the role of Moth despite the character's necessary diminutive stature (as did Kenneth Branagh in his film version). His productions were well received because they looked good and were presented well. However, "they are also among the most heavily shaped and edited of the productions in the BBC series" (Jones 194). His *LLL* is unique in the BBC series because it is not done in period costumes; instead it is set in an eighteenth-century estate, which is undoubtedly the result of Watteau's influence. Despite its beautiful appearance, critics have often complained that in his production of the play the original ambiguities and complexities are lost for the sake of tonal consistency and beauty.

However, ideally television allows for realism and effects not possible on any stage, especially the Elizabethan for which Shakespeare wrote, and in this way the play benefits from its production. In a review of the production in the *Times Literary Supplement,* Peter Kemp noted that "*Love's Labour's Lost* is plugged into its period as into a life-support system. Pulled out of topical context, most of its jokes expire. And even in context, batteries of footnotes are needed to galvanize the play's petrified guyings of defunct absurdities back to life" (Bulman and Coursen 312). This comment inadvertently suggests one of the problems with drama on television: the lack of a live audience. Without that response, there is no way to know with certainty if the jokes or "guyings" are effective. On the other hand, in a live situation, not getting the jokes does not mean not laughing—directors often refer to the phenomenon of audiences laughing because something sounds funny or because the delivery or context suggested it was supposed to be funny. The "flatness" of the television screen removes these factors and makes production all the more important. *Love's Labour's Lost* is especially vulnerable to this problem since, without a festive atmosphere, the play can come across as overly academic. In the words of one critic, Moshinsky illustrated the BBC's tendency to "intervene" much like Restoration adaptations of Shakespeare. He made numerous cuts to the text, including I.ii where the talk between Armado and Moth is omitted and their discussion of love in III.i.7–44 is dropped. In IV.ii some of the "bantering" between

Jaquenetta, Holoferenes, and Nathaniel is cut, and the scene with Moth, Armado, Costard, Holoferenes, and Nathaniel is abbreviated (V.ii.39–72). At I.vi, lines 122–34 are cut. Lines from IV.iii.230+ are also cut as are lines from V.ii.321–324, 462–467, 474–481 and a number of asides in the Masque of the Nine Worthies. Moshinsky also reorders the first two scenes and places the Pageant of Nine Worthies in the library, which has now been transformed into a theater. Finally, rather than Armado, two women sing the final song—Spring dressed in yellow, Winter in grey (72). There was also at least one unusual and daring casting decision. The actress who played the princess of France was Maureen Lipman, who is more famous for her comic timing than her experience in serious drama. Miriam Gilbert notes her qualities of "composure, maturity, and irony, all expressed through a slightly school-marmish tone." This decision reflects the importance of careful casting; this particular decision created a new princess, a woman of more depth whose attraction to the king is based more on intellectual standards than physical beauty. In Moshinsky's own words, "[the play] is a kind of situation comedy using 'love' to explore comedy and reality and what real feelings are" (Gilbert 69).

W.H. Auden's *Love's Labour's Lost*

On February 7, 1973, the Deutsche Opera performed an opera based on *LLL*, with a libretto by W.H. Auden and Chester Kallman and music by Nicolas Nabokov. The libretto was published for the first time by Edward Mendelson in *The Complete Works of W.H. Auden*. As Nabokov noted in his journal at the time, Auden believed that *"Love's Labour's Lost* is the only Shakespeare play that will do as an opera. It is structured like an opera and so much of it is already in rhymed verse" (716). The play was attractive, as Auden noted in a draft of the program that was never printed, because although Italian poets might have turned *Macbeth* or *Othello* into operas, a writer in English would only dare use *Love's Labour's Lost*. (Auden gave passing acknowledgment to *Kiss Me, Kate* and Vaughn Williams' *The Merry Wives of Windsor*, but dismissed them since they were Shakespeare's "weakest works.") *Love's Labour's Lost* made for a good musical because the "euphustic style in which the verse was written would not be destroyed by a modification of the verbal text" (732). However, in their libretto, Auden and Kallman made numerous cuts to the text; in an interview with the *New York Times* on August 8, 1971, Kallman told an interviewer that "we stamped Shakespeare to bits and then put it together again" (717). Mendelson notes that, although full textual notes are lacking, Auden was probably responsible for writing or recasting Act I, scenes i and ii and the opening and closing arias, which are the songs of Winter and Spring, respectively, as well as I.iii through II.i and sections of several later scenes (Mendelson 718). Furthermore, the tone change in the last act with the entrance of Marcade is even more impressive when set to music. To reduce the number of players, the roles of Longaville and Maria were cut and the role of Moth was given to a woman. Also eliminated were Marcade (the news of the king's death is delivered by Boyet), Nathaniel, Holofernes, Dull, Costard, and the forester, leaving five male and five female roles. The play was reduced and restructured to fit the typical three-act opera structure.

The opera opens with the Song of Spring, sung by Moth. In general the stage directions seem to stay true to the spirit of Shakespeare: "A pavilion in the royal park." By opening with the song of Spring, and closing with Winter, Auden and Kallman enclosed the opera in an "opera-time" of one year, progressing from the Spring of the opening to the Winter of the closing and the announcement of the king's death.

As should already be clear, the two writers were not terribly faithful to the original. Auden noted in a letter on August 7, 1969, that "Chester had what I think a brilliant idea, namely to turn Moth into a Cupid-Ariel figure who delivers the letters to the wrong ladies out of mischief. This is more dramatic and has the extra advantage of getting rid of Costard, who could not have been made a character of interest" (719). Furthermore, most of Shakespeare's text is reduced to modernized couplets: Auden and Kallman seemed to admire the formal nature of Shakespeare's language rather than the language itself. Nonetheless, a few passages are true to the original; the songs, for example, are true to Shakespeare, with minor changes to punctuation, and various sections, mainly spoken interludes, are Shakespeare's. For the sake of getting a mixture of voices in early, Auden and Kallman bring in the young ladies in Act I, where they perform a duet around II.i.114–126, "Did I not dance with you in Brabant one?" Armado is generally far less pretentious, probably because the verbal gymnastics of the text are greatly reduced throughout. For example, Armado's soliloquy at the end of Act I is rendered as a song in Act I, scene ii of Auden's libretto:

Quill. Paper. Ink. The love she could not hear
May enter through the eye.
Though love forswears me who forswore

My oath to forswear love. I die!
My heart was at her feet; she trod,
O heartless maid, upon it!
Assist me, some extemporal god
Of rhyme, for I am sure
I shall turn sonnet.
Devise wit, write pen, for I
Am for whole volumes in folio!

Some of Armado's character comes through in these lines, but later Auden and Kallmann have Boyet read Armado's letter, minus the references to Cophetua, Zenelophon, and Caesar. Although much of the Latin is gone, we do see Moth later in the opera reading from a Latin textbook the conjugation for the word "love."

It can be assumed that the critical and popular reception of the single performance were not good—the opera was never revived and at least one review, appearing in the April 1973 edition of *Opera*, solicited a response from both Auden and Kallman, who defended their libretto by distancing it from the stage production, noting that such stage business as the use of real horses in the hunting scene, the stripping of Moth to his codpiece, and showing the ladies changing for a bath was not their work. They conclude by suggesting that the reviewer "seems naive," which they clarify to mean "that he appears to know nothing of contemporary opera production" (735).

Branagh's *Love's Labour's Lost*

As a follow-up to his four-hour, historical *Hamlet*, Kenneth Branagh chose to film *Love's Labour's Lost*, only rather than aiming for the textual accuracy and atmosphere of his previous Shakespeare interpretations, he chose instead to emphasize the musical qualities of the play. For a comedy that contains no songs, *LLL* has often been called "musical," if for no other reason than the fact that it relies on words and sound more than plot or story. Furthermore, Branagh's choice may have been a deliberate acknowledgment of the play's history of productions, starting in the nineteenth century, which have added music to the play. Whatever his motivation, the most successful productions of *LLL* have highlighted its musical qualities. As Dover Wilson wrote in the preface to the 1962 New Cambridge edition of the play, "The abiding impression left in [the Gutherie and Brook's productions] was one of ballet-like speed, tip-toe delicacy, and kaleidoscopic shifts of colour, all in the text rightly conceived, and culminating in the grim shock of the entry of a messenger of Death, clad in black from head to foot." For Branagh's film, what results is an extremely trimmed-down version of the play presented as a 1950s Hollywood musical: the subtitle of the film is *A Romantic Musical Comedy*. In effect, what Branagh has done is to essentially replace the play's emphasis on poetry as the primary mode of romantic conversation with music; more than half of the play's original lines are cut. Thus, the play's structural formality and Lylian groupings are emphasized.

The choice of Hollywood Golden Age musicals as the setting of this adaption is an interesting one in that it reminds us that Shakespeare's play fit into essentially the same entertainment fashion in his sixteenth-century England: the stylized romantic comedy that left little to the intellect or imagination. Although *LLL* is noteworthy for how it unpredictably handles the usual ending of a comedy, it is nonetheless highly traditional in its character types, love-at-first sight plot, and comic banter. Moreover, the inclusion of two plays-within-the-play and the elevated and formal manner with which the lead characters present themselves is a perfect metaphor for the affected nature of 1930s–1950s musicals. Branagh emphasized this similarity, ironically, by cutting both presentations and replacing them with musical numbers; in fact, the Nine Worthies performance is merely alluded to, but is replaced by Costard singing "There's No Business Like Show Business." The film is full of references to Busby Berkeley, Fred Astaire, and Gene Kelly films, and through them creates an overall feeling of nostalgia for a lost, romantic time. Branagh emphasizes the feeling of lost innocence with constant reminders of the coming war (the film is set in the late 1930s, and war-torn Europe serves as the larger context to the confines of Navarre); such a choice could be read as calling attention to the artifice of Hollywood musicals in the same manner Shakespeare's plays called attention to the artifice of Renaissance comedies. The specific setting is September 1939 as the war in Europe is beginning and the gentry is getting its last taste of peacetime. Branagh highlights the isolated nature of the academe and park-like atmosphere of the original by interspersing newsreel footage and Branagh's overvoiced commentary on events in the outside world. This allowed Branagh to retain some of the serious tone of the play, such as its consistent preoccupation with death and final intrusion of the "outside" world without interfering too much on the comedy. For example, the use of Gershwin's "They Can't Take That Away from Me" is an ironic commentary on the events of the film as Branagh chose to jux-tapose it with footage of the bombing of Germany. On the other hand, the use of Jerome Kerr's "I Won't Dance" is a fitting way to have the young women enter the scene in the opening moments of the film.

In all, Branagh includes ten different numbers in the film's ninety-three minutes. As is typical of many modern Shakespeare film adaptations, the cutting is fast and the emphasis is on setting, with much of the film taking place in a library and courtyard. Since many of the Shakespeare film adaptations of the 1990s were aimed at the youth market, Branagh's decision to potentially distance that market by recasting the play as a traditional musical was a brave one, undoubtedly dooming the film to mediocre returns. Only the casting of Alicia Silverstone as the princess and Alessandro Nivola as the king is in any way a nod to the teen market. In one interesting casting decision, Branagh cast a woman, Geraldine McEwan, as Holofernes (here named Holofernia). Predicably, Branagh casts himself in the biggest and most complex role, that of Berowne. In the most fitting casting in the film, the role of Costard was played by Nathan Lane. However, almost all the comic banter be-tween the lower-class characters was cut from the film, with the result that only Costard appeared for more than a few minutes.

In an odd choice for a musical version of a play noteworthy for having no real songs in it, Branagh does away with the closest the play has to offer, the final songs of Winter and Spring. Instead, Branagh ends with the departing plane, carrying the ladies, skywriting, "You that way: we this way," a line included only in the folio and usually given to Armado. Likewise, Branagh chose to use a song instead of the original poems in the sonnet-reading scene. Although one can argue that in the end Bran-agh's scene is still effective, a great deal of the original irony is lost by the exclusion of the poems themselves. Still, the music throughout the play does bring with it a hint of the same kind of beautiful artificiality that the original poems and linguistic acrobatics did for the original play. In a review of the film for *Early Modern Literary Studies*, Debra Tuckett observes that Branagh's choice of songs "are seamlessly woven into the fabric of the play" and that Berowne's speech on the sensual nature of lovers and the power of love at IV.iii.295–361, which ends with "And when love speaks, the voice of all the gods/Makes heaven drowsy with the harmony," is complemented by Branagh singing "Heaven." It is true that these lyrics reflect a theme of the play—namely, that language can-not serve the intentions of lovers—but not all of Branagh's choices are as clearly relevant; for example, one can easily question the appropriateness of having Costard sing "There's No Business Like Show Business" in place of the Nine Worthies pageant or of juxtaposing the bombing of Berlin with "They Can't Take That Away from Me." Nonetheless, Branagh's film served the play well for a modern, popular audience, who would inevitably gather from the film that *Love's Labour's Lost* is one of Shakespeare's most beautiful and entertaining plays.

WORKS CITED

Beckerman, Bernard, and Joseph Papp, ed. *Love's Labor's Lost*. The New York Shakespeare Festival Series. New York: Macmillian, 1968.

Berry, Ralph. *On Directing Shakespeare: Interviews with Contemporary Directors*. London: Hamish Hamilton, 1989.

Bradbrook, M.C. "The Triple Bond: Audience, Actors, Author in the Elizabethan Playhouse." *The Triple Bond: Plays, Mainly Shakespearean, in Performance*. Ed. Joseph G. Price. University Park: Pennsylvania State University Press, 1975. 50–69.

Brooks, Peter. *The Shifting Point: Forty Years of Theatrical Exploration, 1946–1987*. London: Methuen, 1988.

Bulman, J.C., and H.R. Coursen, eds. *Shakespeare on Television: An Anthology of Essays and Reviews*. Hanover and London: University Press of New England, 1988.

Christilles, Dennis, and Delbert Unruh. "The Semiotics of Action Design." *Theatre Topics* 6.2 (1996): 121–141.

Freedman, Gerald. "On Directing *Love's Labour's Lost*—Five Times." *"Love's Labour's Lost": Critical Essays*. Ed. Felicia Hardison Londré. New York: Garland Publishing, 1997. 423–429.

Gilbert, Miriam. *Love's Labour's Lost*. Manchester: Manchester University Press, 1993.

———. "The Disappearance and Return of *Love's Labor's Lost*." *Shakespeare's Sweet Thunder*. Ed. Michael J. Collins. Newark: University of Delaware Press, 1997.

Granville-Barker, Harley. *Prefaces to Shakespeare II*. Princeton: Princeton University Press, 1947.

Grasselli, Margaret Morgan, and Peire Rosenberg. *Watteau, 1684–1721*. Washington: National Gallery of Art, 1984.

Harbage, Alfred. *"Love's Labor's Lost* and the Early Shakespeare." *Philological Quarterly* 41 (1962): 18–36.

Jones, Gordon. "Nahum Tate Is Alive and Well: Elijah Moshinsky's BBC Shakespeare Productions." *Shakespeare on Television: An Anthology of Essays and Reviews*. Ed. by J.C. Bulman, and H.R. Coursen. Hanover and London: University Press of New England, 1988. 192–200.

Londré, Felicia Hardison, ed. *"Love's Labour's Lost": Critical Essays.* New
    York:Garland Publishing, 1997.
Mendelson, Edward. *The Complete Works of W.H. Auden.* Vol. 3. Princeton:
    Princeton University Press, 1988.
Swandler, Homer. *"Love's Labor's Lost*: Burn the Parasols, Play the Quarto!"
    Shakespeare's Sweet Thunder. Ed. Michael J. Collins. Newark: Univer-
    sity of Delaware Press, 1997.
Tuckett, Debra. "Review of Love's Labour's Lost." *Early Modern Literary Stud-
    ies* 6.1 (May, 2000): 23.1–6. URL:http://purl.oclc.org/emls/06-1/tuck-
    rev.htm.
Willis, Susan. *The BBC Shakespeare Plays: The Making of the Televised Canon.*
    Chapel Hill: University of North Carolina Press, 1991.
Wilson, John Dover. *Shakespeare's Happy Comedies.* Evanston: Northwestern
    University Press, 1962.

SELECTED BIBLIOGRAPHY

The following is a bibliography of major sources on *Love's Labour's Lost*. Many of these items are referred to in more depth in the previous chapters. This is by no means an exhaustive list. For a more detailed bibliography, see *Love's Labor's Lost, A Midsummer Night's Dream, and The Merchant of Venice*, ed. by Clifford Chalmers Huffman, a volume in the Pegasus Shakespeare Bibliographies, published by Medieval and Renaissance Texts and Studies, Binghamton, New York, 1995. The most exhaustive bibliography of material until 1981 is found in Nancy Lenz Harvey and Anna Kirwan Carey's *Love's Labor's Lost: An Annotated Bibliography*, published by Garland Press, 1984. For articles only, see Bruce Sajdak's *Shakespeare Index: An Annotated Bibliography of Critical Articles on the Plays 1959–83*, published by Kraus International Publications, 1992.

Love's Labour's Lost: Critical Essays, edited by Felicia Hardison Londré, Garland Publishing, New York, 1997, contains an excellent bibliography and gathers together many of the key critical statements on the play (some of which are listed separately below), as well as collects several essays not available elsewhere.

Acheson, Arthur. *Shakespeare and the Rival Poet*. London: John Lane, 1903.

Anderson, J.J. "The Morality of 'Love's Labour's Lost.' " *Shakespeare Survey* 24 (1971): 55–62.

Arthos, John, ed. *Love's Labor's Lost*. Signet Classic Shakespeare. New York: Signet Classic, 1988.

Asp, Caroline. "*Love's Labour's Lost*: Language and the Deferral of Desire." *Literature and Psychology* xxxv (1989): 1–21.

Babcock, Weston. "Fools, Fowls, and Pertaunt-Like in *Love's Labour's Lost*." *Shakespeare Quarterly* 2.3 (1951): 211–219.

Baldwin, T.W. *Shakespeare's Five-Act Structure: Shakespeare's Early Plays on the Background of Renaissance Theories of Five-Act Structure from 1470.* Urbana: University of Illinois Press, 1947.

———. *William Shakespeare's Small Latine and Lesse Greeke.* Urbana: University of Illinois Press, 1944.

Barber, C.L. *Shakespeare's Festive Comedy: A Study of Dramatic Form and Its Relation to Social Custom.* Princeton: Princeton University Press, 1959.

Barton, Ann. Introduction. *Riverside Shakespeare.* 2nd ed. Ed. G. Blakemore Evans. Boston: Houghton Mifflin, 1997. 208–212.

———. "Shakespeare and the Limits of Language." *Shakespeare Survey* 24 (1971): 19–30.

Beckerman, Bernard, and Joseph Papp, ed. *Love's Labor's Lost.* The New York Shakespeare Festival Series. New York: Macmillian, 1968.

Beiner, G. "Endgame in *Love's Labour's Lost.*" *Anglia* 103 (1985): 48–70.

Berek, Peter. "Artifice and Realism in Lyly, Nashe and *Love's Labour's Lost.*" *Studies in English Literature 1500–1900* 23 (1983): 207–221.

Berger, Thomas L. "The Lack of Song in *Love's Labor's Lost.*" *Shakespeare Quarterly* 26 (1975): 53–55.

Berry, Ralph. *On Directing Shakespeare: Interviews with Contemporary Directors.* London: Hamish Hamilton, 1989.

Bevington, David. " 'Jack Hath Not Jill'': Failed Courtship in Lyly and Shakespeare." *Shakespeare Survey: An Annual Survey of Shakespeare Studies and Production.* Ed. Stanley Wells. Cambridge: Cambridge University Press, 1990. 42.

Binns, J.W. "Shakespeare's Latin Citations: The Editorial Problem." *Shakespeare Survey* 45 (1987): 119–128.

Bird, Christine M. "Games Courtiers Play in *Love's Labour's Lost.*" *University of Hartford Studies in Literature: A Journal of Interdisciplinary Criticism* 11 (1979): 41–48.

Bloom, Harold. *Shakespeare: The Invention of the Human.* New York: Riverhead Books, 1998.

Bonazza, Blaze Odell. *Shakespeare's Early Comedies: A Structural Analysis.* The Hague: Mouton, 1966.

Boughner, Daniel C. "Don Armado and the *Commedia dell'Arte.*" *Studies in Philology* 37 (1940): 201–224.

———. "Don Armado as a Gallant." *Revue Anglo-Americaine* 13 (1935): 16–18.

Bradbrook, M.C. *The School of Night: A Study of the Literary Relationships of Sir Walter Ralegh.* Cambridge: Cambridge University Press, 1936.

———. *Shakespeare and Elizabethan Poetry: A Study of His Earlier Work in Relation to the Poetry of the Time.* Cambridge: Cambridge University Press, 1951.

———. "St. George for Spelling Reform! Social Implications of Orthography—

Cheke to Whythorn; Mulcaster to Shakespeare's Holofernes." *Shakespeare Quarterly* 15 (1964): 129–141.

———. "The Triple Bond: Audience, Actors, Author in the Elizabethan Playhouse." *The Triple Bond: Plays, Mainly Shakespearean, in Performance.* Ed. Joseph G. Price. University Park: Pennsylvania State University Press, 1975. 50–69.

Breitenberg, Andrew. "The Anatomy of Masculine Desire in *Love's Labour's Lost.*" *Shakespeare Quarterly* 43 (1992): 430–449.

Brissenden, Alan. "Shakespeare's Use of Dance: *Love's Labour's Lost, Much Ado About Nothing,* and *The Merry Wives of Windsor.*" *Shakespeare and Some Others: Essays on Shakespeare and Some of His Contemporaries.* Ed. Alan Brissenden. Adelaide: University of Adelaide, 1976. 30–43.

Bronson, Bertrand. "Daisies Pied and Icicles." *Modern Language Notes* 63 (1948): 35–38.

Brooks, Peter. *The Shifting Point: Forty Years of Theatrical Exploration, 1946–1987.* London: Methuen, 1988.

Brown, John Russell. *Shakespeare and His Comedies.* London: Methuen, 1957.

Browne, Ray B. "The Satiric Use of 'Popular' Music in *Love's Labor's Lost.*" *Southern Folklore Quarterly* 23 (1959): 137–149.

Bullough, Geoffrey. *Narrative and Dramatic Sources of Shakespeare.* Vol 1. London: Routledge, 1957.

Bulman, J.C., and H.R. Coursen, eds. *Shakespeare on Television: An Anthology of Essays and Reviews.* Hanover and London: University Press of New England, 1988.

Calderwood, James. "*Love's Labour's Lost*: A Wantoning with Words." *Studies in English Literature 1500–1900* 5.2 (1965): 317–332.

Campbell, Oscar James. "*Love's Labor's Lost* Restudied." *Studies in Shakespeare, Milton, and Donne. University of Michigan Publications in Language and Literature* 1 (1925): 3–45.

———. *Shakespeare's Satire.* London: Oxford University Press, 1943.

Carew, Richard. *The Excellency of the English Tongue.* British Library MS Cott. F. xi, f. 265.

Carroll, William. *The Great Feast of Language in "Love's Labour's Lost."* Princeton: Princeton University Press, 1976.

Cazamian, Louis. *The Development of English Humor.* Durham: Duke University Press, 1952.

Chambers, E.K. *Shakespeare: A Survey.* New York: Oxford University Press, 1926.

Champion, Larry S., *The Evolution of Shakespeare's Comedy: A Study in Dramatic Perspective.* Cambridge: Harvard University Press, 1970.

Charlton, H.B. "The Date of Love's Labour's Lost." *Modern Language Review* 13 (1918): 257–266, 387–400.

Christilles, Dennis, and Delbert Unruh. "The Semiotics of Action Design." *Theatre Topics* 6.2 (1996): 121–141.

Cody, Richard. *The Landscape of the Mind: Pastoralism and Platonic Theory in Tasso's Aminta and Shakespeare's Early Comedies.* Oxford: Clarendon Press, 1969.

Coleridge, Samuel Taylor. *Writings on Shakespeare.* Ed. Terence Hawkes. New York: Capricorn Books, 1959.

Coursen, Herbert R., Jr. "*Love's Labour's Lost* and the Comic Truth." *Papers in Language and Literature* 6 (1970): 316–322.

Cunningham, J.V. " 'With That Facility': False Starts and Revisions in *Love's Labour's Lost.*" *Essays on Shakespeare.* Ed. G.W. Chapman. Princeton: Princeton University Press, 1965. 91–115.

Curtis, Harry, Jr. "Four Woodcocks in a Dish: Shakespeare's Humanization of the Comic Perspective in *Love's Labour's Lost.*" *Southern Humanities Review* 13 (1979): 115–124.

Cutts, John. *The Shattered Glass: A Dramatic Pattern in Shakespeare's Early Plays.* Detroit: Wayne State University Press, 1968.

Danks, K.B. "Love's Labour's Lost." *Notes and Queries* 193 (1948): 545.

Dash, Irene G. "Single-sex Retreats in Two Early Modern Dramas: *Love's Labour's Lost* and *The Convent of Pleasure.*" *Shakespeare Quarterly* 47: 4 (1996): 387–395.

———. *Wooing, Wedding, and Power: Women in Shakespeare's Plays.* New York: Columbia University Press, 1981.

David, Richard W., ed. *Love's Labour's Lost.* Arden Shakespeare. 2nd series. London: Routledge, 1994.

———. "Shakespeare's Comedies and the Modern Stage." *Shakespeare Survey* 4 (1951): 129–138.

Donawerth, Jane. *Shakespeare and the Sixteenth-Century Study of Language.* Urbana: University of Illinois Press, 1984.

Draper, John. "Tempo in *Love's Labor's Lost.*" *English Studies*, 29 (1948): 129–137.

Edwards, Philip. *Shakespeare and the Confines of Art.* London: Methuen, 1968.

Elam, Keir. *Shakespeare's Universe of Discourse: Language-Games in the Comedies.* Cambridge: Cambridge University Press, 1984.

Ellis, Herbert. *Shakespeare's Lusty Punning in "Love's Labour's Lost": With Contemporary Analogues.* The Hague: Mouton, 1973.

Ericson, Peter. "The Failure of Relationship Between Men and Women in *Love's Labour's Lost. Women's Studies* 9 (1981): 65–81.

Evans, Bertrand. *Shakespeare's Comedies.* Oxford: Clarendon Press, 1967.

Evans, Malcolm. *Signifying Nothing: Truth's True Contents in Shakespeare's Texts.* 2nd ed. Athens: University of Georgia Press, 1989.

Flynn, Vincent Joseph. "The Grammatical Writings of William Lily, ?1468–?1523." *Bibliographical Society of America* 37 (1943): 27–42.

Foakes, R.A. "The Owl and the Cuckoo: Voice of Maturity in Shakespeare's Comedies." *Shakespearian Comedy.* Ed. Malcolm Bradbury and David Palmer. *Stratford-upon-Avon Studies* 14. London: Edward Arnold, 1972. 121–141.

Freedman, Gerald. "On Directing *Love's Labour's Lost*—Five Times." *"Love's Labour's Lost": Critical Essays.* Ed. Felicia Hardison Londré. New York: Garland Publishing, 1997. 423–429.

French, Marilyn. *Love's Labour's Lost.* With an essay on the direction of the play by Gerald Freedman. New York: Macmillian, 1968.

———. *Shakespeare's Division of Experience.* New York: Summit Books, 1981.

Gilbert, Miriam. "The Disappearance and Return of *Love's Labor's Lost.*" *Shakespeare's Sweet Thunder.* Ed. Michael J. Collins. Newark: University of Delaware Press, 1997.

———. *Love's Labour's Lost.* Manchester: Manchester University Press, 1993.

Godshalk, William Leigh. "Pattern in *Love's Labour's Lost.*" *Renaissance Papers 1968*: 41–48.

Goldstein, Neal L. "*Love's Labour's Lost* and the Renaissance Vision of Love." *Shakespeare Quarterly* 25 (1974): 335–350.

Granville-Barker, Harley. *Prefaces to Shakespeare II.* Princeton: Princeton University Press, 1946.

Grasselli, Margaret Morgan, and Peire Rosenberg. *Watteau, 1684–1721.* Washington, D.C.: National Gallery of Art, 1984.

Gray, Henry David. *The Original Version of Love's Labour's Lost, with a Conjecture as to Love's Labour's Won.* Stanford: Leland Stanford Junior University Publications, Stanford University, 1918.

Green, Thomas M. "*Love's Labour's Lost*: The Grace of Society." *Shakespeare Quarterly* 22 (1971): 315–328.

Greenblatt, Stephen, gen ed. *The Norton Shakespeare.* New York: W.W. Norton and Company, 1997.

Greg, Walter. *The Editorial Problem in Shakespeare.* Oxford: Oxford University Press, 1942.

———. *The Shakespeare First Folio.* Oxford: Oxford University Press, 1954.

Hamilton, A.C. "The Early Comedies: *Love's Labour's Lost.*" *The Early Shakespeare.* San Marino: The Huntington Library, 1967.

Harbage, Alfred. *As They Liked It: A Study of Shakespeare's Moral Artistry.* New York: Macmillan, 1947.

———. "*Love's Labor's Lost* and the Early Shakespeare." *Philological Quarterly* 41 (1962): 18–36.

Hart, H.C., ed. *Love's Labour's Lost.* The Arden Shakespeare. 1st Series. London: Methuen, 1930.

Hasler, Jorg. "Enumeration in *Love's Labour's Lost.*" *English Studies* 50 (1969): 176–185.

Hassel, R. Chris, Jr. "Armado's Sexual Puns." *University of South Florida Language Quarterly* 9 (1971): 7–8, 42.

———. *Faith and Folly in Shakespeare's Romantic Comedies.* Athens: University of Georgia Press, 1980.

———. "Love Versus Charity in *Love's Labour's Lost.*" *Shakespeare Studies* 10 (1977): 17–41.

Heninger, S.K., Jr. "The Pattern of *Love's Labour's Lost.*" *Shakespeare Studies* 7 (1974): 25–53.

Hibbard, G.R., ed. *Love's Labour's Lost.* The Oxford Shakespeare. Oxford: Clarendon Press, 1990.

Hill, R.F. "Delight and Laughter: Some Aspects of Shakespeare's Early Verbal Comedy." *Shakespeare Studies* [Japan] 3 (1964): 1–21.

Hoy, Cyrus. *The Hyacinth Room: An Investigation into the Nature of Comedy, Tragedy, and Tragicomedy.* New York: Knopf, 1964.

———. "Navarre and His Bookmen." *Shakespeare's Comedies: An Anthology of Modern Criticism.* Ed. Lawrence Lerner. Baltimore: Penguin Books, 1967.

Hunt, John Dixon. "Grace, Art and the Neglect of Time in 'Love's Labour's Lost.' " *Shakespearian Comedy.* Ed. D. Palmer and Malcolm Bradbury. Stratford-upon-Avon Studies 14. London: Edward Arnold, 1972.

Hunter, G.K. *John Lyly, The Humanist as Courtier.* Cambridge, MA: Harvard University Press, 1962.

Hunter, Robert G. "The Function of the Songs at the End of *Love's Labor's Lost.*" *Shakespeare Studies* 7 (1974): 55–64.

Johnson, Samuel. *Samuel Johnson on Shakespeare.* Ed. H.R. Woudhuysen. London: Penguin, 1989.

Jones, Gordon. "Nahum Tate Is Alive and Well: Elijah Moshinsky's BBC Shakespeare Productions." *Shakespeare on Television: An Anthology of Essays and Reviews.* Ed. J.C. Bulman and H.R. Coursen. Hanover and London: University Press of New England (1988): 192–200.

Joseph, Sister Miriam, C.S.C. *Shakespeare's Use of the Arts of Language.* New York: Columbia University Press, 1947.

Kehler, Dorothea. "Jaquenetta's Baby's Father: Recovering Paternity in *Love's Labor's Lost.*" *Renaissance Papers 1990*: 45–54.

Kettner, Eugene J. "*Love's Labor's Lost* and the Harvey-Nashe-Greene Quarrel." *Emporia State Research Studies* 10 (1962): 29–39.

Lamb, Mary Ellen. "The Nature of Topicality in *Love's Labour's Lost.*" *Shakespeare Survey* 38 (1985): 49–59.

Lawrence, Natalie Grimes. "A Study of Taffeta Phrases . . . and Honest Kersey Noes." *Sweet Smoke of Rhetoric: A Collection of Renaissance Essays.* Ed. Natalie Grimes Lawrence and J.A. Reynolds. Coral Gables: University of Miami Press, 1964.

Lee, Sidney. "A New Study of *Love's Labor's Lost.*" *The Gentleman's Magazine* 249 (1880): 447–458.

Leggatt, Alexander. *Shakespeare's Comedies of Love*. London: Methuen, 1974.

Lewis, Anthony J. "Shakespeare's Via Media in *Love's Labor's Lost.*" *Texas Studies in Literature and Language* 16 (1974): 241–248.

Londré, Felicia Hardison, ed. *"Love's Labour's Lost": Critical Essays*. New York: Garland Publishing, 1997.

Lyly, John. *Gallathea. Drama of the English Renaissance I: The Tudor Period*. Ed. Russell A. Fraser and Norman Rabkin. New York: Macmillan, 1976.

Mahood, M.M. *Shakespeare's Wordplay*. London: Methuen, 1957.

Matthew, William. "Language in *Love's Labor's Lost.*" *Essays and Studies* 17 (1964): 1–11.

Maus, Katherine Eisaman. "Transfer of Title in *Love's Labor's Lost*: Language, Individualism, Gender." *Shakespeare Left and Right*. Ed. Ivo Kamps. London: Routledge, 1991.

McFarland, Thomas. *Shakespeare's Pastoral Comedy*. Chapel Hill: University of North Carolina Press, 1972.

McLay, Catherine. "The Dialogues of Spring and Winter: A Key to the Unity of *Love's Labor's Lost.*" *Shakespeare Quarterly* 18 (1967): 119–127.

Memmo, Paul E., Jr. "The Poetry of the *Stilnovisti* and *Love's Labor's Lost.*" *Comparative Literature* 18 (1966): 1–15.

Montrose, Louis Adrian. *"Curious-knotted Garden": The Form, Themes, and Contexts of Shakespeare's "Love's Labour's Lost."* Salzburg Studies in English Literature: Elizabethan and Renaissance Studies 56. Salzburg, 1977.

———. " 'Folly, in wisdom hatch'd;': The Exemplary Comedy of *Love's Labour's Lost.*" *Comparative Drama* 11 (1977): 147–170.

———. " 'Sport by sport o'erthrown': *Love's Labour's Lost* and the Politics of Play." *Texas Studies in Literature and Language* 18 (1977): 528–552.

Mowat, Barbara, and Paul Werstine, ed. *Love's Labor's Lost*. The New Folger Shakespeare Library. New York: Washington Square Press, 1996.

Mulcaster, Richard. *The Elementarie*. Ed. E.T. Campagnac. Oxford: Clarendon Press, 1945.

Neely, Carol Thomas. "Women and Men in *Othello*: "What should such a fool/ Do with so good a woman?" In *The Woman's Part: Feminist Criticism of Shakespeare*. Ed. Carolyn Ruth Swift Lenz, Gayle Greene, and Carol Thomas Neely. Urbana: University of Illinois Press, 1980.

Nelson, Timothy G.A. "The Meaning of *Love's Labor's Lost.*" *Southern Review: An Australian Journal of Studies* 4 (1971): 179–191.

Nevo, Ruth. *Comic Transformations in Shakespeare*. London: Methuen, 190.

Palmer, John. *Comic Characters in Shakespeare*. London: Macmillan, 1946.

Parker, Barbara L. *A Precious Seeing: Love and Reason in Shakespeare's Plays*. New York: New York University Press, 1987.

Parker, Patricia. "Preposterous Reversals: *Love's Labour's Lost.*" *Modern Language Quarterly* 54.4 (1993): 43–482.

Parrot, Thomas Marc. *Shakespearean Comedy*. New York: Oxford University Press, 1949.

Pater, Walter. *Appreciations with an Essay on Style*. New York: Macmillan, 1903.

Perryman, Judith. "A Tradition Transformed in *Love's Labour's Lost*." *Etudes Anglaises* T.XXXVII. no. 2 (1984): 158–162.

Petti, Anthony G. "The Fox, the Ape, the Humble-Bee and the Goose." *Neophilologus* 44 (1960): 208–215.

Phialas, Peter G. *Shakespeare's Romantic Comedies: The Development of Their Form and Meaning*. Chapel Hill: University of North Carolina Press, 1966.

Price, Thomas. "Shakespeare's Word-Play and Puns: *Love's Labour's Lost*. *"Love's Labour's Lost"*: *Critical Essays*. Ed. Felicia Hardison Londré. New York: Garland Publishing, 1997: 71–76.

Proudfoot, Richard. *"Love's Labour's Lost*: Sweet Understanding and the Five Worthies." *Essays and Studies* 37 (1984): 16–30.

Righter, Anne [Barton]. *Shakespeare and the Idea of the Play*. New York: Barnes and Noble, 1963.

Roberts, Jeanne Addison. "Convents, Conventions and Contraventions: *Love's Labor's Lost* and *The Convent of Pleasure.*" *Shakespeare's Sweet Thunder: Essays on the Early Comedies*. Ed. Michael J. Collins. Newark: University of Delaware Press, 1997.

Roesen, Bobbyann [Anne Barton]. *"Love's Labour's Lost."* *Shakespeare Quarterly* 4 (1953): 411–426.

Smidt, Kristen. "Shakespeare in Two Minds: Unconformities in *Love's Labour's Lost."* *English Studies* 65 (1984): 205–219.

Soellner, Rolf. *Shakespeare's Patterns of Self-Knowledge*. Columbus: Ohio State University Press, 1972.

Spurgeon, Caroline. *Shakespeare's Imagery and What It Tells Us*. New York: Macmillan, 1935.

Strathman, E.A. "The Textual Evidence for 'The School of the Night.' " *Modern Language Notes* 56 (1941): 176–186.

Swandler, Homer. *"Love's Labor's Lost*: Burn the Parasols, Play the Quarto!" *Shakespeare's Sweet Thunder*. Ed. Michael J. Collins. Newark: University of Delaware Press, 1997.

Talbert, Ernest W. *Elizabethan Drama and Shakespeare's Early Plays: An Essay in Historical Criticism*. Chapel Hill: University of North Carolina Press, 1963.

Taylor, Rupert. *The Date of Love's Labour's Lost*. New York: AMS Press, 1966.

Thomas, Karl F. "Shakespeare's Romantic Comedies." *PMLA* 67 (1952): 1079–1093.

Thorne, Barry. *"Love's Labor's Lost*: The Lyly Gilded." *The Humanities Association Bulletin* 21 (1970): 32–37.

Traversi, Derek A. *An Approach to Shakespeare*. 3rd ed. Garden City, NY: Doubleday, 1969.

Tricomi, Albert H. "The Witty Idealization of the French Court in *Love's Labour's Lost*." *Shakespeare Studies* 12 (1979): 25–33.

Tuckett, Debra. "Review of *Love's Labour's Lost*." *Early Modern Literary Studies* 6.1 (May, 2000): 23.1–6 URL:http://purl.oclc.org/emls/06–1/tuckrev.htm.

Turner, John. "*Love's Labour's Lost*: The Court at Play." *Shakespeare: Out of Court: Dramatizations of Court Society*. Ed. Graham Holderness, Nick Potter, and John Turner. New York: St. Martin's Press, 1990.

Turner, Robert Y. *Shakespeare's Apprenticeship*. Chicago: University of Chicago Press, 1974.

Ungerer, Gustav. "Two Items of Spanish Pronounciation in *Love's Labour's Lost*." *South Atlantic Quarterly* 63 (1964): 1–9.

Vyvyan, John. *Shakespeare and Platonic Beauty*. London: Chatto and Windus, 1961.

Wells, Stanley. "The Copy for the Folio Text of *Love's Labour's Lost*." *The Review of English Studies* 33 (1982): 137–147.

———. "Shakespeare Without Sources." *Shakespearian Comedy*. Ed. D.J. Palmer and Malcolm Bradbury. Stratford-upon-Avon Studies 14. London: Arnold, 1972. 58–74.

Werstine, Paul. "Variants in the First Quarto of *Love's Labour's Lost*." *Shakespeare Studies*, 12 (1979): 35–47.

West, E.J. "On the Essential Theatricality of *Love's Labor's Lost*." *College English*, 9 (1948): 427–429.

Westlund, Joseph. "Fancy and Achievement in *Love's Labour's Lost*." *Shakespeare Quarterly* 18 (1967): 37–46.

White, R.S. "Oaths and the Anticomic Spirit in *Love's Labour's Lost*." *Shakespeare and Some Others: Essays on Shakespeare and Some of His Contemporaries*. Ed. Alan Brissenden. Adelaide: University of Adelaide, 1976. 11–29.

Wilders, John. "The Unresolved Conflicts of *Love's Labour's Lost*." *Essays in Criticism* (1977): 20–33.

Willis, Susan. *The BBC Shakespeare Plays: The Making of the Televised Canon*. Chapel Hill: University of North Carolina Press, 1991.

Wilson, John Dover. *Shakespeare's Happy Comedies*. Evanston: Northwestern University Press, 1962.

Wilson, John Dover, and Arthur Quiller-Couch, eds. *Love's Labour's Lost*. New Shakespeare. Cambridge: Cambridge University Press, 1923.

Woudhuysen, H.R., ed. *Love's Labour's Lost*. Arden Shakespeare. 3rd series. Walton-on-Thames: Thomas Nelson and Sons, 1998.

Yates, Francis A. *A Study of "Love's Labour's Lost."* London: Cambridge University Press, 1936.

INDEX

About the Author

JOHN S. PENDERGAST is Assistant Professor of English at Southern Illinois University, Edwardsville. His publications have appeared in such journals as *ELH, Studies in Philology,* and *Extrapolation.*